809.3   HAYCRAFT
HAY   Murder for pleasure

MURDER FOR PLEASURE

The Life and Times of
the Detective Story

The Murders in the Rue ~~Trianon~~ ~~Poes~~ Morgue.
By Edgar A. Poe.

It is not improbable that a few farther steps in phrenological science will lead to a belief in the existence, if not to the actual discovery and location of an organ of analysis. If this power (which may be described, although not defined, as the capacity for resolving thought into its elements) be not, in fact, an essential portion of what late philosophers term ideality, then there are indeed many good reasons for supposing it a primitive faculty. That it may be a constituent of ideality is here suggested in opposition to the vulgar dictum (founded, however, upon the assumptions of grave authority,) ~~however~~ that the calculating and discriminating powers (causality and comparison) are at variance with the imaginative — that the three, in short, can hardly coexist. But although thus opposed to received opinion, the idea will not appear ill-founded when we observe that the processes of invention or creation are strictly akin with the processes of resolution — the former being nearly, if not absolutely, the latter conversed.

It cannot be doubted that the mental features discoursed of as the analytical are, in themselves, but little susceptible of analysis. We appreciate them only in their effects. We know of them, among other things, that they are always to their possessor, when inordinately possessed, a source of the liveliest enjoyment. As the strong man exults in his physical ability, delighting in such exercises as call his muscles into action, so glories the analyst in that moral activity which disentangles. He derives pleasure from even the most trivial occupations bringing his talent into play. He is fond of enigmas, of conundrums, of hieroglyphics — exhibiting in his solutions of each and all a degree of acumen which appears to the ordinary apprehension praeternatural. His results, brought about by the very soul and essence of method, have, in truth, the whole air of intuition.

The faculty in question is possibly much invigorated by mathematical study, and especially by that highest branch of it which, unjustly, and merely on account of its retrograde operations, has been called, as if par excellence, analysis. Yet to calculate is not in itself to analyse. A chess-player, for example, does the one without effort at the other. It follows that the game of chess, in its effects upon mental character, is greatly misunderstood. I am not now writing a treatise, but simply prefacing a somewhat peculiar narrative by observations very much at random — I will, therefore, take occasion to assert that the higher powers of the reflective intellect are more decidedly and more usefully tasked by the unostentatious game of draughts than by all the elaborate frivolity of chess. In this latter, where the pieces have different and bizarre motions, with various and variable values, that which is only complex is mistaken (a not unusual error) for that which is profound. The attention is here called powerfully into play. If it flag for an instant, an oversight is committed resulting in injury or defeat. The possible moves being not only manifold but involute, the chances of such oversights are multiplied; and in nine cases out of ten it is the more concentrative rather than the more acute player who conquers. In draughts, on the contrary, where the moves are unique and have but little variation, the probabilities of inadvertence are diminished, and the mere attention being left comparatively unemployed, what advantages are obtained by either party are obtained by superior acumen. To be less abstract — Let us suppose a game of draughts where the pieces are reduced to four kings, and where, of course, no oversight is to be expected. It is obvious that here the victory can be decided (the players being at all equal) only by some recherché movement, the result of some strong exertion of the intellect. Deprived of ordinary resources, the analyst throws himself into the spirit of his opponent, identifies himself therewith, and not unfrequently sees thus, at a glance, the sole methods (sometimes indeed absurdly simple ones) by which he may seduce into miscalculation or hurry into error.

Whist has long been noted for its influence upon what is termed the calculating powers; and men of the highest order of intellect have been known to take an apparently unaccountable delight in it, while eschewing chess as frivolous. Beyond doubt there is nothing of a similar nature so greatly tasking the faculty of analysis. The best chess-player in Christendom may be little more than the best player of chess — but proficiency in whist implies capacity for success in all those more important undertakings where mind struggles with mind. When I say proficiency, I mean that perfection in the game which includes a comprehension of all the sources (whatever be their character) from which legitimate advantage may me derived. These are not only manifold but multiform, and lie frequently among recesses of thought altogether inaccessible to the ordinary understanding. To observe attentively is to remember distinctly; and so far the concentrative chess-player will do very well at whist; while the rules of Hoyle (themselves based upon the mere mechanism

THE FIRST DETECTIVE STORY

First page of the original manuscript of Edgar Allan Poe's "The Murders in the Rue Morgue." (Reproduced by special permission of the Board of Trustees of Drexel Institute of Technology, Philadelphia.)

MURDER
FOR PLEASURE

*The Life and Times of
the Detective Story*

By Howard Haycraft

Newly Enlarged Edition
with
Notes on Additions to a Cornerstone Library
and
The Haycraft-Queen Definitive Library
of Detective-Crime-Mystery Fiction

Illustrated

BIBLO and TANNEN
NEW YORK
1974

Copyright, 1941, by D. Appleton-Century Company, Inc.

Published by arrangement with Appleton-Century,
affiliate of Meredith Press

Copyright, 1951, by Mercury Publications, Inc.

Reprinted by permission of Ellery Queen

Reprinted, 1974, by arrangement with
Hawthorne Books, Inc.

by

Biblo and Tannen Booksellers and Publishers, Inc.
63 Fourth Avenue   New York, N.Y. 10003

Library of Congress Catalog Card Number: 68-25809

SBN 8196-0216-7

Printed in U.S.A. by
NOBLE OFFSET PRINTERS, INC.
NEW YORK 3, N. Y.

To
M.S.H.
and
J.E.H.

FOREWORD

The detective story is the normal recreation of
noble minds.—Philip Guedalla

. . .

My theory is that people who don't like mystery
stories are anarchists.—Rex Stout

When Nazi Luftwaffe squadrons unleashed their wanton
fury on London in the late summer of 1940, initiating to
their own consternation a deathless epic of human courage
and resistance, they also drove a city of eight million souls
beneath the earth's surface for nightly refuge. After the
first shock of a kind of battle new in the annals of war-
fare had passed, life underground began to take on some
of the aspects of normality. One of the earliest harbingers
of rehabilitation was the appearance of books in the fetid
burrows while the bombs rained overhead. What volumes,
asked curious Americans from the comfortable security
of their homes, could men and women choose for their
companionship at such a time? The answer was soon
forthcoming in dispatches from the beleaguered capital,
telling of newly formed "raid" libraries set up in response to popular demand to lend detective stories and
nothing else. The implications contained in this circumstance, as applied to the underlying appeal of the detective
novel, might easily constitute a superior essay in themselves (and are perhaps unfathomable at that). But surely

no more striking illustration could be found of the vital position which this form of literature has come to occupy in modern civilized existence, for whatever reasons.

That detective stories are a mere hundred years old seems, in fact, beyond belief; in the same sense that imagining daily life without the telephone or the radio strains all credulity. For to-day it is a matter of sober statistical record that one out of every four new works of fiction published in the English language belongs to this category, while the devotion the form has managed to arouse in millions of men and women in all walks of life, the humble and the eminent, has become a latter-day legend.

No less a qualified authority than Mr. Somerset Maugham has recently ascribed this state of affairs to the fact that "the serious novel of to-day is regrettably namby-pamby." The charge is outside the province of the present volume and can not be examined here. But Mr. Maugham goes on, at least half seriously, to predict the day when the police novel will be studied in the colleges, when aspirants for doctoral degrees will shuttle the oceans and haunt the world's great libraries to conduct personal research expeditions into the lives and sources of the masters of the art.

Whatever the merits or likelihood of these suggestions, the surprising circumstance is that no adequate factual or analytical history of this movement—so clearly the outstanding literary phenomenon of modern times—yet exists. There have been, of course, the excellent but brief critical studies by Dorothy Sayers, Willard Huntington Wright, and E. M. Wrong; and the longer but relatively inaccessible (and, it must be said, rather academic) treatises of H. Douglas Thomson, Régis Messac, and François Fosca, the first published only in England and now out of print, and the latter two available only in French. These, together with a handful of prefaces, and a larger but widely scattered and uncoördinated body of magazine articles, and one or two "how-to-write-it" manuals, constitute the entire published literature on one of the most vigorous and virile types of all contemporary writing. A form which, to many readers, has come to occupy the solacing spot which *Robinson Crusoe* held in Gabriel Betteredge's affections: a "friend in need in all the necessities of this mortal life"—the one dependable and unfailing anodyne in a world so realistically murderous that fictive murder becomes refuge and retreat! . . . The present book has been undertaken in the hope of at least partially remedying this deficiency: of providing a reasonably readable and useful outline of the main progress of the detective story from Edgar Allan Poe to the present moment.

Throughout the book, the reader will find, emphasis has been placed on the actual and factual rather than the theoretical phases of the subject; with side excursions, when space has permitted, into those fascinating if trivial problems of idiosyncrasy and mannerism so dear to the heart of the true enthusiast. In short, the underlying object of the work has been pleasure—for reader and writer alike.

In making any such book, the problem of exclusion must be, necessarily, more difficult than that of inclusion. The question of just what constitutes a detective story will be considered at some length in the body of the work. For the present we can do no better than repeat again

John Carter's useful and often quoted dictum, as the basis upon which authors and their various works were accepted or rejected: "If we decide, as surely we must, that a detective story within the meaning of the act must be mainly occupied with detection and must contain a proper detective (whether amateur or professional), it is clear that mystery stories, crime stories, spy stories, even Secret Service stories, will have to be excluded unless any particular example can show some authentic detective strain." *

Thus, the volume in hand has been restricted to the bona-fide, the "pure," detective story and its craftsmen —as distinguished (to quote Carter again) from "mere mystery on the one hand, and criminology on the other." Regrettably, it has been impossible to discuss at length all the competent authors who come legitimately under even this rule. Their number has become so increasingly great within recent decades that only a veritable encyclopedia could deal with them adequately. Too, this volume is of necessity concerned less with literary merit per se than with setting forth the history and evolution of detective fiction as a recognizable form. This has made the basis of choice chiefly historical rather than appreciative. Hence, detailed discussion has been limited to those practitioners whose works, in the writer's opinion, have most significantly *influenced* the progress of the police romance throughout the years, either in technique or in popularity. The premise has sometimes meant the inclusion of authors of no very great distinction in themselves, and the omission of others (including many personal favorites) whose

* J. Carter (editor), *New Paths in Book-Collecting* (London, Constable, 1934).

achievements, judged by purely literary standards, might be considered of a higher order. Nevertheless, the attempt has been made to recognize if only in the several lists and indexes most of the authors who have contributed ably and consistently to the form.

In addition to these general premises, a few personal observations may, perhaps, be permitted. It has not been my wish in undertaking this work to set myself up in any sense as an "authority" on the subject of the detective story. Naturally, I own to a strong bias in favor of the police novel among the several forms of recreational and pleasure literature—else I should not have attempted this labor of devotion at all. But I have tried to approach the subject in the spirit of the average friendly reader, and, so far as possible, to synthesize and express that hypothetical individual's opinions and reactions, likes and dislikes, rather than those of professional or formal criticism. If I have succeeded in doing this in any degree, I shall perforce be satisfied.

I should not be honest, however, if I did not confess to certain preferences and antipathies which other readers may or may not share. Some of these predilections and aversions are admittedly of little save personal importance, and have been treated accordingly. But, while I have tried to be fair at all times, I have not spared the horses when discussing any tendencies which seem to me really dangerous to the future welfare of my favorite form of reading and that of several million equally fortunate individuals. On the opposite side, I have conscientiously attempted to avoid over-solemnity about the subject, but have endeavored at all times to consider it only for what it is—a frankly non-serious, entertainment form of literature which, nevertheless, possesses its own rules and standards, its good and bad examples, and at its best has won the right to respectful consideration on its own merits. (But I venture to believe that the demonstrable relationship between the detective story and democratic institutions, discussed in one of the chapters, is not without some serious implication in the present day.)

Acknowledgment is hereby gladly, if of necessity anonymously, expressed to a long list of individuals and corporations who have assisted invaluably by one means or another in the preparation of this book: the personal friends who have listened so patiently and contributed so many helpful suggestions, and the friendly and equally helpful correspondents among authors, editors, and publishers; more specifically, to the magazines in which some of the material has appeared prior to book publication, including the *Saturday Review of Literature*, the London *Spectator, American Cavalcade,* and the *Wilson Library Bulletin.* Special gratitude is also owing to Neal and John Townley of the Beekman Place Bookshop, New York, and to Robert M. and Sarah St. John Trent, without whose combined assistance the "Who's Who in Detection" at the end of the volume could not have been compiled.

In the field of illustration I am happy to acknowledge the coöperation of President Parke R. Kolbe, Dean Marie Hamilton Law, and the Board of Trustees of the Drexel Institute of Technology; Henry B. Van Hoesen, Librarian, and the Library Committee of Brown University; Vincent Starrett and The Macmillan Company; H. T. Webster, Mrs. May Lamberton Becker, and the New York *Herald Tribune;* The H. W. Wilson Company;

Mrs. Winona McBride Oberholtzer and the Estate of Dr. E. P. Oberholtzer; Ned Guymon; Charles Honce; P. M. Stone; Mrs. May Futrelle; the publicity and editorial departments of several publishers, and a number of the individual authors; and, particularly in the case of writers of a past day, the departments and limitless resources of the New York Public Library. In picturing the older authors, incidentally, it has been my whim to show them whenever possible at the prime of their careers rather than in the sunset years of life. The whole matter of illustration has, of course, been governed by the twin considerations of availability and limitation of space.

In conclusion, it is perhaps unnecessary to say that every effort has been made to achieve completeness and accuracy within the bounds laid down. But it is inescapable that in any work exploring a comparatively uncharted field and involving so much detail, some errors and omissions at least will have occurred. (A larger number of these have been avoided than would otherwise have been possible, by the discerning eye of Earle F. Walbridge, who has so invaluably assisted in reading proof.) Some of the interpretations, too, while made with every intention of objective fairness, may be open to question. I shall welcome correspondence from interested readers on any such points, for correction or modification in possible future editions.

H. H.

Old Mastic,
  Moriches, New York

CONTENTS

Contents

ILLUSTRATIONS

MURDER FOR PLEASURE

The Life and Times of
the Detective Story

In September 1941 there appeared in the field of criminological criticism a truly monumental work — Howard Haycraft's MURDER FOR PLEASURE: THE LIFE AND TIMES OF THE DETECTIVE STORY *— the first full-length history of the genre by an American, and still the most outstanding work of its kind ever written. Everybody connected with the detective story — writers, reviewers, and God bless them, readers — went wild about Mr. Haycraft's remarkable book, and pre-publication copies brought forth a flood of enthusiastic testimonials from such connoisseurs as Vincent Starrett, Rex Stout, Erle Stanley Gardner, and the late William Lyon Phelps, and from that beldame of bloodhounding, the late Carolyn Wells (herself a pioneer historian). Your Editors went on record at the time with the following words: "We were so completely fascinated by Mr. Haycraft's* MURDER FOR PLEASURE *that we read clear through in one sitting; it is a landmark in the history of detective fiction — a brilliant, necessary, long-overdue study, written with charm and authority."*

On pages 302–306 of MURDER FOR PLEASURE, *Mr. Haycraft offered what he called "A Readers' List of Detective Story 'Cornerstones' " — the carefully considered highspots published in the United States, Great Britain, and France, from 1845 through 1938. Although it is hard to believe, a full decade has passed since* MURDER FOR PLEASURE *first appeared. So, to help celebrate EQMM's Tenth Anniversary Issue, we asked Mr. Haycraft to go over his notes covering detective stories published between 1938 and 1948, and to select those cornerstones which he thinks should be added to his original list. Further comments at the end of Mr. Haycraft's important critical contribution . . .*

NOTES ON ADDITIONS TO A CORNERSTONE LIBRARY

by HOWARD HAYCRAFT

OF the several events which marked the Centennial of the Detective Story in 1941, two occurred in the same month. One was the first issue of *EQMM*. The other was the publication of the present writer's MURDER FOR PLEASURE: THE LIFE AND TIMES OF THE DETECTIVE STORY, in one of the chapters of which, entitled *A Detective Story Bookshelf*,

I presumed to name some sixty-four writers from Edgar Allan Poe to Mabel Seeley whose first or chief works might constitute the cornerstones of an amateur collector's library. Though the book itself was published in 1941, the latest cornerstone carried the date 1938 — for, I think, fairly obvious reasons of necessary perspective.

It was Ellery Queen's happy idea, which I gladly welcomed, that I should utilize this 10th anniversary issue of *EQMM* as an appropriate forum to bring the cornerstone-list down to date.

Not until I began to review my notes did I fully realize (as no doubt I should have done before) the exceptional difficulties of assembling a definitive list for a decade which witnessed a numerical outpouring unequaled in the history of the form, together with a process of literary osmosis that all but obliterated the old limitations and demarcations. In terms of sheer numbers, between 2,000 and 2,500 detective-mystery-crime titles were published in the United States alone during the period under scrutiny — or more than the entire output of the detective story in its first seventy-five years of existence.

In short, the detective-mystery-crime story (for such is its multiform nature today, and we may as well face it) has come of age, and in the process has left behind it the era of sharply defined frontiers and towering historical landmarks. What the years under consideration *have* produced is some excellent and often polished entertainment, but of a type which in my opinion will require a longer perspective before more than a few of its lasting contributions can be named with any degree of certainty. To spot the pioneers of any movement, literary or otherwise, is comparatively easy (especially in retrospect); but to recognize those members of the succeeding generation most-likely-to-endure is something else again, and needs, I submit, more time.

Enough of this preamble. It should be apparent by now that the present essay will not be the crisp and declarative list of titles for the years between 1938 and 1948 that Ellery Queen and I first envisioned, but rather some preliminary notes pointing to such an eventual end. And which, I hope, may in the meantime suggest a few paths of joy to collectors and readers.

Concerning a few — but only a few — of the new authors and their works of the decennium there can be little doubt. I am certain, for example, that the earlier Philip Marlowe novels of Raymond Chandler ("in and beyond the Hammett tradition," James Sandoe has called them) belong in the charmed circle; though more for their colorful imagery and less for their publicized social content than their author would (and does) contend. As for the representative work, I would leave an open choice between the first and second novels, THE BIG SLEEP (1939) and FAREWELL, MY LOVELY (1940).

Then there are the Lockridges, the creators of that civilized and perennially delightful duo, Mr. and Mrs. North. Today it has become a little the fashion to blame the sins of a host of "wacky" imitators on the Norths. What we are likely to forget, ungratefully, is the fact that the Lockridge novels are among the few domestic productions in which style plays a major part in our enjoyment. Hard-pressed to pick any single title, I would fall back on the curtain-raising tale, THE NORTHS MEET MURDER (1940).

The chief question concerning Dorothy B. Hughes is whether to name her first extravagant but unforgettable study-in-terror THE SO BLUE MARBLE (1940), or such an example of her maturer talent as IN A LONELY PLACE (1947). Cornell Woolrich, at his best a master of sensation fiction almost unrivaled in our day, presents a similar problem of selection; personally, I would choose PHANTOM LADY (1942), published under his pen-name, William Irish. I have a few more reservations about Craig Rice — in the long perspective — but as outstanding examples of typically American humor-cum-detection such of her novels as TRIAL BY FURY (1941), featuring the Justus-Malone team, or HOME SWEET HOMICIDE (1944) win at least conditional consideration.

Fewer than one could wish, Hilda Lawrence's stories have made a major contribution, by shrewd and sensitive writing, toward lifting the American-feminine mystery from its self-induced doldrums; I would choose her BLOOD UPON THE SNOW (1944), introducing Mark East. And though it has had no successor in five years, Helen Eustis's THE HORIZONTAL MAN (1946) is sure of a place on my own shelf as a novel which gave me as much personal enjoyment as any single performance of the decade.

All the authors mentioned to this point have been Americans. The reasons why British newcomers during the period were numerically scarce should be obvious to anyone not wilfully myopic. Nevertheless, a few names and titles stand out. High among them I place Raymond Postgate's ironically compassionate trial story, VERDICT OF TWELVE (1940). Not far behind belongs another modern courtroom classic, Edgar Lustgarten's moving ONE MORE UNFORTUNATE (1947). Space must be found, too, for Josephine Tey's

THE FRANCHISE AFFAIR (1948), a brilliant variation in modern dress on the Elizabeth Canning legend. In the realm of more orthodox detection — once almost the monopoly of our cousins across the sea — it seems to me that Edmund Crispin among the newer writers has best demonstrated the necessary staying-power (though he has grown disturbingly prolix of late). While many devotees of Michael Innes and John Dickson Carr plump for Crispin's THE MOVING TOYSHOP (1946), my own preference is for his less ebullient, better disciplined LOVE LIES BLEEDING (1948).

In a decade dominated by Mars, the spy story inevitably flourished, and with a generally closer relationship to the detective pattern than in previous years. If I were permitted but one author in this category, my vote would go without hesitation to Manning Coles and the two first, inseparable, and incomparable Tommy Hambledon adventures, DRINK TO YESTERDAY and A TOAST TO TOMORROW, both published in the United States in 1941. (Query: why doesn't some enterprising publisher reissue them in a two-in-one volume and earn the gratitude of a new generation of readers?)

Though by definition the discussion thus far has confined itself to new writers, such a distinction would be meaningless in the field of the anthology. Here I think we must reverse the rule and look solely at the works themselves. Imagining again the necessity of a single choice, I would commend to the reader and collector Ellery Queen's centennial 101 YEARS' ENTERTAINMENT (1941), as the decade's contribution certain to stand beside the great pioneer anthologies of Dorothy L. Sayers, Willard Huntington Wright (S. S. Van Dine), and E. M. Wrong on the "definitive" shelf.

Do the foregoing nominations omit large numbers of your favorite mystery writers who blossomed during the decade? They do of mine, too. Authors whose distinction rests less on individual titles than on solid and consistent craftsmanship over many years and books — authors whom the "longer perspective" may well admit to the inner circle in time to come — authors of the stature and accomplishments of, say, Arthur W. Upfield, Elizabeth Daly, A. A. Fair, Cyril Hare, Roger Bax, Charlotte Armstrong, H. C. Branson, to mention only a random handful by way of illustration.

Concerning one deliberate and categorical omission, I want to say a further word. Much as I approve the broadened scope of the modern detective-crime-mystery story, and with no wish to insist on narrow definitions, I am nevertheless unable to go along with some of my colleagues who would claim for the canon virtually every author who has ever touched on crime or violence. I am sufficiently old-fashioned to believe that there is still a distinction of some importance between fiction written for the mystery audience, and psychological novels and character studies which chance to employ crime as a catalyst. For this reason I have purposely not named such essentially non-mystery writers (to my mind) as Graham Greene, James M. Cain, C. S. Forester, and W. R. Burnett — though I am well aware that a case can be made for their inclusion.

If ever they *are* included, if the day arrives when the bars are lowered, then I reserve the right to head my own list of Fringe Benefits with Daphne Du Maurier's REBECCA (1938), one of the finest mystery stories of all time although it was not written as one.

POSTSCRIPT BY ELLERY QUEEN

. . . and now we give you a master-list of all the cornerstones selected by Howard Haycraft, America's foremost historian of the detective story—his original choices covering the period between 1845 and 1938, and the cornerstones he has just recommended from the decade of 1939-1948. In addition, Mr. Haycraft has graciously permitted your Editors to express their own critical judgment, by letting us insert and append those titles which we feel belong in a definitive and historical library of detective-crime-mystery fiction.

Please note that all the titles suggested by Ellery Queen are identified by an asterisk (*), and that all the comments shown in small italic type were written by Queen, and therefore do not necessarily reflect Mr. Haycraft's opinions. As you will see, Queen takes a broader critical view of the mystery field than many of our colleagues. We beg you not to be disturbed by any differences of opinion, implied or overt, which may exist between Mr. Haycraft and ourselves: without a single exception, the differences of opinion are completely honest ones, and honest differences of opinion are not so much the cause of dissension as the basis of true comprehension.

The Haycraft-Queen Definitive Library
of Detective-Crime-Mystery Fiction

TWO CENTURIES OF CORNERSTONES, 1748-1948

1748 Voltaire   *ZADIG
The Great-Grandfather of the Detective Story

1828-9 François Eugène Vidocq   *MÉMOIRES DE VIDOCQ
The Grandfather of the Detective Story

1845 Edgar Allan Poe   TALES
The Father of the Detective Story

1852-3 Charles Dickens   BLEAK HOUSE
                             THE MYSTERY OF EDWIN DROOD, *1870*

1856 "Waters" (William Russell) *RECOLLECTIONS OF A DETECTIVE POLICE-OFFICER
The first English detective yellow-back

1860 Wilkie Collins   *THE WOMAN IN WHITE

1862 Victor Hugo   *LES MISÉRABLES (First edition in English, also *1862*)

1866 Feodor Dostoevsky   *CRIME AND PUNISHMENT (First edition in English, *1886*)

1866 Émile Gaboriau   L'AFFAIRE LEROUGE
                             *LE DOSSIER N° 113, *1867*
                             *LE CRIME D'ORCIVAL, *1868*
                             MONSIEUR LECOQ, *1869*
The Father of the Detective Novel

1868 Wilkie Collins   THE MOONSTONE
The Father of the English Detective Novel

1872 (Harlan Page Halsey)   *OLD SLEUTH, THE DETECTIVE, *1885*
The first Dime Novel detective story

1874	Allan Pinkerton	*THE EXPRESSMAN AND THE DETECTIVE
1878	Anna Katharine Green	THE LEAVENWORTH CASE

The Mother of the American Detective Novel

| 1882 | Robert Louis Stevenson | *NEW ARABIAN NIGHTS
*STRANGE CASE OF DR JEKYLL AND MR HYDE, *1886* |

Was it Maurice Richardson who said of this book that it is the only detective-crime story he knows in which the solution is more terrifying than the problem?

| 1887 | Fergus W. Hume | *THE MYSTERY OF A HANSOM CAB |

An historically important book

| 1887 | A. Conan Doyle | A STUDY IN SCARLET
THE SIGN OF FOUR, *1890*
THE ADVENTURES OF SHERLOCK HOLMES, *1892*
THE MEMOIRS OF SHERLOCK HOLMES, *1894*
THE HOUND OF THE BASKERVILLES, *1902*
THE RETURN OF SHERLOCK HOLMES, *1905*
THE VALLEY OF FEAR, *1915*
HIS LAST BOW, *1917*
THE CASE-BOOK OF SHERLOCK HOLMES, *1927* |

The listing of all the Sherlock Holmes books — the complete works — is sheer idolatry. Surely the first Holmes story, A STUDY IN SCARLET, *is an undeniable cornerstone; also* THE ADVENTURES *and* THE MEMOIRS; *and the best of the novels should also be present in any definitive detective library. Most critics would probably select* THE HOUND *as the best novel; John Dickson Carr's choice is* THE VALLEY OF FEAR.

1892	Israel Zangwill	THE BIG BOW MYSTERY
1894	Mark Twain	*THE TRAGEDY OF PUDD'NHEAD WILSON
1894	Arthur Morrison	MARTIN HEWITT, INVESTIGATOR
1895	M. P. Shiel	*PRINCE ZALESKI

1897	Bram Stoker	*DRACULA

A mystery classic — interpreting "mystery" in its broadest sense

1899	E. W. Hornung	*THE AMATEUR CRACKSMAN

The first Raffles book — "detection in reverse"

1903	(Erskine Childers)	*THE RIDDLE OF THE SANDS

Recommended by Christopher Morley as the classic secret service novel

1906	Godfrey R. Benson	TRACKS IN THE SNOW

1906	Robert Barr	THE TRIUMPHS OF EUGÈNE VALMONT

1907	Jacques Futrelle	THE THINKING MACHINE

1907	Maurice Leblanc	*ARSÈNE LUPIN, GENTLEMAN-CAMBRIO-LEUR
		*"813", *1910*

The Leblanc-Lupin masterpiece
LES HUITS COUPS DE L'HORLOGE, *1922*

1907	Gaston Leroux	LE MYSTÈRE DE LA CHAMBRE JAUNE
		*LE PARFUM DE LA DAME EN NOIR, *1908–9*

1907	R. Austin Freeman	THE RED THUMB MARK

The first Dr. Thorndyke book
*JOHN THORNDYKE'S CASES, *1909*
*THE EYE OF OSIRIS, *1911*
THE SINGING BONE, *1912*

The first "inverted" detective stories

1908	Mary Roberts Rinehart	THE CIRCULAR STAIRCASE

The founding of the Had-I-But-Known school

1908	O. Henry	*THE GENTLE GRAFTER

1908	G. K. Chesterton	*THE MAN WHO WAS THURSDAY
		THE INNOCENCE OF FATHER BROWN, *1911*

| 1909 | Cleveland Moffett | *THROUGH THE WALL |
| | *A neglected highspot* | |

| 1909 | Baroness Orczy | THE OLD MAN IN THE CORNER |

| 1909 | Carolyn Wells | THE CLUE |
| | *The first Fleming Stone book* | |

1910	A. E. W. Mason	AT THE VILLA ROSE
	The first Hanaud book	
		THE HOUSE OF THE ARROW, *1924*

| 1910 | William MacHarg and Edwin Balmer | *THE ACHIEVEMENTS OF LUTHER TRANT |
| | *The first book of short stories to make scientific use of psychology as a method of crime detection* | |

| 1912 | Arthur B. Reeve | THE SILENT BULLET |
| | *The first Craig Kennedy book* | |

| 1913 | Mrs. Belloc Lowndes | THE LODGER |
| | *One of the earliest "suspense" stories* | |

| 1913 | Sax Rohmer | *THE MYSTERY OF DR FU-MANCHU |

| 1913 | E. C. Bentley | TRENT'S LAST CASE (First U. S. title: THE WOMAN IN BLACK) |
| | *The birth of naturalism in characterization* | |

| 1914 | Ernest Bramah | MAX CARRADOS |
| | *The first blind detective* | |

| 1914 | Louis Joseph Vance | *THE LONE WOLF |

| 1915 | John Buchan | *THE THIRTY-NINE STEPS |

| 1916 | Thomas Burke | *LIMEHOUSE NIGHTS |

| 1918 | Melville Davisson Post | UNCLE ABNER |

| 1918 | J. S. Fletcher | THE MIDDLE TEMPLE MURDER |

1920	Agatha Christie	*THE MYSTERIOUS AFFAIR AT STYLES
		The first Hercule Poirot book
		THE MURDER OF ROGER ACKROYD, *1926*
1920	Freeman Wills Crofts	THE CASK
		INSPECTOR FRENCH'S GREATEST CASE, *1924*
1920	H. C. Bailey	CALL MR. FORTUNE
		THE RED CASTLE, *1932*
1920	"Sapper" (Cyril McNeile)	*BULL-DOG DRUMMOND
1920	Arthur Train	*TUTT AND MR. TUTT
1921	Eden Phillpotts	THE GREY ROOM
1922	A. A. Milne	THE RED HOUSE MYSTERY
1923	G. D. H. Cole	THE BROOKLYN MURDERS
1923	Dorothy L. Sayers	*WHOSE BODY?
		The first Lord Peter Wimsey book
		THE NINE TAILORS, *1934*
	—— and Robert Eustace	THE DOCUMENTS IN THE CASE, *1930*
1924	Philip MacDonald	THE RASP
		The first Colonel Anthony Gethryn book
		*WARRANT FOR X, *1938* (English title: THE NURSEMAID WHO DISAPPEARED, *1938*)
1925	Edgar Wallace	THE MIND OF MR. J. G. REEDER
1925	John Rhode	THE PADDINGTON MYSTERY
		The first Dr. Priestley book
		*THE MURDERS IN PRAED STREET, *1928*
1925	Earl Derr Biggers	THE HOUSE WITHOUT A KEY
		The first Charlie Chan book

1925	Theodore Dreiser	*AN AMERICAN TRAGEDY
1925	Liam O'Flaherty	*THE INFORMER
1925	Ronald A. Knox	THE VIADUCT MURDER
1926	S. S. Van Dine	THE BENSON MURDER CASE *or*

The first Philo Vance book
THE "CANARY" MURDER CASE, *1927*

1926	C. S. Forester	*PAYMENT DEFERRED
1927	Frances Noyes Hart	THE BELLAMY TRIAL
1928	W. Somerset Maugham	*ASHENDEN
1929	Anthony Berkeley	THE POISONED CHOCOLATES CASE
		*TRIAL AND ERROR, *1937*
	[Francis Iles]	BEFORE THE FACT, *1932*
1929	Ellery Queen	THE ROMAN HAT MYSTERY

The first Ellery Queen book
*CALAMITY TOWN, *1942*

[Barnaby Ross]   THE TRAGEDY OF X, *1932*

The first Drury Lane book
*THE TRAGEDY OF Y, *1932*

| 1929 | Rufus King | *MURDER BY THE CLOCK |

The first Lieutenant Valcour book

| 1929 | W. R. Burnett | *LITTLE CAESAR |
| 1929 | T. S. Stribling | *CLUES OF THE CARIBBEES |

The only Professor Poggioli book

| 1929 | Harvey J. O'Higgins | *DETECTIVE DUFF UNRAVELS IT |

The first psychoanalyst detective

| 1929 | Mignon G. Eberhart | THE PATIENT IN ROOM 18 |
| 1930 | Frederick Irving Anderson | BOOK OF MURDER |

1930	Dashiell Hammett	THE MALTESE FALCON

The first Sam Spade book
*THE GLASS KEY, *1931**
*THE ADVENTURES OF SAM SPADE, *1944**

1930   David Frome   THE HAMMERSMITH MURDERS

The first Mr. Pinkerton book

1931   Stuart Palmer   *THE PENGUIN POOL MURDER

The first Hildegarde Withers book

1931   Francis Beeding   *DEATH WALKS IN EASTREPPS

Vincent Starrett considers this book "one of the ten greatest detective novels."

1931   Glen Trevor (James Hilton) *MURDER AT SCHOOL (U. S. title: WAS IT MURDER?, *1933*)

1931   Damon Runyon   *GUYS AND DOLLS

1931   Phoebe Atwood Taylor   THE CAPE COD MYSTERY

The first Asey Mayo book

1932   R. A. J. Walling   THE FATAL FIVE MINUTES

1932   Clemence Dane and Helen Simpson   RE-ENTER SIR JOHN

1933   Erle Stanley Gardner   *THE CASE OF THE VELVET CLAWS

The first Perry Mason book
THE CASE OF THE SULKY GIRL, *1933*

1934   Margery Allingham   DEATH OF A GHOST

1934   James M. Cain   *THE POSTMAN ALWAYS RINGS TWICE

1934   Rex Stout   FER-DE-LANCE

The first Nero Wolfe book
*THE LEAGUE OF FRIGHTENED MEN, *1935**

1935   Richard Hull   THE MURDER OF MY AUNT

1935 John P. Marquand   *No Hero
      The first Mr. Moto book

1938 John Dickson Carr   The Crooked Hinge
      [Carter Dickson]   The Judas Window, *1938*
           *The Curse of the Bronze Lamp, *1945*
           (English title: Lord of the Sorcerers, *1946*)

In his original list, Mr. Haycraft chose The Arabian Nights Murder *by Carr and* The Plague Court Murders *by Dickson; but on page 493 of his* The Art of the Mystery Story *Mr. Haycraft wrote: "After careful, and possibly maturer, re-reading I beg to change my vote" to* The Crooked Hinge *and* The Judas Window

1938 Nicholas Blake   The Beast Must Die

1938 Michael Innes   Lament for a Maker

1938 Clayton Rawson   *Death from a Top Hat
      The first Great Merlini book

1938 Graham Greene   *Brighton Rock

1938 Daphne Du Maurier   *Rebecca

1938 Mabel Seeley   The Listening House

1939 Ngaio Marsh   Overture to Death

1939 Eric Ambler   A Coffin for Dimitrios (English title: The Mask of Dimitrios)

1939 Raymond Chandler   The Big Sleep *or*
      The first Philip Marlowe book
           Farewell, My Lovely, *1940*

1939 Georges Simenon   The Patience of Maigret

1940 Raymond Postgate   Verdict of Twelve

1940	Frances and Richard Lockridge	THE NORTHS MEET MURDER
1940	Dorothy B. Hughes	THE SO BLUE MARBLE *or* IN A LONELY PLACE, *1947*
1940	Cornell Woolrich [William Irish]	*THE BRIDE WORE BLACK PHANTOM LADY, *1942*
1940	Manning Coles	DRINK TO YESTERDAY A TOAST TO TOMORROW, *1941* (English title: PRAY SILENCE, *1940*)

The first two Tommy Hambledon books

1941	H. F. Heard	*A TASTE FOR HONEY
1941	Craig Rice	TRIAL BY FURY *or* HOME SWEET HOMICIDE, *1944*
1942	H. H. Holmes (Anthony Boucher)	*ROCKET TO THE MORGUE
1942	James Gould Cozzens	*THE JUST AND THE UNJUST
1944	Hilda Lawrence	BLOOD UPON THE SNOW
1946	Helen Eustis	THE HORIZONTAL MAN
1946	Charlotte Armstrong	*THE UNSUSPECTED
1946	Lillian de la Torre	*DR. SAM: JOHNSON, DETECTOR
1946	Edmund Crispin	THE MOVING TOYSHOP *or* LOVE LIES BLEEDING, *1948*
1947	Edgar Lustgarten	ONE MORE UNFORTUNATE (English title: A CASE TO ANSWER)
1947	Roy Vickers	*THE DEPARTMENT OF DEAD ENDS
1948	Josephine Tey	THE FRANCHISE AFFAIR
1948	William Faulkner	*INTRUDER IN THE DUST

All illustrations appear after page 394.

CHAPTER I

Time: 1841—Place: America

(*Genesis*)

It will be found that the ingenious are always fanciful, and the *truly* imaginative never otherwise than analytic.—EDGAR ALLAN POE, "The Murders in the Rue Morgue"

. . .

As poet *and* mathematician, he could reason well; as mere mathematician he could not have reasoned at all.—EDGAR ALLAN POE, "The Purloined Letter"

. . .

The history of the detective story begins with the publication of "The Murders in the Rue Morgue."—BRANDER MATTHEWS.

I

TIPPECANOE (and Tyler, too) had triumphed at the polls, in an exciting spectacle of red fire and illuminated log cabins. Pigs annoyed visiting European celebrities in the streets of the largest cities. Respectable burghers nodded of an evening over the verses of Mr. Longfellow and the novels of Mr. Paulding and Mr. Simms. Their good wives scanned the pages of *Godey's, The Gift,* and *The Token;* the children had been put to sleep (rather readily, one imagines) with the indubitably instructive works of Peter

Parley. "Society" danced polkas and Prince Albert waltzes, blew its nose on its fingers, and applauded with genteel kid gloves the rival pomposities of Edwin Forrest and Junius Booth. "Elegance" was the watchword of the day. Meanwhile, enterprising tradesmen turned handsome profits in Mineral Teeth, Pile Electuaries, Chinese Hair Eradicators, and Swedish Leeches. Still-new-fangled steam carriages jiggled and bounced adventurously between the more populous centers. The *Great Western* and her sister express packets (now only two weeks the crossing) brought all the news from abroad and the latest British romances for church-going publishers to pirate. In New York, Horace Greeley was busy founding his *Tribune*. In the White House, his term of office but a month old, William Henry Harrison lay already dying—carrying with him a struggling young author's hopes for political preferment. Mr. Brady was soon to open his Daguerrian Gallery. Mr. Morse had forsaken his fashionable portraits to tinker in seclusion with a queer contraption of keys and wires. And on the distant Illinois sod a lanky young giant was riding his first law circuits.

In short—America in 1841.

Philadelphia was a-tingle with the pleasurable sensations of a literary revival. Frankly commercial, often hopelessly lacking in taste, this renaissance nevertheless wore the face of popular and democratic revolt. The concept of "literature" for the few was giving way to the idea of "reading" for the many. Since the days of Ben Franklin, William Penn's city had been famous as a printing center. Now it was realizing its assets. The golden age of cheap magazine publishing was beginning, and Philadelphia was its American Athens. Here were printers and popular journals: the Carey and Lea firms, *Godey's, Atkinson's*, the *Gentleman's, Graham's, Alexander's*, the *Saturday Evening Post*, the *Dollar Newspaper*—among many. Here were editors: Burton, Godey, Graham, the Petersons, Mrs. Hale, the "Reverend" Griswold. Here were artists and engravers: Sully, Sartain, Darley, Neagle, and a host of lesser names. Here were writers of all descriptions: R. M. Bird, T. S. Arthur, Eliza Leslie, "Grace Greenwood," Willis Gaylord Clark, Captain Mayne Reid, George Lippard, "Judge" Conrad, Henry Beck Hirst, "Penn" Smith, Jane and Sumner Fairfield, Joseph and Alice Neal, Thomas Dunn English. And—like a stray cock-pheasant in a sedate domestic fowlyard—Edgar Allan Poe, age thirty-two; critic, poet, and story-teller, currently the guiding editor of *Graham's*.

Tragic Israfel was now at flood tide of success and happiness. The statement is relative and requires explanation. In return for his editorial duties at *Graham's*, Poe was receiving the startling salary of eight hundred dollars a year—more than he ever earned before or afterward. His child-wife, Virginia, was temporarily in good health, as was Poe himself. His salary enabled him for the first, and only, time to provide the necessities of life regularly, and even to add such luxuries as a harp and a tiny piano for Virginia. Faithful, harassed "Muddie" Clemm (Virginia's mother and Poe's foster-mother, surely one of the longest-suffering and noblest women in literary history) could smile for once as she went about her tasks as materfamilias of the little household. Her "Eddie's" bulging head was full of plans for a periodical of his own. Meanwhile, under his editorship *Graham's* became the world's first mass-circulation magazine, leaping in a few short months from a conventional five thousand readers to an unprecedented forty thousand. Poe's own writings were of a uniformly higher standard and greater number than at any other point in his career. The cream of them he contributed to *Graham's,* and they had a large share in its success. An inspiring if unmethodical editor, as well as the most imaginative and stimulating intellect of his time and place, Poe in his own works constantly pointed the way to new fields.

Crime had early claimed his attention. So had puzzles. In *Graham's* for April, 1841, he joined them together. The terrified dreamer of "The Tell-Tale Heart" and "The Fall of the House of Usher" met the analytic solver of cryptograms, the astute completer of *Barnaby Rudge,* on common soil. The result was a new type of tale.

It was a tale of crime, but it was also a tale of ratiocination. It had a brutal murder for its subject, but it had a paragon of crisp logic for its hero. It was "The Murders in the Rue Morgue."

It was the world's first detective story.

II

Puzzle stories, mystery stories, crime stories, and stories of deduction and analysis have existed since the earliest times—and the detective story is closely related to them all. Yet the detective story itself is purely a development of the modern age. Chronologically, it could not have been otherwise.

For the essential theme of the detective story is professional detection of crime. This is its raison d'être, the distinguishing element that makes it a detective story and sets it apart from its "cousins" in the puzzle family. Clearly, there could be no detective *stories* (and there were none) until there were *detectives*. This did not occur until the nineteenth century.

Early civilizations had no police at all in the modern sense of the word. Crime suppression (what there was of it) was a side job of the military, with a little help from private guards. Both relied on bludgeons rather than brains for the meager results they achieved. Consequently, most felony went unpunished. When malefactors grew too audacious, the handiest luckless suspect was gibbeted, roasted, or garroted as an example; and authority was perforce satisfied.

Such crude methods could be effective, of course, only as long as entire nations lived under what to-day would be regarded as martial law. As the complex way of life we call modern civilization gradually developed, the weakness as well as the brutality of the system became increasingly apparent. Enlightened men began to realize that only by methodical apprehension and just punishment of *actual* offenders could crime be adequately curbed and controlled.

So torture slowly gave way to proof, ordeal to evidence, the rack and the thumb-screw to the trained investigator.

And once the investigator had fully arrived, the detective *story* followed, as a matter of course.

This would all seem to be sufficiently plain. Yet a curious misconception regarding the origin of detective fiction has gained currency in recent years. The foundations of this error lie chiefly in the presence of deductive and analytical tales in some of the ancient literatures. This ancestral resemblance (at most) has misled certain otherwise estimable writers, who really should know better, into "discovering" detective stories in Herodotus and the Bible and kindred sources. Fascinating as this game doubtless is, the thoughtful reader can have but scant patience with so manifest a confusion of terms. For the deductive method is only one of a number of elements that make up detection, and to mistake the part for the whole is simply to be guilty of non distributio medii. It would be quite as logical to maintain that the primitive pipings of the Aegean shepherds were symphonies—because the modern symphony includes passages for reed instruments in its scores! As the symphony began with Haydn, so did the detective story begin with Poe. Like everything else in this world, both had precursors; but no useful purpose is served by trying to prove that either flourished before it did or could. The best and final word on the matter has been said by the English bibliophile George Bates: "The cause of Chaucer's silence on the subject of airplanes was because he had never seen one. You cannot write about policemen before policemen exist to be written of."

It is no more than fair to note, however, that the puzzle tales which have come down to us from the comparatively advanced Hellenic and Hebraic civilizations bear a closer *resemblance* to the present-day detective story than do the puzzle tales of any other age before modern times. This circumstance would seem to foreshadow the sharply parallel development of the detective story and the democratic processes: a fascinating subject in itself, which is more fully discussed in Chapter XV of this book.

The first systematic experiments in professional crime-detection were naturally made in the largest centers of population, where the need was greatest. And so the early 1800's saw the growth of criminal investigation departments in the police systems of great metropolises, such as Paris and London. In Paris it was the Sûreté; in London, the Bow Street Runners, followed by Scotland Yard. The men who made up these organizations were the first "detectives," although the term itself was not used until some years later. (According to the Oxford Dictionary the earliest discovered appearance of the word *in print* occurred in 1843, but it was probably in spoken circulation considerably before that date.)

Lurid "memoirs" of the Bow Street Runners had begun to appear in England as early as 1827. And in 1829 the romantic "autobiography" of François Eugène Vidocq, lately of the Sûreté, reached the Paris book-stalls. From about 1830, therefore, it was solely a question of time before the first avowedly fictional detective story would be written. The only surprising circumstance is that it was written by an American, for American police methods at the time were notoriously laggard. The explanation almost certainly rests in Poe's lifelong interest in France and the French: an admiration generously reciprocated by that people in later years. (They have finally stopped writing it "Poë," heaven be thanked!) For, significantly, all Poe's detective tales are laid in Paris and display a remarkable knowledge of the city and its police system. Some chroniclers have gone so far as to suggest that Poe's "lost year," 1832, was spent in France; this, however, can not be accepted without more convincing proof than has yet been discovered. Other critics have ascribed the verisimilitude of the stories to close familiarity with Vidocq's *Mémoires*—which were also to serve Émile Gaboriau so faithfully a quarter of a century later. That Poe was thoroughly conversant with this work there can be no doubt. The extent of his indebtedness will be discussed later when the sources of his detective fiction are examined in detail.

A question of greater interest at the present point is the human paradox that led Poe—the avowed apostle of the morbid and grotesque—to forsake his tortured fantasies, even briefly, for the cool logic of the detective story.

Poe revealed his inner mind in his writings as have few authors in history. And what a mental chamber of terrors that mind was! Horror piles on horror in his early (and later) tales; blood, unnatural lust, madness, death— always death—fill his pages and the "haunted palace" of his brain. Why, then, this sea-change in mid-career, this brief return to temperate realms? Certain events in 1840 had conspired to this end. Poe's periodic jousts with his earthly demons are too well known to need description here. They had at least contributed to his dismissal from the editorship of William Burton's *Gentleman's Magazine*. This disappointment led to additional falls from grace and, eventually, to complete collapse and delirium. At length Poe awoke from the fever, weak but clearer than he had been in months and in a distinctly "morning after" frame of mind. At this opportune moment came prosy, kindly George Graham with his tender of a new editorship—provided the poet would make certain practical guaranties of behavior. A creature of extremes, Poe's reaction was swift and typical. He would accept

Graham's offer and forswear the world of emotion for the sedater climes of reason.

All through Poe's fiction runs his hero—himself. In the earlier tales the hero is a tormented and guilt-driven wretch. Now, by a process of readily understandable rationalization, the puppet reflects the change in the master: he becomes the perfect reasoner, the embodiment of logic, the champion of mind over matter. Instead of bathing insanely in hideous crime, the new protagonist crisply hunts it down. He demonstrates his superiority over ordinary men by scornfully beating them at their own game; by solving with ease the problems which seem to them so baffling. In brief, he is—AUGUSTE DUPIN.

There is assuredly much to be said for Joseph Wood Krutch's brilliant over-simplification: "Poe invented the detective story that he might not go mad."

Men still read them for the same reason to-day.

III

Edgar Allan Poe wrote only three detective stories: "The Murders in the Rue Morgue," "The Mystery of Marie Rogêt," and "The Purloined Letter."

A fourth tale of Poe's, "The Gold Bug," is often carelessly miscalled a detective story. It is a fine story, a masterpiece of mystery and even of analysis—but it is not a detective story for the simple reason that every shred of the evidence on which Legrand's brilliant deductions are based is withheld from the reader until *after* the solution is disclosed! The same objection excludes still another Poe tale, "Thou Art the Man," which, in point of fact, comes much closer structurally to qualifying than

"The Gold Bug." But here again it is the concealment of essential evidence—in this case the all-important factor of the bullet which passed *through* the horse—that rules the story out of court. Judged by any purely literary standards, "Thou Art the Man" is one of Poe's saddest débâcles, for reasons which have no place here; but as a startling prognostication of the mechanics of the present-day detective story it is far too little appreciated.* In addition to the determinative point of evidence already referred to—surely the earliest bona-fide employment of the favorite physical-circumstantial clue—it is remarkable for the following "firsts," at least as applies to the modern tale of crime-cum-detection: the first complete if exceedingly awkward use of the least-likely-person theme; the first instance of the scattering of false clues by the real criminal; and the first extortion of confession by means of the psychological third degree (dependent, in turn, on two lesser devices making their earliest detectival appearance, ventriloquism and the display of the corpse). A correspondent, who prefers to remain anonymous, declares: "My guess is that if Poe hadn't written the three great masterpieces, later-day critics would be doing handsprings over 'Thou Art the Man' as an amaz-

---

* So little is it known, in fact, that when an almost identical central device was employed in a short story a few years ago by the young men who write the excellent ELLERY QUEEN adventures, the resemblance went unnoticed by all reviewers, some of whom praised the ingenuity of the device, and by several thousand readers. It was even, the present writer is reliably assured, unsuspected by the authors themselves until one of them picked up Poe's tale for the first time several months later! The best proof of the anecdote, if any is needed, is that it would remain still a secret to-day save for this gratuitous and good-natured revelation by the Messrs. Queen. The little episode is hereby presented, with compliments, to Vincent Starrett, to add to his collection of unconscious or "psychic" plagiaries.

ing and trail-blazing tour de force." But for Poe's single slip in withholding the vitally conclusive point of evidence —coupled with the tale's unfortunate narrative style— this might still be the case. Detective story or not, it is worth the collateral attention of all serious students of the form equally with the more familiar yarn of Captain Kidd's cipher and the shiny scarabæus.

Before leaving this brief consideration of Poe's more incidental contributions, it is not without some chronological importance to note that virtually all his secondary ratiocinative efforts, including the two tales just mentioned and his analytical treatises on *Barnaby Rudge* and cryptography, were written during approximately the same years as were occupied by "The Rue Morgue," "Marie Rogêt," and "The Purloined Letter." Only the essay on Maelzel's Chess Player belongs to another, and earlier, period.

Poe's three detective tales proper are remarkable in many respects. Not their least extraordinary feature is the almost uncanny fashion in which these three early attempts, totalling only a few thousand words, established once and for all the mold and pattern for the thousands upon thousands of works of police fiction which have followed. The first tale exemplified, loosely, the *physical* type of the detective story. In the second, Poe reverted to the opposite extreme of the purely *mental*. Finding this (presumably) equally unsatisfactory, the artist in him led, inescapably, in the third story to the *balanced* type. Thus, swiftly, and in the brief compass of only three slight narratives, he foretold the entire evolution of the detective romance as a literary form. The types may be.

and of course constantly are, varied and combined, but the essential outline remains unchanged to-day.

Equally prophetic and embracing were Poe's contributions to the internal structure of the genre. In the very first tale he proceeded to lay down the two great concepts upon which all fictional detection worth the name has been based: (1) That the solvability of a case varies in proportion to its outré character. (2) The famous dictum-by-inference (as best phrased by Dorothy Sayers) that "when you have eliminated all the impossibilities, then, whatever remains, however improbable, must be the truth," which has been relied on and often re-stated by all the better sleuths in the decades that have followed. As for the almost infinite minutiæ, time-hallowed to-day, which Poe created virtually with a single stroke of the pen, only a suggestive catalogue need be given. The transcendent and eccentric detective; the admiring and slightly stupid foil; the well-intentioned blundering and unimaginativeness of the official guardians of the law; the locked-room convention; the pointing finger of unjust suspicion; the solution by surprise; deduction by putting one's self in another's position (now called psychology); concealment by means of the ultra-obvious; the staged ruse to force the culprit's hand; even the expansive and condescending explanation when the chase is done: all these sprang full-panoplied from the buzzing brain and lofty brow of the Philadelphia editor. In fact, it is not too much to say—except, possibly, for the influence of latter-day science—that nothing really primary has been added either to the framework of the detective story or to its internals since Poe completed his trilogy. Manners, styles, specific devices may change—but the

great principles remain where Poe laid them down and
left them. Unlike Boy Blue's toys, however, they gather
no dust!

As Philip Van Doren Stern has well said: "Like printing, the detective story has been improved upon only in a
mechanical way since it was first invented; as artistic
products, Gutenberg's Bible and Poe's 'The Murders in
the Rue Morgue' have never been surpassed."

IV

"The Murders in the Rue Morgue," chronologically
the first of Poe's detective stories, was called in the original draft "The Murders in the Rue Trianon Bas," but
happily the more "suggestive" title (to quote a contemporary writer) was substituted before publication. The
circumstance must surely rank high among the magnificent afterthoughts of literature. (How the original manuscript was preserved by chance and rescued for posterity almost half a century after it was written is one
of the fascinating and oft-told legends of American bib-
liophily, which, however, can not occupy us here. It has
been related in print by Dr. A. S. W. Rosenbach and
others.) "The Rue Morgue" made three principal appearances in type in its author's lifetime. First, in
Graham's for April, 1841. Second, as the only number of
a still-born cheap-leaflet series of *The Prose Romances
of Edgar A. Poe* (1843) which has become one of the
greatest rarities of Americana-collecting: published at
twelve and one-half cents, copies have sold in recent
years for as much as twenty-five thousand dollars. And
third, in the 1845 *Tales,* edited by Evert A. Duyckinck.

It was also included, of course, in the "Griswold Edition" of the Collected Works, published in 1850. In addition to these American publications, at least three unauthorized French translations of the tale are known to have appeared in the 1840's.* In an era of international literary freebooting, Poe neither received nor expected any remuneration for them. It may be doubted, in fact, that the world's first detective story ever brought its author a penny in direct financial return—for Poe was the salaried editor of *Graham's* when "The Murders in the Rue Morgue" first appeared; the 1843 leaflet and the 1845 *Tales* alike were failures;† and Israfel was no more when the Griswold collection was issued. Ironically, in the years since Poe's death, the tale has been reprinted with a frequency which, under modern royalty and copyright engagements, would have netted the ill-fed poet a sizable fortune from this single effort; to say nothing of the untold millions which have accrued to his imitators and followers.

These reprints, however, have served to make the paragraphs of "The Murders in the Rue Morgue" thrice-familiar to every school-boy. The story opens with a brilliant but to-day rather outmoded essay on the philosophy of analysis. At length the author introduces

* For an accurate account of this highly involved and usually misunderstood business, see C. P. Cambiaire, *The Influence of Edgar Allan Poe in France* (New York, G. E. Stechert & Co., 1927).

† It would indeed have made little difference to Poe in any immediate financial sense had they been successful. The terms between the author and his publishers virtually pass belief. There is preserved a singularly pathetic letter dated August 13, 1841, from Poe to the Messrs. Lea and Blanchard, proposing (unfruitfully) a volume of tales to include the recent "Rue Morgue," in which he says: "I should be glad to accept the terms you allowed me before—that is—you receive all profits, and allow me twenty copies for distribution to friends"!

his hero, the eccentric and impoverished Chevalier, DUPIN, and his anonymous companion and chronicler, the first of a thousand wondering Watsons. We join in their home-life, if their curious insistence on turning day into night may be designated by so domestic a term, and marvel dutifully with the narrator at DUPIN's powers of deduction. Finally and belatedly, Plot raises its head. A hundred years of imitation have rendered the remainder of the story so much formula: the preliminary account of the crime; the visit to the scene; DUPIN's satisfaction with what he finds, his companion's blank mystification; the methodical stupidity of the official police; the dénouement, arranged by the detective; the inevitable explanation.

Made trite by numberless repetitions, it is yet singularly satisfying.

The reasons why "The Murders in the Rue Morgue" is classified as belonging to the *physical* school of detective story writing may not at once be clear—for the proportions of plot and deduction seem roughly equal in the narrative. Reader, try a simple test for yourself. Without looking at the text, attempt to recall the story, which in all probability you haven't read since school-days. What details stand out most vividly in your mind? The chances are ten to one you will form a mental picture of the murderous ape clutching his victim by the hair, or some related gory incident. Now, ask yourself: *by what train of reasoning* did the detective arrive at his solution? Unless you are a specialist, the same odds prevail that you will not be able to recall. In other words, the story is really dominated by sensational physical event—not by detection, excellently as Poe conceived it.

Poe's second detective story was distinctly a roman à clef. In July, 1841, a beautiful young girl named Mary Cecilia Rogers was murdered in New York under particularly involved and baffling circumstances. If contemporary accounts may be credited, the police bungled the investigation miserably. Poe was frankly contemptuous of their efforts, and more than hinted that he wrote "The Mystery of Marie Rogêt" to expose their ineptitude. For convenience he laid the scene in Paris and put his thoughts into the mouth of DUPIN. The characters were only thinly disguised, however, and in all later publications the story has been printed with footnotes openly identifying the actors, streets, newspapers, and the like with their true American names. Unfortunately, the real crime was never solved (contrary to popular misconception), and we have no means of verifying the soundness of Poe's deductions. The story appeared in three instalments in *Snowden's Ladies' Companion* (of all places!) for November and December, 1842, and February, 1843, and was republished in the *Tales* (1845) and the posthumous Works (1850).*

This longest of Poe's three major excursions into detective literature is, unhappily, the least deserving of detailed attention. It might better be called an essay than a story. As an essay, it is an able if tedious exercise in reasoning. As a story, it scarcely exists. It has no lifeblood. The characters neither move nor speak. They are

* The Mary Rogers legend has been retold by innumerable later writers, with varying degrees of success, and both the crime and Poe's analysis of it have been the subject of much and usually erroneous speculation. For a really scholarly and reliable account of the whole matter, the interested reader is referred to a study by William Kurtz Wimsatt, Jr., of Yale University: "Poe and the Mystery of Mary Rogers" (*Publications of the Modern Language Association*, March, 1941).

present only through second-hand newspaper accounts. A good three-quarters of the work is occupied with Du-pin's (which is to say Poe's) reasoning from the evidence. Only a professional student of analytics or an inveterate devotee of criminology can read it with any degree of unfeigned interest. Applying our simple test again: practically no ordinary reader can relate from memory *either* the facts of the crime *or* the steps by which the detective reaches his rather qualified conclusion. This is the hallmark of the too involved, too dry, too *mental* detective story—and its confession of weakness.

We come now to the last, best, and most interesting historically and bibliographically of Poe's three detective stories.

As the 1840's marked the beginning of the magazine age, so, too, they denoted the crest of an earlier movement in the direction of popular literature: that now forgotten institution, the "gift book" or "literary annual." The gift annual was undeniably commercial and often pretentious, and largely for these reasons it has been slighted by purists. Yet between its gilded calf and morocco covers appeared some of the best work (as well as some of the worst) of the leading writers and artists of the day. Its fees were generous for the times and had the further pleasant effect of coaxing magazine rates upwards to keep pace. And its format, paper, typography, and "embellishments" were in the main far above the era's drab standards of bookmaking.

The American gift annual was customarily published in the autumn months, in advance of the holiday season, and was dated for the *following* year. It is important to understand this circumstance, because one of the most

baseless errors of contemporary bibliography has grown
up around failure to remember it: the habit, even among
eminent authorities, of assigning the initial publication of
Poe's finest detective story to Britain rather than America. (Just why certain *American* bibliophiles should take
the apparent pleasure in the supposed occurrence that
some of them have displayed—while not strictly pertinent
to the present examination—is a puzzle in itself.)

Briefly, the history of the matter is this:

The apex of American gift-annual publishing, by common consent of connoisseurs, was reached in *The Gift:
1845*. The product of the Philadelphia house of Carey and
Hart, this truly handsome volume numbered among its
contributors of prose and poetry such luminaries of the
era as Longfellow and Emerson (two poems each),
Charles Fenno Hoffman, Mrs. Sigourney, N. P. Willis,
Joseph C. Neal, H. T. Tuckerman, Mrs. Kirkland and
Mrs. Ellet, C. P. Cranch, F. H. Hedge, and others of
similar prominence. But, what is of greatest importance,
between pages 41 and 61, *The Gift's* purchasers or recip-
ients could devour (as they presumably chose to do)
"The Purloined Letter," by Edgar A. Poe, no stranger
to the buyers of Carey and Hart's gold-stamped yearly
volumes.

The misapprehension alluded to has occurred because,
at about the same time, solid British heads-of-household
were perusing a sadly abbreviated version of the tale in
that staunch parent of all penny-weeklies, *Chambers'
Edinburgh Journal,* in its issue for November 30, 1844.
This condensation was preceded by an explanatory paragraph so commonly—or wilfully!—overlooked to-day as
to warrant verbatim quotation here:

'THE GIFT'

THE GIFT is an American annual of great typographical excellence, and embellished with many beautiful engravings. It
contains an article which, for several reasons, appears to us so
remarkable, that we leave aside several effusions of our ordinary
contributors to make room for *an abridgment of it.* [Italics
supplied.] The writer, Mr. Edgar A. Poe, is evidently an acute
observer of mental phenomena; and we have him to thank for
one of the aptest illustrations which could well be conceived,
of that curious play of two minds, in which one person, let us
call him A., guesses what another, B., will do, judging that B.
will adopt a particular line of policy to circumvent A. [Poe's
"article" then follows, with its title in smaller type.]

Certainly this unequivocal language would seem to
dispose for all time of the question of priority. Yet within
the present decade a London private press has had the
effrontery to reprint the *Chambers'* abridgment as a
veritable reproduction of the "first publication" of the
story—significantly *omitting* the introductory paragraph!
(This precious bit of spuriosa even misquotes the source
of its "find": ascribing the story to "Chambers' Edinburgh Magazine, November, 1844.") Still more puzzling
is the passive support which has been given to the same
fallacy by several first-rank American Poe-scholars, when
a little obvious if tedious spade-work to ascertain the
publication date of *The Gift* would have removed any
conceivable doubts left by the language of the *Chambers'*
note. The qualified authorities having neglected this duty,
it falls to the present writer to report that *The Gift: 1845*
was "noticed" in at least one American magazine (the
Democratic Review) as early as September, 1844; that
on October 4, 1844, the New York *Tribune* honored it

with a laudatory first-page review more than a column in length; and that its publication was chronicled in autumnal issues of virtually all the leading American periodicals, among them the *Knickerbocker, Peterson's, Graham's,* and *Godey's,* all published many weeks before the transatlantic readers of *Chambers'* were digesting their abridgment on November 30th. On the basis of these incontestable facts, it may now be stated for the first time beyond any reasonable doubt that the Philadelphia publication of "The Purloined Letter" preceded the Edinburgh condensation by approximately two months.*

Bibliography aside, this third detective story of Poe's is far and away the most satisfying, structurally and aesthetically, of the trio. It is simpler, shorter, more compact, more certain of itself than the earlier two. Its quiet superiority appears from the moment it begins. Here is no delayed approach to the subject. A few lines suffice to set the stage, and more plausibly, more naturally than before. DUPIN and his companion sit in their book-closet, *au troisième* (as Poe wrote it), *No. 33, Rue Dunôt, Faubourg St. Germain,* "enjoying the two-fold luxury of meditation and a meerschaum." (How miraculously near is Baker Street!) Almost immediately Prefect G—— enters. The give-and-take of normal conversation replaces the stiff press-cuttings of the earlier tales in revealing the essential facts of the problem. (That is, in the American original. The *Chambers'* abridgment has been squeezed almost as bloodless as "Marie Rogêt.") DUPIN and the Prefect end their colloquy and the latter goes

* For a more extended consideration of this matter, together with some additional points of technical interest, the bibliographically inclined reader is referred to the special Appendix at the end of this volume.

his way. A month later he returns. DUPIN hands him the letter and revels in his open-mouthed astonishment. DU-PIN's explanation to his bewildered comrade follows. A little too detailed, perhaps, for modern tastes ("a little *too* self-evident"), it is nonetheless a true manual of detective logic. The conclusion, moreover, has a mellow touch of humor and humanity lacking in the previous stories. We discover a reluctant fondness for the originally glacial Chevalier as he thaws to mortal vanity and malice for the first time.

To be completely fair, however, we must admit that the tale contains also the one serious logical flaw committed by Poe in the series. As a number of writers have pointed out, DUPIN could not possibly have seen at one and the same time (as he claimed he did) *both* the seal and the address, that is to say both the front and back, of the letter. Even apart from this, the minuteness of his observations—seated as he was across the room, and peering through green spectacles—bespeaks surely one of the most remarkable visions ever recorded!

Our test must serve once more. This time the odds favor the author. Almost every one who has ever read the story can recall something of both essential phases—detection and event. Almost all readers remember DU-PIN's deduction that the letter was hidden by not being hidden at all (still a favorite gambit of the craft); and his ruse of the staged street disturbance to acquire the document (a plot-device directly appropriated by Conan Doyle half a century later in "A Scandal in Bohemia").

Here, at last, we have the *balanced* type—the detective story at its best.

V

Few American authors have undergone such minute inspection and dissection at the hands of scholarship as has Poe. Yet the literary scalpel-wielders have been strangely neglectful of the sources of his detective fiction. Aside from the obvious identifications of "Marie Rogêt," only a few minor "points" have been established. In Pauline Dubourg, the laundress of "The Murders in the Rue Morgue," Hervey Allen (that most readable of Poe biographers) has discovered the name of the maiden-proprietresses of the boarding-school which Poe attended during his boyhood stay in England. (But no one seems to have noted the further occurrence of a *Rue Dubourg* in the latter part of the tale: a repetition so foreign to Poe's usual meticulous workmanship as to suggest a concealed significance.) And some scholars contend that the episode of the escaped orang-outang in the same story grew out of a contemporary incident reported in American newspapers, while others believe that Poe drew on similar material in Scott's *Count Robert of Paris*. But one scans the academic journals in vain for light on so intriguing a problem—for example—as the origin of the first fictional detective's name. (Concerning Dupin's *person* there is no mystery. Unless all perception fails, he can be only Poe's mental self-portrait of the moment in French dress.)

How *did* Poe come to name his hero Dupin? The question may never be finally answered, but the author left at least one important clue when he described his Chevalier as "of an excellent, indeed of an illustrious family." For the name Dupin has in truth been a notable one in

French history. The reader may, if he chooses, discover in the standard French encyclopedias no less than twelve prominent real-life Dupins dating from the fourteenth century to Poe's own years; including several of the presumptive ancestors of George Sand—born herself, a trifle dubiously perhaps, to the *nom*. Of this substantial number of eminent flesh-and-blood bearers of the name, two were even more outstanding than the rest. Both were, suggestively, contemporaries of Poe. Furthermore, they were brothers: André Marie Jean Jacques (1783-1865) and François Charles Pierre (1784-1873). André, the elder, was a statesman of ministerial rank who held the office of Procureur-Général and other high governmental posts for the better part of a generation despite turbulent changes of party and dynasty: a feat which called for no slight degree of political agility—to employ the kindest phrase. As President of the Chamber of Deputies from 1832 to 1840 he was at the pinnacle of his career and consequently prominent in the native and foreign prints during the years immediately preceding Poe's creation of his fictional hero. Besides, André Dupin was a prolific writer on a variety of subjects: among them, French criminal procedure. Several of his works were translated into English; one translation, in fact, was published in Boston in 1839. That his name was familiar to Poe can hardly be doubted. The younger brother (commonly called Charles) was a noted mathematician and economist who also held public office from time to time and was created a baron for his services. His was an even more versatile pen than André's, and he was known to the English-speaking world through numerous translations covering a wide range of topics.

Almost inescapably these brief personal histories will have reminded the informed Poe-student of the Minister D——, the talented villain of "The Purloined Letter." D——, it will be recalled, was not only an accomplished and unscrupulous political intriguant, but, as Poe made a special point of saying, a man-of-letters as well—both "poet *and* mathematician." Moreover, he possessed a brother who had also a "reputation in letters." The parallel is by no means exact, and one would not wish to place too much emphasis on what after all may have been only a coincidence. Yet, in the dual circumstance of Poe's appropriation of the name and his adaptation of the characteristics of the real brothers Dupin, the veriest psychological tyro will be quick to scent a highly logical, if possibly unconscious, "transference." It is, at the least, a fascinating subject for speculation. Perhaps some scholar of the future will uncover more specific evidence: academic hoods have been awarded for contributions less notable!

Of Poe's indebtedness to Vidocq much has been written and more assumed. There can be no doubt that he was closely familiar with that worthy's exploits and memoirs, and that he drew on them for numerous details. But to identify DUPIN, the ageless symbol of amateurism, with Vidocq, the professional—as some critics have done—is to commit a most uncritical error and to miss the whole point and purpose of Poe's ratiocinative stories. For throughout the tales Poe hammers ceaselessly to drive home his acutely personalized thesis of the superiority of the talented amateur mind—meaning, of course, his own. Nowhere is this more graphically brought out than in the patronizing words he places in DUPIN's mouth near the conclusion of "The Rue Morgue." (This, incidentally, is Poe's sole reference to Vidocq in print.)

The Parisian police [DUPIN is made to say], so much extolled for their acumen, are cunning, but no more. Vidocq, for example, was a good guesser, and a persevering man. But, without educated thought, he erred continually by the very intensity of his investigations. He impaired his vision by holding the object too close. He might see, perhaps, one or two points with unusual clearness, but in so doing he, necessarily, lost sight of the matter as a whole. Thus there is such a thing as being too profound.

That the entire passage is a virtual ad hoc rendering of the quotation from Seneca which Poe later chose as the motto of "The Purloined Letter" (*Nil sapientiæ odiosius acumine nimio*) only shows how emphatic at all times was the distinction in his mind between amateur and professional, between DUPIN and Vidocq.

If an identification must be made: a good deal of Vidocq (or of Poe's opinion of him) will be found in the unflattering portrait of the Prefect G—— in the tales. As for DUPIN, he can clearly be no one but Poe— as Poe so obviously considered himself to be DUPIN.*

VI

"The Purloined Letter" was Poe's last detective story, although he lived five more years, to the age of forty.

* In a late issue of *The Pleasures of Publishing* (Columbia University Press, April 14, 1941) the eminent Poe scholar, Thomas Ollive Mabbott, is quoted as saying: "He [DUPIN] is Poe—plus an eccentric French historian I've recently run to earth, who turned day into night. I've been looking for such a character, found him last August." Dr. Mabbott's fuller revelation is anticipated with relish.

Too many historians have argued carelessly that he dropped the genre because it failed to arouse sufficient interest. This is not supported by the facts. While it is true that much of Poe's work was relatively unappreciated in his lifetime, there is no reason to believe that his detective stories suffered more than his fantasies or his poetry. In point of fact, the weight of evidence clearly indicates the opposite situation. Poe not only complained several times in personal correspondence that the public seemed to prefer his ratiocinative tales to what he chose to consider his worthier efforts—he also frequently traded on their popularity in his dealings with editors and publishers. Further, two of the three stories were accounted important enough to be reprinted abroad, in an era when American literature was held in such low esteem that very little of it crossed the water. One of them, even, was the first of his tales to be translated into French, and appeared in no less than three separate versions in that language before his death. And at home, barely a decade after Poe died, young William Dean Howells thought it significant praise to assert of a nominee for President of the United States:

> The bent of his mind is mathematical and metaphysical, and he is therefore pleased with the absolute and logical method of Poe's tales and sketches, in which the problem of mystery is given, and wrought out into everyday facts by processes of cunning analysis. It is said that he suffers no year to pass without a perusal of this author.

Abraham Lincoln subsequently confirmed the statement, which appeared in his little known "campaign biography" by Howells in 1860 and has escaped later attention almost entirely. The instance is chiefly notable, of course, for its revelation of a little suspected affinity between two great Americans—utterly dissimilar save that they shared the same birth year, and that each died tragically before his time. And it serves to establish Lincoln as the first of the countless eminent men who have turned to the detective story for stimulation and solace: a circumstance which also seems, curiously, to have eluded previous mention. At its least, the incident is striking evidence how broadly and powerfully Poe's detective sorcery had captured the popular imagination.

The true reasons for Poe's desertion of the form he created are found in his own life. After 1845 the poet's circumstances, uncertain enough at any time, became increasingly distressing. Little Virginia died. His own end (as he must have suspected) was near. He wrote progressively less, and that little showed a pronounced return to his early morbidity. The last years were a nightmare of poverty, disease, drink, and delusion. In such waking dread there simply was no room for a "perfect reasoner."

The final, shameful curtain fell on the tragedy in October, 1849.

To-day Poe's position in literature is more than secure. He is universally recognized as one of the few poets of consummate genius America has produced, and its finest writer (if not, indeed, the inventor) of the short story. Yet, had he published nothing but the three DUPIN tales, posterity would still award him an eminent and merited niche in Fame's corridors—as The Father of the Detective Story.

CHAPTER II

The In-Between Years

(Development)

Do you feel an uncomfortable heat at the pit of your stomach, sir? and a nasty thumping at the top of your head? I call it the detective fever.—WILKIE COLLINS, *The Moonstone*

I

IT IS a curious fact, deserving of attention by historians, that virtually all the detective stories worth the name have been produced by those (doubly fortunate!) nations that have longest enjoyed the privileges of democracy. The causes and implications of this highly interesting relationship are discussed fully in a later chapter (Chapter XV: "Dictators, Democrats, and Detectives"). For the present, suffice it to say that the relationship does exist, that it is no chance parallelism but direct and causative, and that it is intimately bound up with the whole body of civil and individual rights.

After Poe, the next significant appearance of the detective story occurred in France. This is not the time or the place to examine the violent, often tragic, history of democracy in France, its failures and resurgences, its hopes for the future. It is enough to know that the French love of liberty and the proclamation of civil rights under the First Republic gave direct rise, in the early 1800's, to the first police division organized solely and purposely for criminal investigation—the semi-municipal, quasi-national Sûreté Générale—and that somehow this body managed to survive the multitude of political changes in succeeding years to become one of the world's great crime bureaus. It was the Sûreté that gave the roman policier its next and direct impetus.

Of all the early agents of the Sûreté, the best remembered, if not necessarily the most important, was François Eugène Vidocq (1775-1857). The son of a poor baker, Vidocq became at an early age—if his lively reminiscences are to be credited—a thief, circus performer, vagabond, galley convict, and, above all, a jailbreaker without equal in the annals of crime. Never outside the pages of Dumas, whom he antedated and without much doubt inspired, were such breathless escapes, such gallantry, such daring. Suddenly the prince of felons became the king of thief-catchers, by the simple expedient of making a bargain with the legal authorities to place his wit, ingenuity, and chiefly his knowledge of the underworld at their disposal, in return for absolution of his own offenses. That this made him a sort of glorified "pigeon" seems to have bothered no one. (The plain truth is that he was probably neither the colossal rogue *nor* the great detective that he made himself out to be.) Nevertheless, he served the police for eighteen years and claimed to have placed 20,000 culprits behind the bars in that time. In 1827 he retired at the age of fifty-two, and in 1829 he published his *Mémoires,* in four volumes of better than four hundred pages each, crowding into his dramatic paragraphs more bizarre adventures than any one individual could conceivably have experienced in a single lifetime.

If Vidocq was the colorful liar that this work indicates —if the work itself, as seems only too likely, contained vastly more romance than fact—then perhaps he, rather than Poe, was the actual if fortuitous inventor of the detective story! Certainly, his accounts of his supposed exploits possess most of the essentials of modern detective fiction, with the natural exception of later scientific inventions. Aside from this interesting technical consideration, Vidocq played a major rôle in the genre merely by existing and writing. As Frank W. Chandler has said in his admirable study, *The Literature of Roguery:* "It was necessary that a Vidocq should issue his *Mémoires* for the literary transition from rogue to detective to be definitely effected." A whole generation of later writers became indebted to him as a source. Poe, as we have seen, knew his Vidocq well enough to dispute him; and scores of other authors drew on the *Mémoires* to a greater or lesser degree, including, among many, Hugo, Balzac, Dumas, Dickens, Collins, and Doyle. The fullest and most direct fictional expression of the Vidocq influence, however, occurred in the works of his compatriot, Émile Gaboriau.

II

Émile Gaboriau was born at Saujon, in the Charente-Inférieure, on November 9, 1833, the son of a notary. To escape becoming a lawyer, which his father wished him to be, he enlisted in the cavalry and in seven years advanced to the post of regimental sergeant-major. Despairing of further preferment, he left the army at the expiration of his term of enlistment and made his way to Paris, where he found employment as a clerk in a forwarding office (some authorities say a carriage factory). In his spare hours he earned a few welcome sous by writing mottoes for confectioners' cakes, and popular songs for street singers. Some chance verses addressed to Paul Féval, a popular feuilletonist of the time, brought him to Féval's attention, and he became the writer's secretary.

Now, the feuilleton—meaning literally "leaflet"—was a peculiarly French institution, a sort of "literary supplement" to the newspapers and journals of the day. Originally a hodgepodge of gossip, essays, criticism, puzzles, jokes, and the like, it came more and more to be used by struggling editors as a vehicle for maintaining circulation, by printing in serial form sensational novels of the yellow-back variety, turned out at white heat by literary hacks. Gaboriau's "secretaryship," we may readily imagine, consisted in what a less polite age would call "ghosting" for his hard-driven patron. When he was not writing he was haunting the police courts and the morgue in search of material for his master, whose specialty was the criminal romance.

Eventually the connections he had established enabled him to become a feuilletonist in his own right, and sometime in 1859 he began turning out daily instalments of lurid fiction under his own name for the half-penny press. Each episode had to be written exactly to length, and each was required to end with some suspenseful incident to carry over the reader's interest to the morrow. Gaboriau, in common with his fellow-slaves, wrote on sheets of paper cut to a determined size, with a messenger waiting in the hallway to carry each completed leaf to the printer. Thousands of words came from his pen each day, with no opportunity for revision. It is small wonder that he produced twenty-one novels in thirteen years. It is no more surprising that he died of exhaustion at thirty-nine, on September 28, 1873, just when he seemed to have achieved the ease and security to write as he pleased.

Seven typically artificial and not very successful novels of military and fashionable life had come from Gaboriau's too facile pen before *L'Affaire Lerouge* began its serial career in a dying newspaper called *Le Pays* in 1866. In the sense that it was the first story of novel length to employ detection as an important theme, it is perhaps entitled to the appellation "the first detective novel"— though it bears little resemblance to what we mean by the term to-day. (Of this distinction more will be said later.) *L'Affaire Lerouge* did not save *Le Pays,* which ungratefully proceeded to expire forthwith, but it did attract sufficient attention to win Gaboriau a contract with the newly founded *Petit Journal.* In the seven years that remained of his life he produced fourteen more novels, including four in which more or less detection figures: *Le Dossier 113* (1867), *Le Crime d'Orcival* (1868), *Monsieur Lecoq* (1869), and *Les Esclaves de Paris* (1869).

The reader will notice that a distinction has been implied between the full-blown detective novel, concerned with detection and nothing else, and the novel that merely makes use of detection as one of several themes. Gaboriau's tales all belong to the latter classification. When he sticks to detection, it is excellent detection indeed; but in no one of the five novels which have been named did he succeed in so limiting himself. In *Monsieur Lecoq*, which many critics consider his masterpiece, he put all the detection into the first volume, devoting the entire second half to the narration of a tedious family chronicle. The family, it may be noted in passing, is the basis of most of Gaboriau's novels, as it was of most French fiction of his time. Family scandal is at the bottom of virtually all the problems investigated by his detectives, and the feuilletonist who knew his concierge and shop-girl audience missed few opportunities such a subject presented for melodramatic digression. The proportion of detection is no greater in the other novels. Furthermore, the solution by the detective is seldom the apex of the story. There is no single rise of action to a grand dénouement. We know the guilty party before the book is half through, and from that point forward we read (if we are able!) another story, or several substories, about the same characters.

The chief detective of *L'Affaire Lerouge* is PÈRE TABARET (sometimes called "TIR-AU-CLAIR"), a wealthy bibliophile who finds his inspiration in the memoirs of police agents, thus continuing the Poe formula of the amateur dilettante of crime. Passing reference is made in the early chapters to a police subordinate called LECOQ, whose name and circumstances (he is stated to have entered the detective service after a criminal career) immediately suggest his kinship with Vidocq. So, too, do many of his methods in the later tales, particularly his adeptness at disguise.

LECOQ disappears from *L'Affaire Lerouge* after a few chapters (a distressing habit of feuilleton dummies) but returns to replace TABARET as the detective protagonist of the four remaining novels. Valentine Williams has given an appreciative description of his edifying effect on the turgid narratives: "Through the jostling throng of desperately wicked dukes, of incredibly noble maids, of *banquiers véreux,* Monsieur Lecoq, simple agent of the Sûreté, comes stepping, fresh as a bridegroom, *un beau gars, à l'oeil clair, à l'air résolu,* or, as casual visitors saw him in his careful disguise, a sober personage of distinguished appearance, with his gold spectacles, his white tie, his *mince redingote.* Against a canvas of tiresome puppets he stands out as a living figure." * Truly the stories come to life when Lecoq is on the stage. The difficulty is that he is too often in the wings or hiding behind false faces.

In the conflict, described by Williams, between LECOQ and his background, we find the key to Gaboriau's chief failure according to the standards of modern detective fiction. In his attempt to mix incompatible elements—the lurid unreality of the yellow-back and the cool logic of detection—he violates one of the prime requirements of the form: the semblance, at least, of plausibility. ("A sense of verisimilitude is essential to the detective novel." —Willard Huntington Wright.) The mésalliance he thus unwittingly and unfortunately began has persisted in the French detective story virtually to this day, to its undeniable detriment.†

* Valentine Williams, "Gaboriau: Father of Detective Novels," *National Review* (December, 1923).

† Some one has pointed out that—in addition to his direct leaning on Poe and Vidocq—Gaboriau derived in almost equal portions from two great opposites among his countrymen: Voltaire and his *Zadig,* and Eugène Sue, whose sensational mysteries had their greatest vogue a score of years earlier. As a matter of record, characters designated as detectives appear in some of the Sue stories; though it can scarcely be claimed that the acts they perform are detection, any more than, on the other hand, are Zadig's feats of abstract reasoning.

Nevertheless, Gaboriau's logic—when he does give it rein—is definitely of the better sort; it is only the backgrounds that are at fault. Many of LECOQ's devices are still in use to-day, although of course in altered and generally amplified form. His test to tell whether a bed has been slept in, the example of the striking clock to show that the hands have been set back—to mention but two— have been employed in principle at least by more fictional sleuths of a later day than one would care to estimate. There is nothing really new in LECOQ's reasoning; it stems directly from DUPIN. But Gaboriau, drawing on his well-filled police-court notebooks and on Vidocq's *Mémoires,* elaborated Poe's abstractions with fresh illustrations and variations. (SHERLOCK HOLMES, it is true, scorned LECOQ as "a miserable bungler." But in the same breath he dismissed DUPIN as "a very inferior fellow." For all his exemplary qualities, it is to be feared that the Baker Street seer was not immune to professional jealousy!)

Because of the diverse elements in Gaboriau, it is difficult to classify the ultimate result with any degree of exactitude. He presented plot and detection virtually as separate entities. On the former side, his work was purely *physical;* on the latter, almost as elaborately *mental* as "Marie Rogêt." The issue of this mismating was a *divided* rather than a *balanced* detective story. Any final evaluation of his contribution must therefore distinguish carefully between promise and achievement. By a paradox that would have appealed to his French mind, his reputation to-day rests largely on the fact that he is so seldom read! For Gaboriau is one of those authors whom everybody talks about but whose works (if the truth be told) are virtually unknown. Few modern readers would have the patience to abide the tawdry puppetry, the fustian, the cheap sensationalism, the dull and irrelevant digressions, the dreary and artificial verbiage that are the feuilletonist at his too-frequent worst, in order to get at the few grains of highly competent detection. This is perhaps as well, for (to continue the metaphor) the greatest value of the grain was its germinal quality.

Of the author himself, Valentine Williams has said the kindest and most understanding word: "Running through the coarse woof of plot and counter-plot which the concierges demanded from his stories for their daily sou, we may discern the scarlet thread of a brilliant mind." It is for this implied rather than fulfilled promise that the world honors Gaboriau; for this, and for the impetus he gave the detective story in his own time. Had he lived to write the works that he planned, his honors on both scores would almost certainly have been greater. Even as it is, generations of later detective story writers are in his debt. He blazed no really new trails, but he tilled in honest peasant fashion a great deal of virgin soil.

III

During almost identically the same years that Gaboriau was reintroducing the detective story to France, another young man, geographically removed by only a narrow channel of water, but oceans distant in literary stature, was making a single but memorable contribution to the genre in England.

William Wilkie Collins was born January 8, 1824, in Tavistock Square, London, the eldest son of William

Collins, R.A., a well-known artist. His younger brother, Charles, also a writer, married Charles Dickens' sister. Wilkie's schooling was of a random nature, several years being spent with his parents in Italy and in travel. The boy took some interest in painting, was apprenticed to a tea firm, and was called to the bar. He never married. When he was twenty-four he published a two-volume memoir of his father. In 1850 his only historical novel, a forgotten and rather inept romantic piece called *Antonina,* with an Italian background based on his travels, made its appearance. A year later he met Dickens, an event of the utmost significance to both men. Not only did they collaborate in a number of works; their influence on each other was great. This is remarkable in itself. Though Dickens affected almost every other writer of his time, Collins has been declared the only writer who influenced *him.*

In the opinion of many able critics, in fact, Collins was almost Dickens' equal in characterization and was often his superior in technical plot construction. The vital difference between them was one of background and breeding. Dickens had the "common touch," Collins was "genteel"—and the words spelled the distinction between greatness and near-greatness. Collins recognized the discrepancy (but not the cause) and tried to overcome it, but without success. Ironically, it was his attempt to write polemic and reformist novels in the manner of Dickens that marked his popular and literary downfall. From high esteem in his early career, when he was sticking to his last, he fell to obscurity in his last years and died ungratefully forgotten in his own lifetime. Recent decades have seen a deserved revival of interest in Collins, and his true stature as a major Victorian novelist is slowly coming to be recognized; but it is significant of human fallibility that there still exists no adequate biography of him.*

Collins died on September 23, 1889. At sixty-five he had already outlived his fame. This fame, so gratifyingly reascendant to-day, rests principally and sufficiently on two works. In 1860, six years before Gaboriau produced *L'Affaire Lerouge,* Collins published *The Woman in White.* It was, however, a mystery rather than a detective novel. It remains to-day one of the finest examples of its own genre, but it need not concern us here save as it helped pave the way for what was to come. Early in 1868 the magazine *All the Year Round* (Charles Dickens, Editor) began serial publication of *The Moonstone.* In July of the same year the nine-hundred-page novel made its appearance between covers, in three stout volumes. T. S. Eliot has called it "the first, the longest, and the best of detective novels." Purists may question the strict accuracy of at least the first two adjectives, but few who have read this astonishingly modern masterpiece will quarrel with the spirit of Eliot's magnificently unqualified estimate.

One distinction, however, should and must be made for the sake of technical probity. Excellent and predominant

* Alexander Woollcott—who has done such notable work in bringing Collins to the attention of present-day readers—is authority for the statement that Dorothy Sayers, the eminent English detective novelist, has been working for some years on such a biography. "But," he adds (in his foreword to the Modern Library's combined edition of *The Moonstone* and *The Woman in White*), "I am oppressed by a doubt that she will ever get around to finishing it." Mr. Woollcott's reputation as a prophet seems in this instance unfortunately only too safe. His statement was made in 1937, and no announcement of the biography has yet come from Miss Sayers or her publishers.

as are the detectival elements in *The Moonstone,* Collins
—like Gaboriau before him—stopped just short of creating a really new form. What he did, essentially, was to
write a full-bodied novel in the fashion of his time, using
detection as a central theme to catalyze the elaborate in-
gredients; much as another novelist of the same era
might have employed a love or revenge motif as the uni-
fying factor for the crowded canvas of his three-decker.
Collins accomplished the amalgamation far more tact-
fully than did poor Gaboriau. He did not try to mix oil
and water. He chose compatible elements. Yet the position of the two writers with respect to the detective novel
is strongly analogous. Both embodied the theme in an
already existing form, rather than creating a new type of
literature. The story of the theft and fate of the Yellow
Diamond is *in itself* as perfect a detective plot as the
world has known. But it is only a part, if a highly important and integral one, of the novel *as a whole.* Detection is the plum in the pudding, but it is by no means the
entire pudding. . . . And Collins' detective is only a subordinate character, not the principal actor in the drama.

(Paradoxically, however, the outstanding trend in the
present-day detective story, as will be discussed in later
chapters, is the abandonment of rigid formulas in favor
of blending the detective elements with the novel of manners and character, much as Wilkie Collins did three-
quarters of a century ago. Furthermore, *The Moonstone*
has achieved the distinction of being directly paraphrased
in several modern works, including, among others, two
of the finest detective novels of this generation: Dorothy
Sayers' *The Documents in the Case* and Michael Innes'
Lament for a Maker. Thus does the wheel revolve!)

To describe here the wonderfully imaginative plot of *The Moonstone* would be an insult to those who have met that affection-inspiring work, and an act of distinct unfriendliness toward those who still have the delectable experience ahead of them. But it will betray no vital secret to say that Collins drew both inspirationally and directly from the English criminal *cause* of the decade, the controversial Constance Kent or "Road Murder" case of 1860. The episode in *The Moonstone* of the paint-stained nightgown and the washing-book is taken almost bodily from the Kent trial. So, too, Superintendent Seegrave in the novel is the real-life Superintendent Foley, and SERGEANT CUFF is no one but Inspector Whicher in slight disguise; the roses were Collins' own contribution.

If the book were notable for nothing else, it would be memorable as the first novel of detection to include real humor in the writing—and humor not of the forced, injected variety, but springing logically and naturally (as it should) from situation and character. The characterization itself is the quality, even more than the plot, which makes the book the thing of joy it is. In all fiction there will be found few more delightful personages than Gabriel Betteredge, a figure who can hold his own with the best of Dickens' creations. One must wonder, too, what the Drusilla Clacks of the day thought of Collins' acid and revealing sketch of their sister busybody—but no Clack of any era would be likely to read anything as wholesome as *The Moonstone*! The portrayal of the pious villain would lead modern readers to suspect him rather quickly, through wishful thinking if nothing else; yet this would scarcely have been true in Collins' time. It is perhaps an additional commentary on the author's essential subordination of the detective element that SERGEANT CUFF, in spite of the roses, is the least vivid character in the narrative. Ezra Jennings, who is not generally regarded as a detective, but whose contribution some readers consider truer sleuthing than anything the professional CUFF did, is far more unforgettably drawn. Franklin Blake, Rachel Verinder, Rosanna Spearman, Matthew Bruff— all are living beings, valued friends, and the prototypes of a long lineage of detective dramatis personæ. Psychology the novel certainly has, as well as physiology of a high order. Both are represented in the great laudanum experiment, a tour de force that has seldom been surpassed in the literature. The setting of the story is thoroughly natural and contemporary to its date, eschewing the Gothic trappings so much in favor when Collins wrote.

On the purely technical side, the handling of the "least-likely person" theme (i.e., with regard to the identity of the thief) is the most ingenious—with the possible exception of Agatha Christie's debatable *Murder of Roger Ackroyd*—in detective fiction. The pace of the narrative may at first seem slow by modern standards; when considered in relation to the subject-matter it is leisurely and rich in detail without being unduly prolix or digressive; the very deliberateness heightens and enhances the moments of excitement when they arrive. Of Collins' skill at conveying suspense, Arthur Compton-Rickett has written: "[He] excites us not by what he tells us, but by what he does not tell us." Truly enough, Collins' power lies less in frontal assault than in suggestion, an effective auctorial asset in any type of fiction. In a formal sense, *The Moonstone* belongs midway between the romance of incident and the novel of character. The detective portion, judged by itself, is an almost perfect example of the *balanced* type—a consummate blending of narrative and logical deduction.

Wilkie Collins made one masterful contribution to detective literature. We regret his subsequent apostasy, laudable as were his motives, much as we deplore the ambition of a fine comedian or character-actor to play Hamlet. His single, superb novel will live as long as detective stories are read and enjoyed. Numberless grateful readers will agree with the jurist Oliver Wendell Holmes' verdict, at ninety-two: "The best there is."

IV

Two works by Charles Dickens are sometimes included in historical listings of detective fiction: *Bleak House* (1853) and the uncompleted *Mystery of Edwin Drood* (1870). They will not detain us long. Both were even more indirect and casual contributions than those of Gaboriau and Collins.

In *Bleak House,* only fourteen of the sixty-six chapters have any bearing on the investigations of Inspector Bucket, who is said to have been based on the author's personal friend, Inspector Field of the London Metropolitan Police Force. Furthermore, the topic of the inquiry is no more than a sub-plot in the novel as a whole.*

---

* However, Julian Hawthorne in his anthological *Lock and Key Library,* published some years ago, made an ingenious and on the whole surprisingly successful attempt to create from these materials a bona fide detective story in Dickens' name. He separated the fourteen chapters from the rest of the book, arranged them in sequence, and gave the resulting work the title *Inspector Bucket's Job*. Barring a not unexpected jerkiness, the *Job* is not at all a bad one. Nevertheless, this interesting experiment scarcely makes the parent novel anything but what it was

As for *Edwin Drood,* which is supposed to have been prompted by Dickens' desire to outglitter *The Moonstone,* there is puzzle enough; but several authorities have pointed out the absence of a determinable detective. (While another school of thought holds out for Datchery.) It is possible, of course, that the author may have had an indisputable detective in mind for the later stages of the story. Dickens lived to complete only twenty-three chapters, and for a Dickens novel this was a bare beginning; there was ample space for the later introduction of a bang-up sleuth if he wanted one. There is room for belief, too, that the rivalry which inspired the book in the first instance would have produced such a conclusion. What the Sage of Gad's Hill might have accomplished had he lived to create an important fictional detective is a no less intriguing literary mystery than the unrevealed solution of the story itself, which has occupied so many minds. That distinguished writer on criminology, the late Edmund Pearson, called the latter puzzle "the foremost problem in fiction," though he admitted that "it is perfectly futile to some folk," while "perfectly fascinating to others." G. K. Chesterton accorded *Edwin Drood* and its author an even more double-edged compliment when he wrote: "The only one of Dickens' novels which he did not finish was the only one that really needed finishing. He never had but one thoroughly good plot to tell; and that he has told only in heaven." A sizable literature has grown up on the subject of *Edwin Drood,* and a good score of attempts have been made by

before—a typical Dickens full-canvas work, including an incidental detective tale in the manner of a "play within a play." But BUCKET himself remains, if nothing else, the first English fictional detective; and as such he needs no apologies.

various hands to complete it, but with consequences thus far more curious than significant. So far as we are concerned in the present volume, it must remain only a *potential* detective story.

*   *   *

Gaboriau, Collins, Dickens. Each contributed something *toward* fictional detection. Jointly, they kept the form alive: saved the theme, perhaps, from premature extinction. And Collins dropped, in passing, a single, matchless pearl. But the creation of a really great detective character, the writing of full-length detective stories concerned with detection and nothing else, was still two decades away—locked in the questing brain of a red-cheeked school-boy in Edinburgh.

CHAPTER III

Profile by Gaslight

(Renaissance)

"Excellent!" I cried.
"Elementary," said he.
    —A. CONAN DOYLE, "The Crooked Man"

I

PICTURE a winter's morning in Edinburgh sixty years ago. It is dark and bitterly cold. The crowded lecture theater of the Royal Infirmary is lit murkily by flickering oil lamps. There is a pungent odor of chemicals in the chill air.

Through the thick gloom rasps the crisp, nasal voice of the lecturer on the rostrum. He is Joseph Bell, consulting surgeon of the Infirmary and idol of the students, though they fear his caustic tongue. His powers of observation and analysis are the wonder of pupils and fellow-medicos alike. In five minutes' time, it is said, he can deduce the occupation and past history of any person brought before him.

Beside him this morning stands a clinic patient, whose case is to be diagnosed. Bell calls one of the students to the platform.

"What is the matter with this man, sir?" he barks at the trembling undergraduate. "No! You mustn't touch him. Use your eyes, sir! Use your ears, your brain, your bump of perception, your powers of deduction."

The unhappy tyro makes a wild guess. "H-hip-joint disease, sir," he stammers weakly.

"Hip-nothing!" Bell snorts. "The man's limp is not from his hip, but from his feet. Were you to observe *closely* you would see that there are slits, cut by a knife, in those parts of the shoes where the pressure is greatest against the foot. The man is a sufferer from corns and has no hip trouble at all.

"But he has not come here to be treated for corns, gentlemen," Bell continues. "His trouble is of a much more serious nature. This is a case of chronic alcoholism. The rubicund nose, the puffed, bloated face, the blood-shot eyes, the tremulous hands and twitching face muscles, the quick, pulsating arteries—all show this.

"My diagnosis," he concludes dryly, "is confirmed by the neck of a whisky bottle protruding from the patient's right-hand coat pocket.

"Never, gentlemen, neglect to ratify your deductions."

Verily, the words are the words of Dr. Bell. But the voice, gentlemen, is that of SHERLOCK HOLMES.

II

Arthur Conan Doyle—known throughout the civilized world as the creator of SHERLOCK HOLMES—was born in Edinburgh on May 22, 1859, of mixed Anglo-Irish blood. His family traced its descent on both sides from distinguished ancestry, but in circumstances it was anything but affluent. Nevertheless, the boy received a good education, though not without great struggle and sacrifice: first in a series of Jesuit schools in Great Britain and on the Continent (he was born a Catholic but left the faith later in life) and later at the Royal Infirmary in Edinburgh, where he came under Joseph Bell's influence. The keen intellect of the older man quickly recognized kindred qualities in the younger, and a helpful appointment of Doyle as Bell's out-patient clerk followed. Despite this assistance, Doyle was forced from time to time to leave classes behind for a term to work as helper to some parish sawbones for the funds to continue his studies. But the bulldog determination which characterized his whole life enabled him to finish his medical course only slightly behind his regular class.

His love of literature, too, manifested itself at an early age. Even in the days when every shilling looked as big as a pound, the thin coppers intended for his daily lunch often found their way to the two-penny book-stalls in the Grassmarket in exchange for tattered editions of Tacitus, Homer, Swift, Addison—and Poe and Gaboriau.

The story of Doyle's almost accidental creation of SHERLOCK HOLMES has been told so frequently and so well that a brief recounting here will suffice.

In 1882 the young practitioner hung out his red lamp in Southsea, a suburb of the southern seacoast city of Portsmouth, and in 1885 he married. He had chosen the Southsea location with high expectations. An anecdote told many years later in his autobiography reveals what he actually found. After he had been in practice some time he received a letter from the tax authorities informing him that his income report for the previous year had been found "most unsatisfactory." The debt-ridden young doctor with a sick wife scrawled two bitter words across the face of the communication and posted it back. The words were: "I agree."

But the faulty judgment that took Doyle to Portsmouth ranks high in the list of literature's disguised blessings. Not many months at Bush Villa, Southsea, were needed to tell the mustached, pugnacious, young physician the nature of his plight. With virtually unlimited time to sit, puff his cheap shag, and ponder in his waiting-room, barren of furnishings and patients alike, he had begun to send out short stories to the cheaper magazines. A modest success in this direction only served to show that his time was wasted—that if any really substantial return were to be expected from his pen, only a full-length book could be the answer. Accordingly one was written and went forth to the wars, until the day arrived when its tattered sheets had been rejected by every possible publisher. Perhaps the ultimate rebuff came by the same post as the tart complaint from the tax office.

At any rate, Doyle was on the verge of despair and surrender when, by some providential trick of the brain, "Joe" Bell's eagle-beak came before his mind's eye, and the Great Idea took glimmering shape. Feverishly he began to write, and a few weeks later *A Study in Scarlet,* with a hero surnamed for an admired American poet,* and a foil and narrator to be immortally known as Watson, took its turn in the mails. For many weary months it seemed destined for the same fate as the earlier manu-

---

* Doyle revealed his source of the name in later years. Whether the elder Oliver Wendell Holmes, who was born in the same year as Poe but lived until 1894, knew either the stories or the circumstances of the nomenclature is not revealed. But his son, the great jurist, was to the end an unregenerate SHERLOCKIAN, who could still find delight in the Baker Street saga at well past ninety....But see Appendix B at end of volume.

script. (It was not, in all truthfulness, a very good story.) At length came an offer. Twenty-five pounds "outright" —less by far than the price of a single copy in the auction rooms to-day. Discouraged and disgusted, the author accepted Ward, Lock and Company's terms and resigned himself to waiting a full year to see his offspring in print.

Even when *Beeton's Christmas Annual* provided one of the most incredible first editions in history, in December, 1887, the battle was far from won. Unlike Byron, the Southsea physician failed to awake to find himself famous. The event, in fact, went to all outward appearances unnoticed; and Doyle in his chagrin had determined never to think of HOLMES again, and probably would not have done so but for an unforeseen piece of fortune. On a day in 1889, almost two years after the *Beeton* fiasco, Doyle was summoned to meet a representative of the American magazine, *Lippincott's,* whose editor had admired *A Study in Scarlet* sufficiently to make a substantial offer for another HOLMES story. (Thus the world's most renowned detective owes not only his name but his very perpetuation to America—a fact which his grateful creator never forgot.) Encouraged by a substantial advance payment, Doyle worked with much greater care, and in due course *The Sign of the Four*—oh, magical words!— made its bow in *Lippincott's* for February, 1890, was published in London later in the year, and scored an immediate popular success on both sides of the water. Fame had knocked at last. Doyle's poverty had made the world immeasurably richer.

The saga begun in 1887 was to continue for a round forty years, though Doyle made numerous and varied attempts to bring it to an earlier end. The narrative of those years has been so brilliantly chronicled by Vincent Starrett and other devoted worshipers at the shrine that it would be sheer effrontery to repeat more than the outline here.

The success of *The Sign of the Four* brought the editor of the young *Strand Magazine* camping on Doyle's doorstep with an assignment for a dozen HOLMES short stories. They began in July, 1891. A second twelve tales followed in the same publication some two years later. In America, the first series appeared simultaneously in a large number of daily newspapers (no small item in HOLMES' early and wide American renown) through the agency of the newly organized McClure's Syndicate; the second series in *Harper's Weekly*. The initial twelve tales were collected between covers as *The Adventures of Sherlock Holmes,* published in England and America in 1892; and eleven of the second twelve (the recalcitrant disciple is preserved in *His Last Bow*) as *The Memoirs of Sherlock Holmes,* published in 1894. If any reader be prepared to name two other books that have given more innocent but solid pleasure, let him speak now—or hold his peace!

At the end of the second series Doyle made his most determined attempt to rid himself of his sleuth. Even to-day one shudders at the enormity of the deed. He killed HOLMES! The outcry was instant, sincere, and voluminous. (A letter from the distaff side began, "You Beast!") In his own mind Doyle began to wonder if there might not have been an error in his information. The first sign of weakening was the appearance, in 1902, of the full-length HOLMES novel, *The Hound of the Baskervilles*. Watson, to be sure, explained carefully that the events antedated the affair of the Reichenbach by some years and that the work was by way of being a posthumous memoir. But the seed of doubt was planted.

The momentous tidings of the colossal mistake came first to the readers of the *Strand* for October, 1903. (It is no apocryphal exaggeration, but a matter of sober publishing record, that queues formed at the London stationers' on publication date.) "The Adventure of the Empty House," the episode chosen to bring the exciting news to the world, was the first of a new series of thirteen tales about the resurrected investigator. In America they appeared in *Collier's Weekly,* with the famous Frederic Dorr Steele illustrations. The collected book version, entitled—inevitably—*The Return of Sherlock Holmes,* was purchasable on both sides of the Atlantic in 1905.

The reading public was properly grateful and would not for any known worlds have had matters otherwise. And yet—the reception of the new tales was not entirely unmixed. Doyle enjoyed relating a homely incident that expressed the state of the popular mind neatly. "I think, sir," he quoted a Cornish boatman as saying to him, "when HOLMES fell over that cliff he may not have killed himself, but he was never quite the same man afterwards." Thus did opinion that deplored the slackening in the quality of the stories at the same time demand their continuance.

In response to this demand, Doyle, with evident and proper reluctance, produced three more HOLMES books: *The Valley of Fear* (1915), *His Last Bow* (1917), and *The Case-Book of Sherlock Holmes* (1927). The first of these was a full-length novel, and one which it is to be feared posterity will pronounce sadly inferior to anything else in the saga; the last two were the familiar groupings of short stories that had previously appeared in a number of English and American journals over a period of years.

As the *Adventures* were somewhat fresher and more original than the *Memoirs,* so were the *Memoirs* better than the *Return,* and the tales in the *Return* to be preferred to the books that followed. No one knew better than Doyle that each new series and volume marked a perceptible retrogression in his and HOLMES' powers—yet in the face of popular clamor he was helpless. One exception may be made to this chronological diminution: *The Hound of the Baskervilles,* which, despite the date of its publication, is definitely Early HOLMES in both conception and execution. One can not quarrel, in fact, with those idealists who maintain that Doyle's knighthood in the same year must have been a grateful government's recognition of this masterpiece, rather than the author's Boer War services which were publicly assigned.

The remainder of Sir Arthur's life was largely pleasant and mildly eventful. The Baker Street saga was translated into virtually every known written language and brought prosperity in its wake. Doyle wrote and traveled much. Of his other works, many of them notable in their own right, *Micah Clarke* and *The White Company* may be mentioned particularly as two of the best historical novels in English. But everywhere he went he was associated with HOLMES, a good deal to his annoyance, and he was constantly expected to solve every sort of great and small puzzle and problem. Controverting the popular belief that fiction and fact are widely separated, he took a successful part in two major causes célèbres, the Slater and Edalji affairs. His brilliant analysis of the evidence in each case aided materially in preventing grave injustice.

It is interesting to note that on several occasions in later years Joseph Bell suggested plots to Doyle for HOLMES stories, but the author was forced to confess his old teacher's ideas "not very practical."

As more than one writer has pointed out, Bell may have been the model from whom HOLMES was drawn, but the real detective was Doyle himself. In appearance, with his beefy British frame and walrus mustache, he was much closer to Watson than HOLMES. Ruggedness was his predominant characteristic. He had the Englishman's traditional fondness for sports of all kinds and an equally typical partisanship for the underdog. He was an unusual combination of the militant and the gentle, a dauntless fighter in any cause he believed to be right, and an adversary to be feared; but in his heart, said his friends, there was no room for malice. The great sorrow of his life was the death of his son Kingsley in the First World War. The tragedy intensified an earlier interest in spiritualism, and both he and Lady Doyle (who lived until 1940) became ardent converts. Ignoring denunciation and ridicule, he spent the last years of his life in travel to all parts of the world lecturing on the subject. Of the passionate sincerity of his convictions there could be no doubt.

Arthur Conan Doyle's life ended, after seventy-one active and fruitful years, at his home at Crowborough, Sussex, July 7, 1930.

III

The rôle of Doyle and HOLMES in resuscitating and rejuvenating the Poe-Gaboriau formula was enormous and far-reaching. It is something of a paradox, therefore—but one which can not be ignored—that by modern standards the tales must often be pronounced better fiction than detection. They undeniably gave new life-blood to the form; they established a pattern which was to endure for a generation; yet it is certainly no disparagement to point out that they live to-day for the two immortal characters who move through their pages rather than for any particular excellence of plot or deduction. Subjected to purely technical analysis, in fact, they will be found all too frequently loose, obvious, imitative, trite, and repetitious in device and theme.

All the longer stories (with only the partial exception of *The Hound of the Baskervilles*) rely on painfully Gothic and antiquated treatment of the revenge motif. In two instances, *A Study in Scarlet* and *The Valley of Fear,* Doyle not only used without apology the creaking "flash-back" device, but did it so embarrassingly in the manner of Bertha M. Clay at her worst as to make the most ardent SHERLOCKIAN blush and hastily change the subject. The *Study in Scarlet,* in addition, violates two of the most sacred tenets of the detective story: the culprit is revealed to be one who has not, properly speaking, appeared previously in the story; and the solution is in large part based on information acquired secretly by the detective and not revealed to the reader until after the dénouement. The latter fault, in fact, tends to crop out in an embarrassing degree in many of the narratives.

Aside from his masterly creation of character, little real originality or inventiveness can be claimed for Doyle. Even *The Sign of the Four* bears a strong family resemblance in certain of its principal features to an older classic—Wilkie Collins' *Moonstone*. (Curiously enough,

Doyle, who was ever ready to bow to Poe and Gaboriau as his masters in the craft, never properly acknowledged his indebtedness to his own compatriot.) The similarity of "A Scandal in Bohemia," among the shorter stories, to Poe's "Purloined Letter" has been mentioned in an earlier chapter; and certainly "The Dancing Men" could have been written only by an author who was familiar with "The Gold Bug."

On the whole, Doyle was happier in the short story than the longer form. Yet so faithful a disciple as Vincent Starrett pairs a sizable group of earlier and later tales, bearing plot resemblances that seem more than accidental: "A Scandal in Bohemia" and "The Norwood Builder"; "The Blue Carbuncle" and "The Six Napoleons"; "The Greek Interpreter" and "The Solitary Cyclist"; "The Naval Treaty" and "The Second Stain." Any discerning reader can easily expand the list. Repetitions of stock-characters, implements of crime and of detection, and similar minutiæ are even more numerous throughout the long saga. All these are integral weaknesses that can not be explained away, as certain others may be, by the obvious fact that HOLMES came first in his particular field and has suffered from his imitators.

The detective himself has not escaped his share of just criticism. His frequent empiricism, his intolerance of others, his self-esteem got occasionally under even Watson's devoted hide. It was not without cause that E. W. Hornung, Doyle's brother-in-law and the creator of RAFFLES, once punned: "Though he might be more humble, there's no police like HOLMES."

No offense is intended by these remarks; and none, one trusts, will be taken by even the most religious of Baker

Street apostles. For SHERLOCK HOLMES is a character who magnificently transcends the need for apology. What is it that has given him this opulent estate? For what excellent reasons do we forgive shortcomings we could condone in no one else? Why do we call his very absurdities beloved? The quality is at once simple and difficult to define—and one that many abler technical achievements sorely want. Lacking a single mot juste we may speak tentatively of "flavor." Or, to choose a hardier word, "gusto." One hesitates to use the overworked phrase "born story-teller"; yet Doyle's almost naïve zest was certainly a factor.

For it is not intricacy or bafflement that causes the tales to be read and re-read with a never diminishing thrill, when the slick product of to-day is forgotten in an hour. It is the "romantic reality" of their comfortable, nostalgic British heartiness. It is the small boy in all of us, sitting before an open fire, with the winter wind howling around the windows, a-wriggle with sheer pleasure. It is the "snug peril" of fin de siècle Baker Street, with hansom cabs rumbling distantly on wet cobblestones, and Moriarty and his minions lurking in the fog. It is the warmth behind drawn curtains, the reek of strong tobacco, the patriotic "V" done in bullet-pocks on the wall, the gasogene, the spirit lamp, the dressing-gown, the violin—and the "needle." It is the inevitable bell, the summons to duty and high adventure. It is "Sherlockismus," in the happy Carrollism of Father Knox:

> "...How do you know that?"
> "I followed you."
> "I saw no one."
> "That is what you may expect to see when I follow you."

It is the detective on all fours, nose to the ground, tracing a criminal's spoor with small animal sounds of happiness, like the human bloodhound he is. It is the triumphal return to 221-B, the "mission of humane vengeance" accomplished, the chase at end, the task well done. It is HOLMES, beginning the explanation over one of Mrs. Hudson's late suppers. It is Watson's wide-eyed and penultimate, "Marvelous!" It is SHERLOCK's final and superb, "Elementary!"

William Bolitho came close to the heart of the secret when he wrote of HOLMES: "He is more than a book. He is the spirit of a town and a time." Vincent Starrett has suggested the mood and the emotion even more imaginatively:

Granted the opportunity, gentlemen—one might cry, in paraphrase of Dr. Bell—of recovering a single day out of the irrecoverable past, how would you choose to spend that sorcerous gift? With Master Shakespeare in his tiring room? With Villon and his companions of the cockleshell? Riding with Rupert or barging it with Cleopatra up the Nile? Or would you choose to squander it on a chase with SHERLOCK HOLMES after a visit to the rooms in Baker Street? There can be only one possible answer, gentlemen, to the question.*

IV

To the devotion SHERLOCK HOLMES has inspired in his readers, from the great to the humble, there are testimonials without end. None of these is more touching than the belief, held for years by thousands, that he was an actual, living human being—a circumstance that consti-

---

* *The Private Life of Sherlock Holmes* (New York, The Macmillan Company, 1933); by special permission of the author and publisher.

tutes one of the most unusual chapters in literary history.

Countless troubled letters, by the testimony of the postal authorities, have been addressed with appealing faith to "Mr. Sherlock Holmes, 221-B, Baker Street, London." Early in the century a party of visiting French school-boys was taken on an educational tour of the metropolis. Asked what historic sight they chose to see first, they replied with one accord: "The house where SHERLOCK HOLMES lives." When Doyle announced in one of the later stories that HOLMES was retiring from London to keep bees in Sussex, the mail was swelled with applications from would-be housekeepers and friendly advice from apiarists, amateur and professional. During the First World War, Doyle (in his late fifties, a government observer and propagandist) was introduced to a French general who shall be nameless. What rank, the general suddenly demanded, did SHERLOCK HOLMES hold in the English army? Searching vainly for humor in his questioner's face, Sir Arthur could only stammer in halting French that the detective was "too old" for active service.

The legend of HOLMES' reality has been swelled by other enthusiastic if more sophisticated readers who know well enough that their hero never lived in flesh and blood, but who like to keep up the pretense that he did: high tribute in itself. Already a railway locomotive—running, of course, out of the Baker Street Station—has been named in his honor; and movements are frequently set on foot to erect a statue to his memory. Countless readers have visited Baker Street and photographed and mapped it end-to-end. Prolonged debates have raged over the most likely location of the mythical 221-B. (Good cases may be made out for several sites, but the weight of SHER-

LOCKIAN authority seems to favor the present No. 111.)
And in far off New York to-day an assorted group of
devoted HOLMES enthusiasts, headed by bonhommous
Christopher Morley as Gasogene and Tantalus, and calling themselves the Baker Street Irregulars, foregather
at appropriately uncertain intervals to dine and hear reports of scholarly research in the Sacred Writings and
other matters of Conanical import.* "221-B Culture" is
the Morleyesque phrase for the nostalgic pastime.

Some one has accurately said that more has been written *about* HOLMES (exclusive of the stories themselves)
than any other character in fiction. A good half-dozen
full-size published volumes are already given to his career
and personality, and the number grows constantly, while
the essays and magazine articles amount literally to hundreds; even Watson is achieving a respectable list of
memorabilia in his own right. As Harry Hansen has
pointed out, there is no other instance in literary annals
where the *character* rather than the author is the subject
of such fervid admiration.

But if, as these circumstances would seem to suggest,
HOLMES-worship has become something of a cult in late
years, it is certainly defensible as the most innocent and

---

* To mention, among many, Dr. Felix Morley's unique but entirely
plausible theory that Moriarty survived as Hitler; and Rex Stout's un-
manning hypothesis—not generally, it must be said, accepted by the
membership—that Dr. Watson was really Mrs. Holmes and that "her"
name was Irene Watson!...In more serious vein, it is necessary to
report that the English counterpart, the Sherlock Holmes Society of
London, has undergone what one trusts will be only a cæsura since the
tragic death of its moving spirit, Mr. A. G. Macdonell, well known to
the New York group, in an air raid early in 1941. Late word comes also
of the formation of a Boston "chapter," christened The Speckled Band,
whose essential official, the treasurer, bears the correctly HOLMESIAN if
euphemistic title of the Cheetah.

least harmful of all its kind. Its unashamed insistence that what-never-was always-will-be stands in oddly human fashion for a Higher Sanity in a too-real world.

Two solid external factors that have contributed to the unequalled fame of HOLMES are the illustrations and the numerous stage and screen plays made from the stories. Of these, special mention must be accorded the closely related conceptions of Frederic Dorr Steele, on the easel, and the late beloved William Gillette, in his own famous dramatizations, behind the footlights. (Gillette's one original venture into detection, *The Astounding Crime on Torrington Road,* written in his later years, should be better known to connoisseurs as an unorthodox but gripping tour de force.) These two, perhaps, have done more than any one else save Doyle himself to make the angular features and pipe and deerstalker cap that signify the sleuth more readily recognizable around the globe to-day than the face of many a living statesman or titan of affairs.

It is a pleasure to urge once more, upon all readers who may be interested in delving further into HOLMESIAN lore, Vincent Starrett's both inspired and restrained *Private Life of Sherlock Holmes,* happily still in print at the date of this writing. A mellow and imaginative handbook of SHERLOCKIAN research in itself, it is supplemented by an equally valuable bibliography of the subject.

Too many ecstatic superlatives—and the present writer has no doubt been guilty of his share—have been heaped on the gaunt brow of the Southsea physician's chance creation. Yet when all these are removed, SHERLOCK HOLMES still remains the world's best-known and best-loved fictional detective. But for the tales in which he appeared, the detective story as we know it to-day might never have developed—or only in a vastly different and certainly less pleasurable form.

CHAPTER IV

England: 1890-1914

(*The Romantic Era*)

I

"VIXERE *fortes ante Agamemnona*," wrote E. M. Wrong
in his admirable Introduction to the Oxford collection of
Crime and Detection stories, "but we have forgotten them,
and tend to think of the pre-HOLMES detectives as of the
pre-Shakespearean drama; to call them precursors only."
And mere precursors they were, for the most part, though
recent attempts have been made to disinter their literary
bones, chiefly for the benefit of those aficionados of the
esoteric, the edition collectors. John Carter has performed
particularly able investigation in this field, uncovering a
sizable list of writers in the form who flourished after
Gaboriau and Collins but before Doyle. The specialist
whose interests lie in collecting is referred to this valuable authority (see Chapter XIII). The rest of us can
have little concern with authors who neither influenced
the development of the detective story seriously in their
own time nor are remembered for themselves to-day. The
few pre-HOLMESIANS who were exceptions on either
ground will be discussed in due course.

One pre-HOLMESIAN (by a few months) who neither
influenced others nor is remembered for himself to-day,

but who deserves our brief attention for a unique cause, is the Anglo-Australian fiction writer, Fergus Hume (1859-1932). Although he published more than 130 hack works in his long lifetime, at least half of them in the mystery-detective category, his sole bid for fame rests on his first story, *The Mystery of a Hansom Cab,* written while he was a barrister's clerk in Melbourne, and first published there.* For some unfathomable reason this shoddy pot-boiler received vastly more contemporary attention than Doyle's *Study in Scarlet,* issued about the same time. It was dignified by a full-length parody only slightly worse than the original; and by the time of its author's death it had sold more than half a million copies —making it, according to Willard Huntington Wright and other authorities, the greatest commercial success in the annals of detective fiction. Scarcely readable to-day, *The Mystery of a Hansom Cab* belongs among the famous "freak books" and is mentioned here for its historical interest only.

II

After the sensational triumph of SHERLOCK HOLMES in the late 1880's and early 1890's, England experienced a veritable epidemic of detective stories. The majority of

* Bibliographers have hitherto unanimously given the date of the Melbourne publication as 1887. However, an article in the *London Illustrated News,* October 6, 1888, discovered by the present writer, places it a year earlier. This is confirmed by E. M. Miller's recent *Australian Literature From Its Beginnings* (Melbourne University Press, 1940), which gives a detailed account of the writing of the story and further states that the only known copy of the 1886 imprint is preserved in the Mitchell Library, Melbourne. Nevertheless, the *real* fame of the book dates from its London printing of 1887, so that the usual comparisons of it with *A Study in Scarlet,* issued in that year, are not without good basis.

them, as could only be expected, were cheap imitations, long since forgotten. A few, however, deserve consideration on their own merits.

The first important English writer of detective fiction after Conan Doyle was Arthur Morrison. Born in Kent in 1863, he entered journalism after a short career in the civil service; to-day he is the last living survivor of the old *National Observer* staff, the famous "Henley group." Aside from his detective stories, which he belittles, he is well known for his sketches and novels. His graphic pictures of nineteenth-century London slum life in *Tales of Mean Streets* were classics of their time and place and have been credited with strongly influencing contemporary housing legislation (in which Britain has led America by so many years). His *Painters of Japan,* published in 1911, is still a leading work on that subject, and the British Museum acquired his collection of Chinese and Japanese paintings in 1913. In the First World War he held an important post in the civilian defense and personally telephoned the earliest warning of the first Zeppelin raid on London. An only son fought through the entire war and died in 1921 as the consequence of his service. To-day Arthur Morrison lives in quiet retirement at his rural home in Buckinghamshire, surrounded by his art treasures, a mellow septuagenarian survivor of what may well have been a better age. He is a Fellow and Member of Council of the Royal Society of Literature.

It was in 1894 that Arthur Morrison began his series of stories relating the adventures of MARTIN HEWITT, a barrister-turned-sleuth. HEWITT bears a resemblance both to HOLMES, who preceded him, and to R. Austin Freeman's medical-legal expert, DR. THORNDYKE, whom he antedated by a little more than a decade. He is less dramatic than the former and less scientific than the latter, but the tales in which he takes part (most of them of the short variety) are good if conventional detection, set against HOLMESIAN backdrops. He has his Watson, of course: one Brett, a journalist. Despite his similarity in many ways to Doyle's hero, he represents the first symptomatic reaction against the eccentric detective in fiction: the author lays considerable stress (which is not always borne out) on the investigator's commonplaceness.

For the most part the stories are well written (one must except a few unfortunate occasions when Morrison attempted to employ the argot of the underworld), and the problems, if not too baffling to-day, still make pleasant reading nearly half a century after they first saw print. The HEWITT books are four in number: *Martin Hewitt: Investigator* (1894), *Chronicles of Martin Hewitt* (1895), *The Adventures of Martin Hewitt* (1896), and *The Red Triangle* (1903). The first three are collections of short stories, the fourth, an episodic novel. They are almost impossible to find in their original state to-day, but HEWITT is well represented in the more carefully compiled anthologies.

Arthur Morrison added little that was new to the HOLMES formula, but his quiet and literate touch helped the detective story to survive an era when too many of its practitioners were second-rate workmen, content to imitate the more obvious and less admirable characteristics of the Doyle romances.

III

A less direct contributor to the detective story in the HOLMES era, but·one of some technical importance, was Robert Barr (1850-1912). Born in Glasgow, he was taken to Canada by his parents at an early age. He grew up to become headmaster of a school in Windsor, Ontario, at scarcely twenty, and then drifted across the border to join the staff of the Detroit *Free Press* as a reporter. The exuberant American journalism of the 1870's was to his liking, and in 1881 his services were rewarded when the *Free Press* sent him to London as its representative. His facile pen quickly won him admission to the English popular magazines with his light and humorous tales, of which he wrote and sold hundreds. He died at sixty-two, at the height of his career.

As a writer, Robert Barr was literally that dubious entity, "a born story-teller," with little art in composition save an effortless narrative style. (Yet Stephen Crane, on his death-bed, chose Barr to complete his *The O'Ruddy;* and so acute a critic as Vincent Starrett has pronounced the touching collaboration "perfectly performed.") The public eagerly absorbed his ephemeral works, which were written first for magazine consumption and later made into books, only to forget them almost immediately. He would be virtually unknown to-day except for the presence in historical anthologies of some of the episodes from his *Triumphs of Eugène Valmont* (1906), his lone excursion into the detective field.

VALMONT was as Gallic as his name presumes, ludicrously pompous, and exceedingly fallible. His only present-day significance is as the first humorous detective of any standing. Creation of such a type was inevitable, as a reaction against the "master-mind" school of sleuthing. But, as many authors have discovered, it is a device that is singularly difficult to handle; for the instant that a detective becomes ridiculous or stupid, he is ipso facto a failure within the meaning of the act. A fictional sleuth may have his little vanities, he may even come to wrong conclusions; but, by the unwritten rules of the form, he must retain sufficient underlying dignity and skill in his profession to hold the respect of his readers: otherwise the whole structure falls. A successful modern example of the humorous detective is Agatha Christie's popular HERCULE POIROT (who, incidentally, bears a pictured resemblance to VALMONT that seems more than accidental). But VALMONT himself was too broadly drawn. Only one or two of the stories in which he figured are at all readable to-day, and it must be concluded that Robert Barr was more important for the style he founded than for his own success within that mode.

IV

From the earliest days of the police novel there has been a vast deal of high-flown talk about the "scientific" detective. The plain truth is that few of the sleuths of fiction wearing this designation would know which way to turn if they found themselves in a real-life laboratory. The shining exception for all time is R. Austin Freeman's DR. JOHN THORNDYKE. No other literary criminologist, so far as this writer knows, has been paid the tribute of having his fictional methods put into use by the real police.

One good reason for this unique situation lies in Freeman's training and background. Born in London in 1862, he attended private schools and took up the study of medicine. Like Conan Doyle he was impressed by the methods of one of his medical school instructors (in Freeman's case a specialist in medical jurisprudence, Dr. Alfred Swayne Taylor), and also like Doyle he was later to "sit" his mentor as model.

After taking his medical degree, Freeman went to the Gold Coast of Africa, where he acquired the material for his first (non-detective) books and a case of blackwater fever that permanently impaired his health. Invalided home to England, he practised his profession in various not very profitable capacities—one comprehends the presence of the forlorn "locum tenens" in so many of his tales—including a term as medical advisor at Holloway Prison, where he learned to know his "old lags." Eventually his health made further active practice of any sort inadvisable, and he turned to fiction and the creation of the medico-legal detective story, in which he stands preëminent to this day.

The Red Thumb Mark (1907) was the book which marked his début in the form, at the age of forty-five. In respect to puzzle-and-solution, this remarkable volume remains one of the undisputed milestones of the genre. What is of but slightly less importance, it served to bring into existence the immortal THORNDYKE and his delectable associates, Jervis and Polton. To-day the bombs of the barbarians have written physical finis to the familiar chambers in King's Bench Walk; but in some happier and imperishable country of the mind, one likes to believe, the admirable trio still serve the cause of abstract justice with insufflator and micrometer.*

A shy, modest man, looking the solid Britisher he is, Dr. Freeman makes his home at Gravesend, Kent. There, in the heart of "Hell's Corner," he was reported still to dwell in 1941, aged seventy-nine, philosophically pursuing his writing and numerous hobbies in a personally designed bomb-shelter in his garden. He is known to be an expert bookbinder, a capable wax and clay modeler, and an amateur painter of the academic school, as well as his own laboratory technician. To prospective interviewers he invariably replies: "I have no desire for personal publicity." Unlike his famous character, he is married, and has two sons.

The numerous Freeman books, still happily appearing at yearly intervals at this writing, are of a uniform detectival excellence, if slightly monotonous in their resemblance to each other. Special significance, however, attaches to *The Singing Bone* (1912), in which the author made the experiment of revealing to the reader the full stories of the crimes *first,* then describing the steps leading up to the solutions by the detective. This rather dangerous departure—perilous in that it dispenses almost entirely with the puzzle and suspense elements—Freeman never repeated in toto; but in all the Thorndyke stories the revelation of the criminal will usually be found subordinated to the *means* of detection. In another writer

---

* A particularly timely and delightful "reconstruction" of the Thorndyke legend and surroundings, in the best Baker Street Irregular manner, has recently been provided by P. M. Stone, the American collector and authority on Freeman, in his essay "5A King's Bench Walk," published in the omnibus volume *Dr. Thorndyke's Crime File* (New York, Dodd, Mead, 1941).

this might be grounds for criticism, but in Freeman's skilled hands so fascinating is the business of investigation (based on actual experiments worked out in the author's extensive laboratory) that we scarcely notice the absence of mystification.

As a craftsman in the more literary sense, Dr. Freeman presents an interesting anomaly. His narrative style is so often that of late-Victorian romanticism that it is not unusual to find him unconsciously classified in the Doyle period. Indeed, the domestic trappings of a typical Freeman tale bring to the fire-lit chambers in King's Bench Walk much the same mood of snugness and nostalgic bachelor bonhommie which is destined to bespeak Baker Street to the end of time. But in his pioneer insistence on the fair-play method, the creator of JOHN THORNDYKE, M. D., was a Modern before the Moderns. He was the true and undoubted "parent" of the scientific detective story in the highest meaning of the phrase, and remains to-day the living dean of that form—if not, indeed, of all detective story writers of whatever style or persuasion.

v

A perennially favorite device of writers of detective fiction is the "arm-chair" detective, who solves crimes without visiting the scenes, by the application of his invariably bulging brow to the recounted facts. In real life such detection could not be taken seriously, but used occasionally in fiction it makes a welcome if never too plausible variant of the conventional methods. One of the first writers to employ the formula extensively was Baroness Orczy (1865-), with her OLD MAN IN THE

CORNER tales. (The convention had been used earlier by M. P. Shiel in his PRINCE ZALESKI stories; which, however, qualify only somewhat dubiously as detection.)

Emmuska, Baroness Orczy, was born in Hungary, the only child of Baron Felix Orczy, a composer and conductor of some note, and Emma Orczy, née Comtesse Wass. As a child she knew Wagner, Liszt, Gounod, and Massenet, all friends of her father. Though she spoke no word of English until she was fifteen, all her writings are in that language. After early studies in Brussels and Paris, she enrolled in the Heatherley School of Art in London, where she met a young English student, Montagu Barstow, whom she married. Some of her paintings were hung at Royal Academy shows and she had a modest success as an illustrator, both alone and in collaboration with her husband, who had become a well-known artist. He in turn collaborated with her in the creation of her colorful hero, the "Scarlet Pimpernel," with whose numerous and popular romantic adventures she is chiefly identified in the public mind. It was at his suggestion also that she decided to try her hand at detective stories, which both husband and wife were fond of reading.

The nameless OLD MAN IN THE CORNER, who solves crimes as he sits at a corner table of a London ABC tea shop, tying and unraveling complicated knots in a piece of string as he talks, made his appearance in a book of the same title in 1909, returning in 1926 in a second volume called *Unraveled Knots*. A danger inherent in the "arm-chair" method, and frequently illustrated by the OLD MAN stories, is the tendency of the plots to become static; too often, also, they mistake intuition for deduction. Nevertheless, some of the more readable of the

OLD MAN tales have found their way into anthologies, where they represent a mildly diverting but essentially minor and rather archaic sub-development in the literature.

For some years now, Baroness Orczy has made her home in Monte Carlo, where she is surprisingly youthful and vigorous in her middle seventies. The outbreak of war in 1939 found her in England and nearing seventy-five; characteristically, she hurried home to Monte Carlo to do relief work among her neighbors. At latest reports she is still there.

Her contribution to the detective story has been neither large nor significant, but it is essentially pleasant and entertaining.

VI

For a good generation after HOLMES, virtually every fictional detective of consequence was either an outright amateur or, at the least, a private consulting agent, engaged in outshining and humiliating the minions of the law. With A. E. W. Mason's M. HANAUD, of the Sûreté, we come for the first time since Gaboriau to a really notable *police* detective. In this single sense HANAUD may loosely be called a descendant of LECOQ. But there the resemblance ends, for in contrast to the lumpish sensationalism of Gaboriau, the HANAUD adventures are among the most subtly conceived and described in the genre. Mason, though he chooses a Gallic mise-en-scène, and though he handles French judiciaire procedure like a native, is an Englishman, and is thus not under the compulsion most French writers of detection seem to feel, of following literally in the footsteps of the feuilletonist.

Born in London in 1865, Alfred Edward Woodley Mason was educated at Dulwich College and Oxford. An early career as an actor gave him a sense of theater that may well account for the adaptation of so many of his books to the stage and screen. He turned to literature at the age of thirty. In illustration of his many notable popular and critical successes, *The Four Feathers* may be mentioned among his novels and *The Witness for the Defence* among his works for the theater. The most painstaking of craftsmen, he often travels half-way around the globe to absorb at first hand authentic color and detail for a single elaborately conceived and executed story. A term in the House of Commons inevitably produced a political novel; experiences during the First World War as the civilian Chief of the British Naval Intelligence gave him material for a number of volumes of superior adventure and intrigue.

The first HANAUD book was *At the Villa Rose* (1910). The second, *The House of the Arrow,* did not appear until fourteen years later. The large-bodied, rapier-witted detective and his Greek Chorus, the wine-loving Mr. Ricardo, have appeared in three other full-length novels and one rather obscure short story, published at long intervals. Despite this relatively small representation, HANAUD easily stands out as one of the indisputable "greats" among fictional sleuths.

A favorite topic of debate among the cognoscenti is whether *At the Villa Rose* or *The House of the Arrow* is the greater achievement. Granting the former the advantages of priority, the present writer nevertheless alines himself with those who hold that the reader must go to *The House of the Arrow* to experience the full flavor of the Mason-HANAUD combination: the wealth of atmosphere, the effortless portrayal of character, the brooding sense of evil, the mordant and brilliant humor. But whichever title we choose, it will be amply evident that Mason was the first writer after Collins to make significant use of the *psychological* element in the detective story. Like R. Austin Freeman—whom he resembles in no other respect—he was far ahead of his time. Mr. Mason is still writing to-day, at well past seventy. It is surely permissible to hope for at least one more of the matchless HANAUD tales before he chooses to lay down his pen.

VII

It would be both impractical and unnecessary in a volume of the present scope and purpose to go into any detail concerning the career or the multitudinous and varied works of Gilbert K. Chesterton (1874-1936), one of the genuinely distinguished English men-of-letters of this century. Our interest here is confined to only one of his many phases, but one that for its protagonist may possibly outlive his more pretentious and "serious" writings. Chesterton's love of paradox is too well known to require comment. He must have delighted in the fact that by the creation of his erstwhile meek, round-faced priest-detective, FATHER BROWN, he gave body to one of the most famous and best loved of detective *characters* —while writing tales that often are not detective *stories* at all!

The FATHER BROWN series is composed exclusively of short stories, of which there are fifty, collected in five volumes: *The Innocence of Father Brown* (1911), *The*

Wisdom of Father Brown (1914), *The Incredulity of Father Brown* (1926), and *The Secret of Father Brown* (1927), and the belated and definitely inferior *The Scandal of Father Brown* (1935). Chesterton also created two lesser quasi-detectives: HORNE FISHER of *The Man Who Knew Too Much* * (1922) and MR. POND of *The Paradoxes of Mr. Pond* (1936). Both imitated the BROWN formula, but neither one equaled or amplified it in any significant way.

The best BROWN stories, from a detectival standpoint, are found in the first two volumes. In the final three the artificiality and fantasticism that tinge all the tales to a certain extent are even more pronounced. To say that FATHER BROWN is the greatest of "intuitive" detectives is to suggest by the same word the most serious failure of his adventures by deductive standards: for deduction, not instinct, is the root of all convincing criminal investigation. Chesterton partly circumvented the difficulty by explaining (a trifle too frequently and insistently) that BROWN's magician-like ability to produce full-fledged solutions out of his globular head was only the logical operation of his profound knowledge of human wickedness, acquired in his priestly calling. Many critics have objected also to the backgrounds of the stories. Far from meeting the verisimilitude test of plausible fictive detection, they are often too abstruse to carry conviction even as fantasy (which also needs some connecting link with reality to achieve its purpose). Nevertheless, there are numerous points in the little priest's favor, as detective as well as man of wisdom. And Chesterton's vivid imag-

---

* Related only by title to the remarkable Alfred Hitchcock film-melodrama of the same name.

ination, on the occasions when he kept it within the range of plausibility, greatly enriched and revivified the stereotyped form into which the detective story was beginning to fall when he started writing.

Nearly all the problems in the Brown stories are problems of character. But Chesterton's approach was philosophical, where A. E. W. Mason's (for example) was psychological. As Willard Huntington Wright points out, FATHER BROWN is chiefly concerned with the moral and religious aspects of crime. In fact, it may well be Chesterton's chief contribution to the genre that he perfected the *metaphysical* detective story. Though not particularly suited to the métier, and for that reason seldom found in its pure state among other writers of detection, influential traces of it are present in the works of many of the better Moderns. A few of the individual stories are undeniably brilliant, whether judged as detective tales or as that problematical thing called Art. Chesterton is at his best when he states a problem in apparently supernatural terms and then resolves it by philosophical paradox—see such tales as "The Hammer of God," "The Invisible Man," and that anthologists' favorite, "The Queer Feet." Unfortunately, the explanations are sometimes as fantastic as the premises, and too frequently the author seizes the occasion to intrude personal dogma and mysticism.

But such faults are largely forgivable in the light of the greater achievement. When Chesterton began to write the FATHER BROWN narratives, the detective story had only two main classifications: increasingly heavy-handed romanticism on the one side, and the new scientificism on the other. (Mason, it is true, had re-introduced the element of psychology, but he did not follow it up until well after the War.) Chesterton's brilliant style and fertile imagination brought new blood to the genre; gave it a needed and distinctly more "literary" turn that was to have far-reaching effect. His great reputation and the instant response to FATHER BROWN as a character combined to create an aura of prestige and respectability which detective fiction at the time was beginning to require if it was to survive and progress.

Too many of Chesterton's tales will not meet the full test of good detection, but he can not be lightly dismissed. He belongs definitely among the important innovators.

VIII

The next significant English name, in any chronological consideration of the post-Doyle years, is that of E. C. Bentley, whose epoch-making novel, *Trent's Last Case,* appeared in 1913. Detailed discussion of this author and book are reserved to a later chapter, however, for reasons which will appear at that point. Suffice it to say here that though Freeman and Mason and Chesterton were ahead of their time, they were logically enough precursors; but Bentley, despite his dates, definitely *belongs* to a later period, the era we call Modern.

The last important English author of the HOLMES period proper (which may be said, approximately, to have ended with Sarajevo) is Ernest Bramah, whose blind detective MAX CARRADOS appeared in the London bookstalls in 1914, on the eve of the First World War. (This may account for the fact that the first CARRADOS book, entitled simply *Max Carrados,* was never published in the

United States, but only in England.) Later books in which the sightless investigator appears are *The Eyes of Max Carrados* (1923) and *Max Carrados Mysteries* (1927), together with a single story in *The Specimen Case* (1924). All are collections of short stories: there is no CARRADOS novel.

Mr. Bramah, who is also widely known for his humorous works, including the delightful pseudo-Chinese parables, "The Kai Lung" tales, is one of the most self-effacing of modern authors. "I am not fond of writing about myself," he explains diffidently, "and only to a less degree about my work. My published books are about all that I care to pass on to the reader." So successful has he been in this objective that not even the year of his birth is certain—though his autobiographical first book, *English Farming and Why I Turned It Up* (1894), places the event inferentially in the 1860's or early 1870's. Described by his friends as "the kindest and most amiable of men," the author lives to-day in quiet retirement in Hammersmith. A small bald man with twinkling black eyes, he is an authority on numismatics (an attribute shared by CARRADOS), while the knowledgeable backgrounds of the Kai Lung books suggest a sometime residence in the Far East. Aside from these few circumstances, little is known of him save that he writes under a partial pseudonym (he was born Ernest Bramah Smith).

The blindness of MAX CARRADOS, in the skilful Bramah stories, is never the meretricious bid for popularity that it would become in the hands of a less able or conscientious author, but a unique and legitimate adjunct to detection. Drawing on the well-known fact that a disability of one of the senses often enhances and sharpens the others, Bramah endows CARRADOS with the entirely believable capacity of "seeing" by other means than with his eyes. This gives him as a criminologist (at least as a fictional one) an advantage that more than compensates for his handicap. Occasionally the tales lean a little too far in the direction of intuition, and at other times they partake of the monotony of the arm-chair method; but for the most part they have a basis of sound investigation and deduction, imaginatively set forth.

Wise, witty, gentle MAX CARRADOS is one of the most attractive figures in detective literature—and a worthy protagonist to bring the epoch to an end.

IX

No discussion of the era will be complete, however, without brief mention of the "one-book" authors—those writers better known in other fields of literature, who made a single contribution to the detective story—and a few of the outstanding "border-liners."

Israel Zangwill's (1864-1926) partly satiric novelette, *The Big Bow Mystery* (1891), clearly deserves a better fate than its present obscurity; perhaps some enterprising publisher may be persuaded to bring it back into print in a format suited to the present day. Lord Charnwood (1864-   ), the distinguished British biographer of Abraham Lincoln, wrote a modern and eminently readable detective novel in *Tracks in the Snow* (1906). Produced before his elevation to the peerage, it was originally issued under his family name of Benson, and has been republished in recent years under his present title. *Grand Babylon Hotel* (1904), by Arnold Bennett (1867-1931), reveals at least a strong vein of detectivism. Some critics include *The Wrong Box* (1889), by Robert Louis Stevenson (1850-1894) and his stepson Lloyd Osbourne, in lists of police fiction.

Among the earliest attempts to create feminine sleuths we must recognize Catherine Louisa Pirkis' *Experiences of Loveday Brooke: Lady Detective* (1894), George R. Sims' (1847-1922) *Dorcas Dene: Detective* (1897), and M. McDonnell Bodkin's *Dora Myrl: The Lady Detective* (1900). *Michael Dred: Detective* (1899), by Robert and Marie Connor Leighton (parents of Clare Leighton, the artist), has some interest as perhaps the first story to make the detective the murderer. Hesketh Prichard's (1876-1922) woodsman-sleuth NOVEMBER JOE finds place also among the oddities and curiosities.

The "border-liners"—authors whose fiction falls somewhere between the undoubted detective story and such related forms as mystery, criminal adventure, or intrigue—can not occupy us long. The adventures of Louis Tracy's (1863-1928) INSPECTOR FURNEAUX and M. P. Shiel's (1865-   ) PRINCE ZALESKI were claimed by their respective creators to be detection, but seem in retrospect somewhat closer to mystery; the disputed collaborations of the two as "Gordon Holmes" present the same objection. Another collaboration, that of L. T. Meade (1854-1914) and Clifford Halifax, in the 1890's, produced some early examples of the scientific method. "Robert Eustace" has lent his medical knowledge to a number of professional fictionists. *John Silence* (1908), by Algernon Blackwood (1869-   ), is now and then included in lists of this sort. Vincent Starrett calls Grant Allen's (1848-1899) *Hilda Wade* (1899), completed by Conan Doyle from Allen's notes, "one of the great stories of pursuit and detection and one that is too little known"; some others of Allen's stories also qualify in some part. A few of the "Johnny Ludlow" tales of Mrs. Henry Wood (1814-1887), better known as the genteel authoress of *East Lynne,* disclose a strain of domestic sleuthing against Cranfordian backgrounds. The countless spy-and-intrigue novels written by E. Phillips Oppenheim (1866-) occasionally approach detection, as do the rather imitative secret service tales of William LeQueux (1864-1927). While Thomas W. Hanshew's (1857-1914) CLEEK stories, beginning with *The Man of the Forty Faces* (1910), must, in John Carter's words, "be read to be believed."

Mrs. Belloc Lowndes (1868-) made two notable contributions to the fringe of detective fiction with *The Chink in the Armour* (1912), a psychological study from the point-of-view of the unsuspecting object of a murder plot, and *The Lodger* (1913), a masterly fictional analysis of the Jack-the-Ripper murders. Mrs. Lowndes has published many later novels, repeating and varying the formulas of her two memorable tours de force, but none of them has ever had the success of the originals. Her HERCULES POPEAU stories represent a legitimate, if rather slight, approach to detection per se. RAFFLES, the Robin Hood-ish and once highly popular crime-hero created by E. W. Hornung (1866-1921), Conan Doyle's brother-in-law, sometimes varied his burglarious career with investigation, and even when he played an unrelieved criminal rôle, his adventures were good detection in reverse. The RAFFLES stories are worth re-reading to-day—if only to discover what Earle F. Walbridge, an American aficionado of "the blood," means when he says that over them hovers "a faint suggestion of decadence." To the modern reader they frequently present aspects of humor not intended by the author. Hornung's *The Crime Doctor* (1914), is "straight" if forgotten detection. Barry Pain's (1862-1928) Constantine Dix stories also view the problem through the culprit's eyes. In their respective métiers, Mrs. Lowndes and the Messrs. Hornung and Pain all bear a discernible ancestral relationship to the Inversionist school of the following generation: Francis Iles, Richard Hull, Anthony Rolls, et al.

These are only a few, e pluribus. The list could be continued indefinitely. But it is not the obligation of this book to recognize *every* author who has at one time or another approached the hem of detection. Our work is sufficiently cut out to suggest and trace a few of the principal trends and study in some detail the really influential contributors.

CHAPTER V

America: 1890-1914

(*The Romantic Age*)

I

UNLESS the reader is prepared to admit Nick Carter and his confrères and the semi-fictional Pinkerton reminiscences and their ilk to the dignity of detective novels, it must be said that the American field lay fallow from Poe's "Purloined Letter" (1844) to Anna Katharine Green's *The Leavenworth Case* (1878). Any number of reasons may have contributed to the length of the hiatus, not the least of which was a major internal war, more disrupting than any upheaval that England or even volatile France underwent during most of the same period. But the silence is of less interest or significance than the circumstances of its breaking.

For there are sufficient aspects of uniqueness about *The Leavenworth Case* to make it, despite some incredibly bad writing, one of the true historical milestones of the genre. It beat HOLMES to the post by almost a decade; it sprang full-fledged from its author's head, without traceable antecedents; it contained a sound police detective, EBENEZER GRYCE, and a remarkably cogent plot; it was one of the all-time best-sellers in the literature; and above all it was written by a woman (the first, in fact, to practice the form in any land or language) at a time and place when feminine literary output was slight at best and confined chiefly to sentimental verse and similar lady-like ephemera.

Anna Katharine Green (1846-1935), variously called the mother, grandmother, and godmother of the detective story, was born in Brooklyn and was educated at Ripley Female College in Vermont. The only explanation she gave in later years for her unprecedented invasion of the detective field was that she made the experiment as preparation for a poetic career! But the fact that her father was a well-known criminal lawyer of the day undoubtedly had something to do with it. In 1884 she married Charles Rohlfs, a furniture designer and manufacturer. Most of her life was spent in Buffalo, where she died in her ninetieth year.

During her long career Anna Katharine Green published between thirty and forty works of fiction. Most of them were mystery or detective stories, but only a handful (contrary to journalistic misstatements at the time of her death) had GRYCE for their central character. (Her feminine detective, VIOLET STRANGE, is best forgotten.) Aside from *The Leavenworth Case,* perhaps the best of the GRYCE stories is the novelette, *The Doctor, His Wife, and the Clock.* Of her other books, Mrs. Rohlfs' own favorite was *The Hand and the Ring,* but connoisseurs prefer *The House of the Whispering Pines* and *The Filigree Ball,* both of which, however, classify as period pieces to-day—as, for that matter, does all her work. For no one can pretend that Anna Katharine Green's stories are distinguished literature: she is best met with, as some one has remarked, at the impressionable age. Her style is unbelievably stilted and melodramatic by modern standards, her characterizations forced and artificial. But her plots are models of careful construction that can still hold their own against to-day's competition. For this quality, and by virtue of precedence and sustained popularity, she occupies an undisputed and honorable place in the development of the American detective story.

II

Anna Katharine Green's best work occurred in the field of the novel and novelette. The American detective story did not revert in important measure to the shorter form in which it was conceived by Poe, and which is still considered by many critics the theoretically perfect compass for its narration, until the appearance of Jacques Futrelle (1875-1912), the creator of THE THINKING MACHINE. Despite his French-sounding name, Futrelle was a native American, born in Pike County, Georgia, of old Southern stock. In his twenties he became a theatrical manager, and in 1895 he married L. May Peel, also a writer. For several years he was a member of the editorial staff of the Boston *American,* in which many of his tales first appeared, proceeding from newspaper work (like Earl Derr Biggers, who also had his start in Boston journalism a few years later) to the successful writing of detective fiction. He died, tragically and heroically, at thirty-seven in the *Titanic* disaster.

THE THINKING MACHINE, Futrelle's amusing and believably eccentric contribution to the ranks of fictional sleuths, made a somewhat incidental first appearance in the closing chapters of an adventure novel, *The Chase of the Golden Plate* (1906). His complete name, we are told, was AUGUSTUS S. F. X. VAN DUSEN, Ph.D., LL.D., F.R.S., M.D., and M.D.S., and he was cast as a professor in an unnamed university near a large American city strongly resembling Boston. He wore a number eight hat, and his life was dedicated to the blunt proposition that two and two equal four—not sometimes but all of the time. Next to John Rhode's DR. PRIESTLEY, he is probably the most truculent of all the detectives of fiction.

The best of the short stories in which THE THINKING MACHINE performed his feats of mental wizardry were collected in two volumes: *The Thinking Machine* (1907) and *The Thinking Machine on the Case* (1908). The first named was re-issued in 1918 as *The Problem of Cell 13,* the title of the first story in the book. This notable tale, found in many anthologies, is Futrelle's chief single claim to remembrance. Exemplifying detection-in-reverse (the theme is THE THINKING MACHINE's attempt, on a wager, to escape from the death cell of a penitentiary), it is an unforgettable tour de force that no devotee should miss. Nearly all THE THINKING MACHINE stories, for that matter, will stand re-reading to-day. Except for occasional "dating" incidents inherent in the mise-en-scène, there is little in the writing to indicate their pre-war vintage. The concept of the problems is essentially fresh and modern, and the style is straightforward and agreeably free of the pomposity which characterized too much of the detective fiction of the time.

Had Jacques Futrelle lived beyond his thirty-seventh year, he might well have become one of the two or three leading names in the development of the American detective story. As it was, he brought to the genre a lightness of touch in advance of his time, and even by present-day standards his plots are still artful and his narratives readable.

III

The dividing line between the *physical* type of detective story and the pure mystery story is often difficult to distinguish. The conclusive test might well be whether, in the final analysis, the solution is accomplished by incident (mystery story) or deduction (detective story). Even by this test, it is not easy to decide in which of these categories the dramatic and highly popular murder stories of Mary Roberts Rinehart belong. They fall almost exactly on the border-line. (But it is possibly not without some significance that the average uncritical American reader, asked to list important writers of the "detective story," will almost invariably place Mrs. Rinehart's name first.) Examined in the light of careful scholarship, some of the Rinehart tales would likely be found to belong to the one type, some to the other. One day, perhaps, the academic world will forego its preoccupation with the dead bones of the past long enough to perform this practical service to literature!

Born in Pittsburgh, in 1876, Mary Roberts studied to become a nurse. At nineteen she married Dr. Stanley Marshall Rinehart; of their three sons, one has become a writer and two are associated to-day with the firm of Farrar & Rinehart, Mrs. Rinehart's present American publishers. A stock-market slump in 1903 wiped out the Rineharts' small savings and left them $12,000 in debt. In a vague hope of contributing to the family support, Mrs. Rinehart began to write short stories in the intervals of bringing up her family of growing boys. Considerably to her surprise, her first story sold to *Munsey's Magazine* for thirty-four dollars, and in her first year of writing she earned eighteen hundred dollars. While convalescing from an operation she wrote her first long story, and her first crime story, *The Man in Lower Ten,* which was published serially in 1907 but not in book form until 1909. Her first work to appear between covers was *The Circular Staircase* (1908), another murder tale.* It was an immediate success and the forerunner of a long list of mystery-detective fiction to come from Mrs. Rinehart's pen in succeeding years. Before long she was credited with being the highest-paid author in America.

During the First World War she made two trips to Europe as a correspondent, and several books eventuated from the experience. After the Armistice she and Dr. Rinehart made their home in Washington. Since his death in 1932 she has lived in New York. In recent years she has written comparatively little, chiefly because of ill health, against which she has had to struggle for most of her life; but her work still commands top prices and a huge circle of readers whenever it makes its too-infrequent appearances in print. In addition to her crime fiction she is the author of a sizable shelf of romances and humorous tales, the Tish stories in the latter category being especially popular. She has been called primarily a "woman's author," although numerous masculine readers delight in her books, without apology.

* In a record-breaking stage version entitled *The Bat,* written by the author and Avery Hopwood in 1920, the plot was altered to make the supposed official detective the culprit—an adaptation but not necessarily an imitation of Gaston Leroux's successful device in *The Mystery of the Yellow Room.*

Virtually all the Rinehart crime novels have detectives of a sort, which is one reason they are so difficult to classify. Most of them have two: an official detective of more or less astuteness; and the first-person narrator, usually a woman, most often a romantic spinster engaged in protecting young love from unjust suspicion, who alternately complicates the plot and aids detection in unpremeditated fashion—a combination of participating (usually interfering!) Watson, and detective-by-accident.

This is the readily recognizable "Rinehart formula," still delightful when practised by its originator, but becoming increasingly tedious in the hands of her far-too-numerous imitators among American women writers. It is, in fact, only Mrs. Rinehart's superlative talent as one of the great story-tellers of the age (and the intensely human quality of her writing) that induces us to overlook in her own tales breaches of detective etiquette we could excuse in nobody else: what Waldo Frank calls her "carpentry." Foremost in any catalogue of these flaws must be the manner in which romantic complications are allowed to obstruct the orderly process of puzzle-and-solution. Similarly, the plots are always being prolonged by accidents and "happenstances"—not honest mistakes of deductive judgment by the investigator, which would be a legitimate part of the game, but unmotivated interferences and lapses on the part of the characters, who are forever blundering into carefully laid traps and springing them prematurely, or "forgetting" to tell the official detective of important clues. ("Four lives might have been spared if I had only remembered. . . .") Only too frequently, it must be confessed, these clues turn out at the dénouement to have had no bearing on the puzzle anyway!

We can excuse, perhaps, the interminable "Had-I-But-Knowns" as a harmless but irritating species of auctorial mannerism. Much more serious is the writer's tendency to abuse the least-likely-person theme, to pin the crimes on psychologically (and sometimes physically) impossible characters. A final and vital flaw is the painful stretching of the long arm of coincidence which would have us believe, in utter defiance of the laws of probability, that Fate will obligingly and repeatedly bring together without other cause whole groups of persons who, usually unknown to themselves, are intimately related through some complex pattern of antecedent events. (Suggested mental exercise for bored readers: Try to chart—or even figure out—the relationships of the characters in the author's *The Great Mistake*!)

Unfortunately, it is too often these weaknesses that Mrs. Rinehart's imitators are prone to mimic, rather than her points of strength—of which there are many. For the "formula" she devised possesses immense technical advantages, quite apart from its inventor's personal narrative skill. Chief among them, as pointed out by the late Grant Overton, are the reader's participation in the adventure by self-identification with the narrator; and the "forward action" of the plot, the direct antithesis of the over-intellectualized puzzle story. In a Rinehart murder novel the initial crime is never the be-all and end-all but only the opening incident in a progressive conflict between the narrator and the criminal. As Overton further observed: "Here [is] no put-the-pieces-together formula; here [is] an out-guess-this-unknown-or-he'll-out-guess-you, life-and-death struggle." Sometimes this dramatic approach goes too far and carries the story past the border-line of detection and into the realm of mere mystery-adventure; but kept within bounds it is a technique that practitioners of the cut-and-dried Static School might profitably study. In Mrs. Rinehart's own skilled hands it results in a mood of sustained excitement and suspense that renders the reader virtually powerless to lay her books down, despite their logical shortcomings.

Whether mystery or detection, Mary Roberts Rinehart's works have played an incalculable rôle in introducing women, both readers and writers, to puzzle fiction. She represents the quintessence of the romantic mood in the literature. She is the unquestioned dean of crime writing by and for women.

IV

Thirty years separated the first novels of Anna Katharine Green and Mary Roberts Rinehart, but only a year intervened between Mrs. Rinehart's bow and the initial appearance between covers of the next popular American woman writer of detective stories.

Carolyn Wells was born in Rahway, New Jersey, sometime in the 1870's, of early New England ancestry. Travel abroad constituted an important part of her haphazard but eclectic education. At the turn of the century she was contributing light verse and sketches to humorous journals on both sides of the water, and at about the same date she was briefly connected with the Rahway Library Association. These twin experiences led her into the department of literature for which she will probably remain longest known, the field of anthology. Her *Nonsense Anthology*, compiled in 1902, is still a classic of its kind.

From that date to the present writing Miss Wells has published something more than 170 books of all descriptions. She has also been active in many fields, and among her friends she has numbered the great and near-great of two continents. Her achievements are the more remarkable for the fact that she has been almost totally deaf since an attack of scarlet fever at the age of six. In 1918 she married Hadwin Houghton, a member of the American publishing family; their married life, terminated by Mr. Houghton's death a few years later, was brief but happy. To-day Miss Wells lives in a pleasant apartment overlooking New York's Central Park.

FLEMING STONE, Carolyn Wells' best-known detective character, made his first appearance between book covers in *The Clue*, published on September 27, 1909.* Exactly thirty years later to the day, Miss Wells' publishers observed the anniversary by bringing out her seventy-fourth mystery novel, also a FLEMING STONE adventure. STONE had figured in most, though not all, of the intervening volumes, which probably gives him the distinction of more full-length appearances than any other detective of fiction —though his laurels are currently beginning to be threatened by Georges Simenon's modern French sleuth, INSPECTOR MAIGRET. (Edgar Wallace, J. S. Fletcher, and E. Phillips Oppenheim, each with more than one hundred volumes of soi-disant mystery fiction to his credit, have all surpassed Miss Wells in *total* output in the general field, but no one of these authors has consistently followed a *single* central character through more than a handful of stories at most.)

---

* His very earliest bow in print, for those readers who may be interested, occurred in a short story in *Lippincott's Magazine* in 1907.

The best and most workmanlike STONE stories are, in general, the sleuth's earlier investigations. In recent seasons Miss Wells has written on a definite schedule calling for the publication of three FLEMING STONES, on fixed dates of the calendar, each year. The surprising fact, perhaps, is not that some of the stories scarcely rise to the mark, but that they have not perceptibly diminished in popularity. Carolyn Wells is in many ways a remarkable woman—gracious, well loved, gallant. She would presumably be the last to maintain that FLEMING STONE belongs in the company of the immortals of detective literature. The fact that his adventures have given harmless pleasure to many thousands of readers she undoubtedly considers full and sufficient reward.

Miss Wells' informative volume *The Technique of the Mystery Story* will be discussed in a later chapter.

v

Certain years stand out as mile-posts in the history of detective literature. The palm of annus mirabilis is usually awarded, by common consent, to 1887: the date that recorded not only the "birth" of SHERLOCK HOLMES but also the effective launching of Fergus Hume's *Hansom Cab* on its sensational and unexplained cruise as the best-selling detective story of all time. High place must also be accorded to 1907, marking as it did the first significant appearances of Freeman's DR. THORNDYKE in England, Leroux's ROULETABILLE and Leblanc's LUPIN in France, and Futrelle's THINKING MACHINE in America. Less notable for quantity, but yielding to none in quality, was 1911, the year that saw the creation of both G. K. Chesterton's English FATHER BROWN and Melville Davisson Post's UNCLE ABNER—a character as distinctively American as the rugged Virginia mountains that form the setting for his adventures—the outstanding contribution of the United States to detective fiction between AUGUSTE DUPIN and PHILO VANCE.

Melville Davisson Post (1871-1930) was born near Clarksburg, West Virginia. He worked on his father's farm, attended rural schools, and received a degree in law from West Virginia University in 1892. Several years spent in the practice of criminal and corporation law in his native state gave him the background for *The Strange Schemes of Randolph Mason* (1896), a volume of short stories dealing with an unscrupulous lawyer who used his knowledge of legal loopholes to defeat justice. The book created something of a furor, moralists objecting that it gave too much advice to criminals. Post retorted in the preface to a sequel, *The Man of Last Resort* (1897), that nothing but good could come of exposing the law's defects. As if in proof of the contention, at least one of the MASON stories, "The Corpus Delicti," is credited with having hastened a long needed change in criminal procedure. In *The Corrector of Destinies* (1909), however, Post was forced to follow the course of Leblanc with LUPIN in France and Hornung with RAFFLES in England—to heed popular demand and finally put his hero on the side of law and order. Though one notes with a sort of perverse satisfaction that the dour old renegade never became wholly benevolent: "Sir, I had no interest in your life. The adjustment of your problems was the only thing of interest to me," he barks at an effusive client in one of the *Corrector* tales.

The MASON stories qualify as detection only in an oblique sense, if at all. But there is no doubt that they helped to pave the way in Post's mind for UNCLE ABNER, whose sleuthing is of the purest ray. A rockhewn Virginia squire of the Jeffersonian era, whose position as protector of the innocent and righter of wrongs in his mountain community compelled him to turn detective with some of the most convincing results known to the short story form, UNCLE ABNER (who never appeared in a novel) had a long career in the popular magazines, beginning in 1911. The book collection of the tales, *Uncle Abner: Master of Mysteries,* did not appear until 1918, but has been in print continuously ever since.

Post, who received record prices for his magazine work, considered himself the champion of plot-technique in the short story. Indeed, he is probably the most creditable exponent of the formularized short story that America has developed; and his skill in this direction, however detrimental it may have been to his "artistic" reputation, brought to the detective story a new technical excellence that was to have far-reaching effects. His clipped, economical style was admirably suited to the form, and his deft, selective plot manipulation was a strong and healthy contrast to the rambling diffuseness of most of his countrymen who were active in the field at the time.

Nevertheless, in his preoccupation with plot formulas, Post underestimated some of his own greatest talents. The ABNER stories are still read and re-read after more than a quarter-century less for the intensive plots of which their author was so proud—strikingly original in their time but mostly hackneyed by imitation to-day—than for the difficult-to-define quality that separates the sheep from the goats in any form of literature: in Post's case, as nearly as can be expressed, his richly sentient realization of character, place, and mood. Had he been willing to emphasize this side of his talent more, his stature as a true literary artist might have been greater than now seems likely. As it was, his never quite expressed serious abilities were sufficient to set him, in the less pretentious form of the detective story, head and shoulders above his contemporaries and to make him the peer of almost any practitioner of the genre who has written since.

After the success of his early tales, Post abandoned the legal profession entirely for literature. The story of his later life is principally synonymous with his writing career, though he traveled extensively abroad and was active in the councils of the Democratic party at home. He fell from a horse at the age of fifty-nine and died two weeks later at his West Virginia home.

Superlatively fine as they are, the UNCLE ABNER stories have not altogether escaped criticism. Their most serious fault, in the opinion of certain critics, is the author's failure in a few of the tales to make all the evidence explicit. In at least one instance this criticism is justified beyond any doubt.* But in other cases, one wonders if a basic misunderstanding on the part of the critics themselves may not be at fault? Certainly, we must insist on fair play. But the detective story, whether long or short, does not exist in which there is not *some* "off-stage" work—if only in the detective's mind. To have matters otherwise would

---

* In the ABNER story, "An Act of God," Post proves by a phonetic misspelling the forgery of a document purportedly written by a deaf-mute. The brilliant solution is spoiled by the fact that he does *not* allow the reader to scan the document. Had he done so, the tale might well be ranked as one of the most nearly perfect in all the literature.

be to deprive us of our puzzle in mid-career. In nearly every case, Post's offense is merely the logical extension of this principle; and one feels, somehow, that the writer of the *short* detective story (handicapped and restricted in ways that the author of a novel never knows) should be allowed the widest possible discretion and latitude in this respect. Had Post met the demands of the quibblers to catalogue and label every clue, there would in many instances have been no mystery and no story. . . . It is not without relation that, for all Post's genius in physical device, ABNER's detection in the final analysis nearly always hinges on *character*. It is his judgment of men's souls that leads him to expect and therefore to find and interpret the evidence, where lesser minds (including, perhaps, the literal ones of his decriers) see naught.

In all, Melville Davisson Post created the surprising total of six detective characters: UNCLE ABNER; RANDOLPH MASON (to some degree); SIR HENRY MARQUIS of *The Sleuth of St. James's Square* (1920) and *The Bradmoor Murder* (1929); MONSIEUR JONQUELLE of *Monsieur Jonquelle: Prefect of Police of Paris* (1923); WALKER of *Walker of the Secret Service* (1924); and COLONEL BRAXTON of *The Silent Witness* (1930). All are good in their kind, but none of the others seriously challenges the immortal Virginia squire.

No reader can call himself connoisseur who does not know UNCLE ABNER forward and backward. His foursquare pioneer ruggedness looms as a veritable monument in the literature. Posterity may well name him, after DUPIN, the greatest American contribution to the form.

VI

Recognition comes slowly to some writers, rapidly to others; some grow in stature after their deaths, others fade into obscurity. Melville Davisson Post's detective stories are if anything more highly regarded to-day than they were in his lifetime. Quite the opposite fate was reserved for Arthur B. Reeve (1880-1936), the creator of CRAIG KENNEDY, whom it was once the fashion to call "the American SHERLOCK HOLMES." For older readers the KENNEDY name still holds nostalgically pleasant memories; to the younger generation it will mean nothing at all. It is to be doubted if any other fictional sleuth, of similar temporal prominence, has fallen so completely into limbo. An attempted re-reading of the KENNEDY stories to-day will quickly disclose the reason. KENNEDY was cast as a scientific detective: he is said to have been inspired by a Dr. Otto H. Schultze, sometime medical adviser to the district attorney of New York. But his "science," as some one has remarked, was largely the ephemeral pseudo-science of the "Sunday supplements"; and even in Reeve's more restrained moments the stories dramatized the mechanical wonders of their own day. This undeniably gave them a momentary journalistic pertinence, which may well be the reason for their once great popularity, but not even the fond author could expect ' tales dependent solely on the novelty of the acetylene torch, the dictograph, or the Maxim silencer to retain their interest for more than a brief era.

Arthur Benjamin Reeve was born at Patchogue, Long Island, New York. After graduation from Princeton University he attended law school but never practised, turn-

ing instead to journalism. Editorial connections with a
number of magazines led to a series of articles on scientific
crime detection, and, in turn, to the score or more of
KENNEDY books, beginning with *The Silent Bullet* (1912),
a collection of short stories. (The individual stories had
begun to appear in magazine form in 1910.) For about a
decade thereafter Reeve was the best known detective-
story writer in America. But with changing fashions and
fresh blood (no pun intended!) after the First World
War, KENNEDY's popularity began to wane, and in his
later years Reeve devoted himself seriously to the topic
of crime prevention, directing a radio series on the subject
and writing for the newspapers as a specialist. He also
wrote serials for the silent moving pictures. He died of a
heart ailment at fifty-six, at his home at Trenton, New
Jersey.

So inescapably "dated" are the KENNEDY stories in
their subject matter, so nearly forgotten to-day, that it is
easy to underestimate their contemporary importance. To
give Reeve his due, he had a mobile narrative style and a
journalistic ability to hold interest. If his detection was
seldom brilliant, neither was it ever wholly bad. In their
time his tales gave innocent pleasure to multitudes of
readers. Thousands of Americans of a generation now
growing sparse of hair and short of breath met their
"first detective" in his pages.

VII

The American scene in detective literature was not, of
course, exclusively represented in these years by the foregoing names. As in the English field, there were minor and

incidental contributors and the inevitable "border-liners."

We can not go quite so far as those rather literal critics who would nominate Fenimore Cooper's Red Indians as the first American sleuths. But at least one later and major "legitimate" novelist, Mark Twain (1835-1910), wielded a strong if somewhat oblique influence in predisposing his countrymen toward the detective story. The reference is less to the burlesque *Tom Sawyer: Detective* than to certain events in *Huckleberry Finn* and *Pudd'nhead Wilson*: in the latter novel, published in 1894, occurs what may possibly be the first use of fingerprints in fiction. Brander Matthews (1852-1929) and Mary E. Wilkins Freeman (1852-1930) both took a keen interest in the form, and both wrote tales which have found their way into anthologies, though neither developed a significant detective. Julian Hawthorne (1846-1934) produced crime and near-crime fiction near the turn of the century which some connoisseurs feel has been unfairly neglected. Charles Honce writes, "He was half a century too soon." *The Achievements of Luther Trant* (1910), by Edwin Balmer (1893-   ) and William MacHarg (1872-   ), is a volume deserving more than passing attention. Based on contemporaneous methods of the psychological laboratory, the episodes have suffered inevitably from the passage of time. But the writing was of a superior order, and at least one tale, "The Man Higher Up," is notable for the first appearance in fiction of the principle of the modern "lie-detector." Samuel Hopkins Adams (1871-   ) made one excursion into the field with his Average Jones stories in the volume of the same name, published in 1911. The tales were well above the level of their era, both in conception and style, and it is a source of perennial regret that this excellent story-teller has shown no inclination to revive his attractive hero. Burton E. Stevenson (1872-   ), the only ac-knowledged librarian-writer of detective fiction (and the distinguished compiler of the *Home Books* of verse and quotations), has contributed several competent volumes to the genre, of which *The Mystery of the Boule Cabinet* (1912) is frequently singled out for the jig-saw quality of its puzzle. After a silence of several years, Mr. Steven-son has recently re-entered the field. It is usually for-gotten that John T. McIntyre (1871-   ), best known in recent years for his realistic novels of the underworld, was also the author of the quite *un*realistic Ashton Kirk books, beginning in 1912. Gelett Burgess (1866-   ) now admits authorship of the single volume of Astro tales, *The Master of Mysteries,* published anony-mously in 1912; it is not too much to say that he fares better when judged by his non-detective writings. Cleve-land Moffett's (1863-1926) *Through the Wall* (1909) still has ardent partisans.

Numerous other authors, though they did not actually write detective stories, touched on the fringes of the sub-ject during the years under consideration and thus in-directly influenced either the form or the public, or both. Of many, we may mention: C. N. and A. M. Williamson, H. M. Rideout, Harold McGrath, Irvin Cobb, Arthur Train, Louis Joseph Vance, and Frank L. Packard.

It can not be pretended that the American detective story revealed anything like the quantity or the level of quality of its English counterpart in the years up to the first world conflagration. So far as the land of Poe was concerned, any general flowering of the form was still far away. But the time was not entirely an empty or an idle one. An era that produced only a Melville Davisson Post—if nothing more—needs no apology.

CHAPTER VI

The Continental Detective Story

THE marked inferiority of the Continental detective story—even that of France, with a few exceptions—when measured against the English and American product must be largely ascribed to origin and tradition. In America the detective story was founded by one of its greatest men of letters of all time. In England it was fostered and advanced by such literary giants and near-giants as Dickens, Collins, and Doyle. But in France the form began with a hack-writer, and the florid sensationalism injected into it by Gaboriau continues to mar the usually excellent logic of the French roman policier to this day. As for the remainder of the Continent, it simply lacked the essential political and legalistic backgrounds of the established democracies, and was consequently able to produce at best feeble imitations of the real thing. Recent world events make it necessary to refer to even this limited development in the past tense.

Nearest to Gaboriau in the French detective story, both chronologically and stylistically, was another feuilletonist, Fortuné Hippolyte Auguste Du Boisgobey (1821-1891). Du Boisgobey was Gaboriau's avowed disciple, even to the extent of writing a novel intended to perpetuate LECOQ after his creator's death. His most successful book was *Le Crime de l'Opéra*, which, however, is not a detective story but a mystery novel. Of his work in the roman policier proper, *Le Forçat Colonel* (1872) is usually cited as his most representative effort. He followed no continuing detective character through his novels. The best that can be said for Du Boisgobey (who, indeed, is recalled only as a name to-day, even in his own country) is that he was a lesser Gaboriau.

No further proponent of any importance appeared in France until almost two decades after Du Boisgobey's final, forgotten police novel. Gaston Leroux (1868-1927) was already well known as a journalist and author of popular fiction when he turned in 1907 to the detective story with *Le Mystère de la Chambre Jaune* (*The Mystery of the Yellow Room*), the first of half a dozen "aventures extraordinaires" featuring JOSEPH ROULETABILLE, reporter. But the only one of the succeeding novels to approach the popularity of the initial volume was its immediate sequel, *La Parfum de la Dame en Noir*.

The Mystery of the Yellow Room is generally recognized, on the strength of its central puzzle, as one of the classic examples of the genre. For sheer plot manipulation and ratiocination—no simpler word will describe the quality of its Gallic logic—it has seldom been surpassed. It remains, after a generation of imitation, the most brilliant of all "locked room" novels. The author's use of the official detective as the culprit (though an outworn device to-day) was also in its time a highly original conception. Moreover, Leroux, unlike most of his compatriots, played religiously fair with his readers.

But on the debit side, one regrets to say, the score is also high. The author's narrative method can be compared only to the serial thrillers of early moving-picture days. The dialogue stems directly from the "Hist!" and "Aha!"

school. The aged theme of family scandal is dragged from its mothballs to serve once again. The characters are still the incredible puppets of Gaboriau's feuilletons. (One wonders, in passing, if Leroux's employment of the name Stangerson for two of his chief actors was an intentional or an unconscious tribute to Conan Doyle: see *A Study in Scarlet;* he openly borrowed Doyle's Watson convention, giving ROULETABILLE his admiring Sainclair.) Disguises and aliases abound; the long arm of coincidence is stretched beyond all credibility; and mere probability is ever the least of the novelist's anxieties. We are expected, for example, to believe that ROULETABILLE was little more than sixteen years old at the time of the *Yellow Room* problem—and that he could interrupt a criminal trial and virtually take over its conduct from the constituted officials of justice. As a crowning touch, the chubby hero is revealed (in the second novel of the series) as the *son* of his arch-foe!

No, for all his excellence as a contriver of adroit puzzles, Leroux is simply not the modern reader's dish. He was an influence and an important one, but his position is chiefly historical and technical.

Leroux's name is usually coupled with that of Maurice Leblanc, the creator of ARSÈNE LUPIN, who flourished during virtually identical years. Leblanc was born in Rouen, in 1864, of Franco-Italian descent. His sister, the actress Georgette Leblanc, was for many years the companion of Maurice Maeterlinck, who wrote many of his plays for her. Like Leroux, Leblanc was a journalist. He wrote fiction for some time without important success until, on a day in 1906, he was asked by the editor of a new journal, *Je Sais Tout,* to supply a short story of crime. Without an idea in his head and with no previous knowledge of crime or criminals, Leblanc took up his pen, and his impudent hero sprang into spontaneous being. From this almost accidental beginning came one of the most successful careers in contemporary French letters, culminating in the ribbon of the Legion of Honor for the author. Until the Nazi occupation Leblanc was known to be living in retirement near Paris; no word has come from him since. (But he definitely did *not* die in 1926, as Willard Huntington Wright erroneously stated in *The World's Great Detective Stories*.) He is described as a quiet, friendly man of medium height, with a large, cheerful face, bright, kindly eyes, and a large mustache over a humorous mouth. Much of his writing in his productive years was done in the open air. He is said to have a taste for chess and the works of Poe and Balzac.

The first collection of Lupin stories, *Arsène Lupin: Gentleman-Cambrioleur*, was published in 1907. Other volumes followed in rapid succession until the early 1930's. Most of them were collections of short stories, a few loosely episodic novels. Lupin himself has undergone a curious history. In all the earlier books he is the gentleman-burglar of the original title. Then, as more and more readers clamored for him to turn his brilliant talents to the pursuit of crime, a transitional period sets in, and he devotes himself to correcting the blunders of the official police, usually without their knowledge and to their discomfiture. In the final volume he is often openly on the side of law and order. (An early parody by Leblanc in the worst vein of Gallic satire, involving Lupin and Sherlock Holmes in unequal combat, deserves mention as a historical curiosity; but as a work of fiction it is best forgotten.)

The disguises and aliases complained of in Leroux are, if anything, even more tedious in Leblanc. His narrative style, too, tends toward the exclamatory. And as a logician LUPIN is scarcely a match for ROULETABILLE. Yet the casual modern reader will be likely to pronounce Leblanc's stories fresher, livelier, definitely more readable, and in many instances more believable than Leroux's. Paradoxically, it is probably their very picaresque quality which produces the latter effect; for once the reader is induced to accept the premise of deliberate unreality—"anything goes." Fantasy, as some one has remarked, writes its own rules, and the unabashed escapism of the LUPIN adventures *seems* somehow more credible to us than the ROULETABILLE investigations, which, making a greater pretense of realism, too often end by being merely sensational.

LUPIN himself is responsible in no small degree for the success of the stories. Few readers will disagree with the tribute paid the scamp-detective by Charles Henry Meltzer: "To the skill of SHERLOCK HOLMES and the resourcefulness of RAFFLES, ARSÈNE LUPIN adds the refinement of a casuist, the epigrammatic nimbleness of a La Rochefoucauld and the gallantry of a Du Guesclin." *The Eight Strokes of the Clock* (1922) is named by virtually all critics as the work containing the best examples of LUPIN as detective and deserves the attention of every discriminating reader. The earlier volumes, for the most part, belong in quite a different category.

To sum up: Leblanc is perhaps not quite the equal of Gaboriau or Leroux in the realm of pure ratiocination, but he is an infinitely more resourceful and convincing story-teller, a finer master of plot and situation, than either of them was capable of being. He is still a rewarding author for those who will meet him half-way.

French writers of soi-disant detective fiction in more recent years have been numerous and prolific, but for the great part singularly undistinguished as compared with the bright particular stars of the English and American firmament during the same period. Even François Fosca, leading contemporary French writer on the subject, has found but two of his compatriots in all the years since Leblanc and Leroux whom he deems worthy of specific mention in his *Histoire et Technique du Roman Policier*. One of these, Pierre Véry (1900-), is unknown in translation. The other, Georges Simenon (1903-), creator of INSPECTOR MAIGRET, has recently come into his belated own in England and America.

Simenon's name was originally Georges Sim, and he is really a Belgian (born in Liége) rather than a Frenchman. Here is his own characteristically terse account of his career:

At sixteen years of age, reporter on the Liége *Gazette*. At seventeen, published my first novel, *Au Pont des Arches*. At twenty, marriage; moved to Paris. [His later home, at least until the German invasion, was at Nieul-sur-Mer.] From twenty to thirty, published about two hundred novels under sixteen pseudonyms, and traveled, chiefly in a small boat, all over Europe. At thirty, on board his yacht, the *Ostrogot*, then in the north of Europe, wrote his first detective novels and created the character of MAIGRET. For two years wrote a novel of this series every month. At thirty-three abandoned mystery novels, and was at last able to write more personal works. That's all.

Several of the MAIGRET novels were translated and published in America in the early 1930's, when they were taking France by storm, but for some reason they failed to catch on with the public. The series was discontinued for some years only to be revived again by an enterprising publisher, who, sensing that the novelettes (which is really their nature) were too slight to be acceptable to American readers as complete books, fell upon the happy idea of issuing them two to the volume. A contract was announced for the publication of some twenty-five of the MAIGRET tales in this manner.

The series thus begun in 1940 scored an immediate success and brought Simenon a recognition that was long overdue. Characteristically, he is now as greatly overpraised in America as he was unfairly ignored previously. He has been called the indubitable spiritual heir of virtually every writer from Conan Doyle to Edgar Wallace (whom he resembles solely in quantitative output and energy). He is actually none of these things. He is a young writer of great zest and resourcefulness, with a flair for quick characterization and atmosphere-painting, whose unfailingly diverting short novels must be pronounced a little better as straight fiction than as detection.

Sometimes his deductive feats are no less than brilliant; often they are missing entirely as MAIGRET plods and puffs his sleepy way through criminal investigations in all parts of the pre-1939 Continent. Nevertheless, MAIGRET —who represents a sort of ingratiating synthesis of HANAUD, JIM HANVEY, and INSPECTOR BULL, but with a great deal of flavor and individuality in his own right— must be set down as one of the few really distinctive and original detective creations of recent years. As John Peale

Bishop has said in the *New Republic:* "There are times when, with his comprehending pity and his patience in applying power, MAIGRET comes close to being what was best, what was most human, in the Third Republic." And, as Miriam Allen deFord remarks, Simenon's own "wit, suavity, and mastery of style are beyond question."

George Bernanos (1888-   ), best known as the author of the memorable *Diary of My Times,* is sometimes mentioned in connection with the roman policier, but his position in the field—if any—is on the psychological fringe, as a Gallic and even more remote Francis Iles. . . . One or two of Claude Aveline's (1901-   ) INSPECTOR RIVIÈRE stories have been translated into English, but without repeating the success of MAIGRET.

Continental contributions to the detective story, aside from the French, have been so few, so indirect, and so unimportant that there would be no sensible object in discussing them here: the result would be only a list of authors obscure at best and for the great part untranslated and unavailable in England or America. The interested collector and the specialist in foreign literature are referred to Willard Huntington Wright's brief section on the subject in his introductory remarks to *The Great Detective Stories* (1927). One title and author should perhaps be added to the Wright list: *The Black Box Murder* (1889) by Maarten Maartens (1858-1915), the only detective story of more than passing note produced by The Netherlands. Also, in the years since the Wright summation, the police novel is reported to have made new strides in the Scandinavian nations. In fact, no less distinguished a spokesman than Knut Hamsun pronounces the works in this field of a younger Jonas Lie—not to be confused with the novelist of the last century or with the contemporary artist—as the best in any language. But translations again are lacking, and the explosion of the totalitarian cataclysm over Europe would seem to have halted effectively further development in any part of the Continent for at least a number of years.

CHAPTER VII

England: 1918-1930

(*The Golden Age*)

It should be possible, I thought, to write a detective story in which the detective was recognizable as a human being.—E. C. BENTLEY, *Those Days*

I

AN interesting speculation for the literary theorist is what the course of the detective story would have been had the First World War failed to occur when it did. On the one hand, the genre, especially in England, seemed on the eve of a new and more naturalistic flowering, of its own making. On the other, without the catharsis of catastrophe which influenced all literature so profoundly, this incipient trend toward a more credible form and style might have died a-borning. Of this much we may be certain: that the War marked, whether fortuitously or not, an effective period to the romantic tradition that stemmed from Baker Street. Before 1914, the difference between detection and mere mystery was clear in the minds of only a few. After 1918, we find a new and distinct cleavage, with the tinseled trappings of romanticism relegated for the most part to the sphere of mystery, and a fresher, sharper detective story making bold and rapid strides on its own stout legs. How much of this change was the effect of the awful years of interruption, how much a logical development that would have occurred anyhow, can never be completely determined. Certainly it must be said that the germinal seed, at least, of the new growth was planted well in advance of the conflagration.

History often refuses to be neat and tidy—to the infinite annoyance of those who deal in chronological categories. Thus it was that, though the War of 1914-1918 marked both a hiatus and a boundary between the old-style detective story and that which we call Modern, the first tale fully to deserve the fresher adjective made its lithe and fair-faced bow a full year *before* the explosion at Sarajevo that set the world aflame. None of the initiated needs to be informed that its title was *Trent's Last Case* or its author E. C. Bentley.

The son of an English government official and a Scottish mother, Edmund Clerihew Bentley was born into a typical upper-middle-class family in Shepherd's Bush, London, in 1875. His early education was at St. Paul's School, where he began a lifelong friendship with another student and future author, G. K. Chesterton. At Merton College, Oxford, to which he won a history scholarship in 1894, he "did as many things as possible," this procedure being his "idea of what a University meant." He was an enthusiastic oarsman and president of the University boat club; he founded a literary magazine; and he served as president of the Oxford Union, the famous undergraduate debating society, often called "the cradle of Parliament." But politics was not to be his sphere. Called to the bar at the Inner Temple in 1901, he left the profession of law for journalism after only one year, joining first the editorial staff of the *Daily News,* which he preferred because it was the English paper most strongly opposed to the South African war. "I believed earnestly," he writes, "in liberty and equality; I do still."

For twenty-two years, from 1912 to his retirement in 1934, Bentley was chief leader-writer for the independent *Daily Telegraph,* specializing in foreign affairs, always his favorite political study. (The Hitler War forced his return to active journalism in 1940, to succeed Harold Nicolson as literary editor of the *Telegraph,* "after six years of happy freedom.") In 1902 he married Violet, daughter of General N. E. Boileau of the Bengal Staff Corps; of their two sons, the younger, Nicolas Clerihew Bentley, is well known as a humorous writer and illustrator. The elder Bentley began his own literary career in similar vein, contributing light verse, sketches, and parodies to *Punch* and other humorous periodicals from university days onward, and even indulging in a little drawing. His first book publication was a volume of nonsense verse, *Biography for Beginners* (1905), illustrated by his friend, Chesterton, and signed by the author as "E. Clerihew." The formless four-line verse which it originated is called a "clerihew" to this day. It was in 1913 that the leader-writer and humorist turned his pen and talents to crime, with what results grateful readers of all nations fondly recall: the full circumstances will be discussed a little later.

Though *Trent's Last Case* was a pleasant financial success as well as a literary triumph—it has been translated into nearly every written language—it in no way changed the even tenor of its author's life, and for nearly a quarter of a century all indications were that it had been but too accurately named. It was not until 1936, after Bentley's

retirement from active editorial work, that likable, decent
PHILIP TRENT (by profession an artist and journalist,
and unconsciously more than a little reminiscent of his
creator) took his long deferred encore bow. *Trent's Own
Case* (written in collaboration with H. Warner Allen,*
1881-   ) did not have, understandably, the epoch-making
success of the earlier work, but discriminating readers
rejoiced to find in it much of the urbane naturalism, suf-
fused wit, and rich bouquet which had made its rejuvenating predecessor so notable. A few iconoclastic souls
even give it preference. A volume of characteristic short
stories, *Trent Intervenes,* appeared in 1938. These three
slight but significant volumes constitute the entire Bentley
contribution to the detective story to the date of the
present writing. It is perhaps unnecessary to say that
thousands of readers join in hoping that many more of
the incomparable TRENT narratives may appear before
his kindly inventor decides to put down his pen.

To-day Mr. Bentley lives quietly and modestly with his
wife in Paddington: a large, graying, essentially simple,
idealistic, and generous man who symbolizes the finer side
of an England that—for better or worse—may never be
known again. "The main influence in my life," he writes,
"has been my association with G. K. Chesterton; for the
rest, my outlook was established by the great Victorians,
who passed on to me the ideas of the Greeks about essential values, namely, physical health, freedom of mind, care
for truth, justice, and beauty." At Chesterton's death in
1935, Bentley was elected to succeed him as the second
(and present) president of the Detection Club, the re-

* Author of crime fiction in his own right, and also—literary detectives
please note!—of a work called *Mr. Clerihew: Wine Merchant.*

nowned association of England's best detective authorship. He has continued to write in leisurely fashion himself, and in 1940 published a mellow volume of reminiscence, *Those Days*, which he calls "by far the best thing I have ever produced—according to me."

Like Conan Doyle before him, he regrets, by implication at least, the obscuring of his other works by his best known hero: he has hinted with typical diffidence that he would prefer to be remembered by posterity for his several humorous books, which, indeed, have considerable reputation in his native land, though American readers are likely to find them a little too *Punch*-like for their tastes. This is unconscious ingratitude, for Mr. Bentley has a particular fondness for Americans and American slang, including a special admiration for the Broadway tales of Damon Runyon. In fact, his attempt on one occasion to write a Preface in imitation of Runyon's colorful New Yorkese amused reviewers in the United States for reasons that he could scarcely have intended. Topical humor apparently transmits poorly in either direction!

It was in 1910, Bentley reveals in the autobiographical *Those Days* (unfortunately not published in America), that he first began thinking of writing a detective novel. From its inception, he says, it was a conscious reaction against the combined austerity and absurdity into which the form had increasingly sunk. "It does not seem to have been noticed that *Trent's Last Case* is not so much a detective story as an exposure of detective stories." The tale, however, was *not* written as the result of a wager with Chesterton, contrary to accepted legend, though Bentley did have his friend's encouragement. After many months of "thinking out" the plot, the actual writing began. "Almost all of the work was done on my feet," says Bentley. "The thinking out was done while walking [from Hampstead] to Fleet Street; the writing was done at a standing-up desk."

A particularly interesting circumstance in the history of *Trent's Last Case* is the part played by American publishing—much as SHERLOCK HOLMES owes his perpetuation to Britain's erstwhile colonies. Bentley had entered the completed manuscript—then known as "Philip Gasket's Last Case"—in a prize contest for first novels conducted by a London publisher, but it had failed to be considered for the award. Again like Doyle, he had virtually abandoned hope of publication. Then, at a dinner in London in 1912, he chanced to be seated next to a young man "of winning personality," the representative of the American publishing firm, the Century Company. As the result of their conversation the manuscript was submitted and in due course accepted for New York publication. The American firm required two changes, of contradictory wisdom: the author was asked to alter his hero's name from Gasket to the shorter and more euphonious TRENT, and the title to *The Woman in Black*. In both the English publication and the later American re-issues, however, the novel appeared under its better known and unique title. Bentley's explanation of his choice of adjective, incidentally, is that "the labor of writing the story, in my leisure from a regular newspaper job, had been so crushing that I meant never to attempt a detective novel again." After the American acceptance the encouraged author went to his friend John Buchan, then a partner in the firm of Nelson, for advice in finding a British publisher. Buchan read the manuscript and accepted it himself, and virtually simultaneous publication occurred on both sides of the Atlantic in March, 1913.

The plot of *Trent's Last Case* is at once unorthodox and cunningly contrived. To outline it here would be superfluous for those who have read the masterpiece and unfair to those who still have that abounding pleasure ahead of them. The style is adept, light, and entertaining: "I know no more than the man in the moon," says Bentley to-day, "how it happened that I made TRENT adopt that particular line of preposterous talk." The detection is of a highly superior brand—but the detective's conclusions are happily far from the truth. To complicate matters still further (and this is where the greatest unorthodoxy enters) the detective breaks all the rules by humanly falling in love with the supposed culprit. The eventual revelation of the murderer is almost as startling as in Agatha Christie's *Roger Ackroyd* but is accomplished without resort to debatable devices. The character-drawing is the subtlest in the form since *The Moonstone*. The whole performance, in fact, is pervaded by an indescribable flavor of literacy and naturalness that can be conveyed only by first-hand acquaintance.

Yet a word of caution is advisable. *Trent's Last Case*, like every epochal work, must be regarded in its own historical spectrum to be fully appreciated. Compared to the highly developed product of to-day, it is competent, literate, and ingenious enough—but in no sense of the word pyrotechnic. Its deceptive *un*-remarkableness, in fact, is the chief reason for its uniqueness in an era in which flamboyance and over-writing were the hallmarks of the crime novel. Contrasted with the turgid narratives of its own period, its civilized effortlessness and engaging humor are as twin beacons in a fog, and its real worth becomes apparent. Judged by this, the only fair standard, *Trent's Last Case* stands truly first among modern examples of the genre. It is one of the great cornerstones of the detective story, and if any contemporary writer is heir to the mantle of Wilkie Collins, the honor could not fall on worthier shoulders than those of E. C. Bentley.

In John Carter's words, he is truly "the father of the contemporary detective novel."

II

Another English author who overlapped the two eras, but in quite a different sense from Bentley, was J. S. Fletcher (1863-1935). The paradox of Bentley is that he wrote the first truly modern detective novel—in the romantic period. The anomaly of Fletcher is that, though his greatest popularity came in the 1920's, his works belong in spirit to the HOLMESIAN era of gas illumination and horse-drawn transportation. In some respects it is a mistake to call Fletcher a detective story writer at all, for by far the larger share of his prolific output belongs in the category of mystery. Yet he did turn out a few pleasant examples of legitimate if highly romanticized detection, and to countless uncritical members of the reading public in the 1920's he symbolized (albeit quite erroneously) the "new detective story," then at the crest of its recently won respectability.

Joseph Smith Fletcher was born at Halifax in Yorkshire (the background of so many of his books), the son of a Nonconformist clergyman. Orphaned at an early age, he was brought up by his grandmother. At eighteen, the same year in which he set out to conquer the journalistic world, he issued a volume of youthful verse; at twenty-nine, he published his first novel, a forgotten three-decker historical romance. Shortly he was earning enough money from his books, which numbered well over a hundred by the time of his death, to leave newspaper drudgery behind. Among his more "serious" works, his several volumes of antiquarian research still have genuine reputation, and furnished him, besides, with excellent background material for his fiction.

Although Fletcher had turned his hand to mystery-detection of a sort as early as the turn of the century, his real prominence in the field dates from 1918, when he was "discovered" by President Woodrow Wilson, an ardent devotee of puzzle and crime fiction. The volume that pleased the President, and which still remains Fletcher's topmost achievement, was *The Middle Temple Murder*. From 1918 to the date of his death at seventy-two his works poured from the presses at an unbelievable pace. In justice to Fletcher it must be said that a good share of the spate of books that appeared over his name in 1920's consisted of re-issues of earlier works; but apart from these he was accountable for three or four actually new volumes a year. For all this quantity of words and plots, he never produced a really significant single detective character, with the possible exception of ROGER CAMBERWELL, the hero of a series of inferior adventures written in the author's last years, long after his best work was done.

It goes almost without saying that in any such output much of the result was bound to be haphazard and unequal. Yet Fletcher could disclose genuine talent when he took the pains, particularly in the construction of richly tapestried English backdrops, the reflection of his antiquarian studies. The difficulty was that too often his carefully begun and elaborately set narratives turned out to be peopled by pasteboard puppets and degenerated into sheer—and mere—melodrama in lieu of anything resembling conscientious detective procedure. The once great popularity of the Fletcher stories has waned virtually to the vanishing point since their author's death, but in their time, careless and hasty as they often were, they played an important part in creating the modern vogue for the form.

J. S. Fletcher was once an indisputably Big Name in what was loosely called the detective story. For this reason he can not be ignored by serious students of the literature, though he has long since been superseded by fresher and better writers.

III

Some of the characteristics that distinguish the new-style detective story from the old- have already been implied. Briefly, the new-style story is more natural, more plausible, more closely related to real life than the old-style—and is generally better written. The author is more careful to play fair with his readers; attempts to startle and amaze are fewer; there is less hokum, to borrow an expressive term from the theater, or at least the hokum is less obvious and obtrusive. The detectives are less eccentric and more human, less omniscient and more fallible. They act in the manner of ordinary mortals and sometimes even make mistakes. The cult of infallibility is to-day as out-of-date as Nick Carter; the "super-sleuth" is found only in the comic supplements. All these differences do not mean that the new-style story is necessarily less thrilling or adventurous than the old-. They simply mean that the thrills and adventures are more believable.

An interesting sidelight on the changing fashions of the detective story is the pronounced trend since the Armistice toward the police detective as hero: a trend entirely in keeping with the wider movement in the direction of naturalism and realism in the genre. For reasons both atavistic and technical, the amateur will probably continue to hold first place among fictional sleuths as long as the form endures. But the observant reader requires no reminder of the increasing emphasis that the present generation of writers has placed on truthful depiction of police procedure, if not, indeed, on the professional detector of crime himself.

The first of modern writers to find fictional possibilities in the step-by-step methods of actual police routine was Freeman Wills Crofts (1879-   ). In the opinion of a vast number of readers and critics he has never been equaled, much less surpassed, in his particular field. The son of a doctor in the British Army, Mr. Crofts was born in Dublin and lived a great part of his life in Northern Ireland. Educated at the Methodist and Campbell Colleges, Belfast, at seventeen he entered on his professional career as a civil and railway engineer, a vocation which contributed no little to his later almost mathematical detective plots. The first of these, however, had to await the author's fortieth year.

"In 1919," he writes, "I had a long illness, with a slow recovery, and to while away the time I got pencil and exercise book and began to amuse myself by writing a story. It proved a splendid pastime and I did a lot of it before getting about again. Then I put it away, never dreaming that it would see the light of day, but a little later I re-read it, thought that something might be made of it, and began to alter and revise. Eventually ... to my immense delight it was published."

This story, as every devotee knows by now, was that masterpiece of practical crime detection, *The Cask* (1920). Mr. Crofts will presumably not object if one hazards the statement that not even he has succeeded in topping this well-nigh perfect example of its kind. In its quietly documented thoroughness, it is one of those timeless stories that improve rather than lose by the test of re-reading—preferably with pocket-atlases and maps of pre-Hitler London and Paris by the reader's side. Its central theme has become the trade-mark of Mr. Crofts' work in the field: the painstaking demolition of the "unbreakable" alibi. In fact, it has become almost a truism that the one character in a Crofts' story who could not *possibly* have committed the crime will in the end be shown to have done just that!

If *The Cask* has a flaw, it is its failure to introduce INSPECTOR FRENCH, the modest, believable police hero of most of the author's later works. This difficulty was remedied, however, with the appearance of *Inspector French's Greatest Case* (1924), a volume worthy in almost every way to find its place on the shelf beside *The Cask*. Unfortunately, not so much can be said of quite all the later Crofts books, for in recent years some impatient readers claim to have noticed evidences of weariness in the methodical Inspector's adventurings. Others feel that his narrator occasionally becomes too greatly preoccupied with time-tables and menus to serve the best interests of fiction. These complaints, one fears, are at one and the same time justified and inherent in the factual method when it gets out of hand. The detective story may not be an "art form," but in common with all fiction it partakes of the axiom that art can reproduce life only by being *selective*.

That Mr. Crofts carries his chosen method sometimes a little too far is regrettable but by no means fatal to the enjoyment of any of his numerous works, even the least of which are rewarding to the reader who is willing to meet the author half-way with time and attention. Certainly, fellow-practitioners and readers alike owe him a very considerable debt for his conscientious pioneering in the early 1920's, and for his contribution of several of the most enduring stories in the genre. It is a pleasure to record that this contribution has not gone unrewarded. *The Cask* has sold more than 100,000 copies in two decades, with *Inspector French's Greatest Case* only a little behind, and Mr. Crofts' more-than-a-score of works have been translated into at least ten languages. In 1929 he was able to retire from engineering and in 1939 he was made a Fellow of the Royal Society of Arts. At latest reports he and his wife were living quietly in the Guildford region of Surrey, which has served as the locale of several of his stories.

Whatever he may or may not produce in the future, Freeman Wills Crofts' permanent place in the history of detective fiction is already more than secure.

IV

Scarcely a month passes in normal years without some reference in the British press to the "Big Five" of living English detective story writers. The exact composition of this semi-mythical inner circle of the craft has long puzzled and eluded American readers, accustomed as they are to carefully tabulated "best" lists of everything from books to football players. As present knowledge serves, no definite compilation of the group has appeared in print.* It seems safe to say, however, that any impartial statistical poll of the sentiments of readers on both sides of the Atlantic would assure a position high on the list to H. C. Bailey (1878-   ), the creator of plump, drawling REGGIE FORTUNE.

Henry Christopher Bailey describes himself as "a Londoner born and bred and by habit." He was a classical scholar (First Honors) at Corpus Christi College, Oxford, and was coxswain of his college boat. At Oxford, also, he wrote his first book, a historical novel, *My Lady of Orange*. "Discovered" by Andrew Lang, it was published both in England and America while its author was still an undergraduate. A series of similar novels followed, the product of Bailey's part-time labor as he earned his livelihood by journalism. He has been employed for many years by the London *Daily Telegraph* in a variety of capacities, including those of dramatic critic, war cor-

* Even an appeal through the columns of the august *Sunday Times* of London has failed to produce an authoritative listing. But, with the help of Mrs. May Lamberton Becker of New York and Herbert B. Grimsditch of London, the writer *believes* the generally accepted constituency of the elusive quintet to be as follows: Dorothy Sayers, Agatha Christie, R. Austin Freeman, Freeman Wills Crofts, and H. C. Bailey. (This is not necessarily an expression of personal preference.)

respondent, and, currently, leader-writer. A small, wiry, bespectacled, dark-haired man in his sixties, Mr. Bailey to-day makes his home in Highgate with his wife; they were married in 1908 and have two daughters.

It was during his term as war correspondent in the years 1914-1918 that Bailey turned to detective stories, "as a relief." MR. FORTUNE, a doctor by profession and a detective by accident, made his first public appearance in *Call Mr. Fortune* (1920), a collection of longish short stories: the form by which the author is best known, although in recent years he has entered the field of the full-length novel, both with MR. FORTUNE and with JOSHUA CLUNK (of whom more later). For more than two decades, further FORTUNE adventures have appeared in a steady flow of one to two volumes each year. They are virtually as popular in America as in England and have been translated into several languages.

A good deal of resemblance has been noted between the Bailey-FORTUNE stories and the FATHER BROWN tales of G. K. Chesterton which began a decade earlier. Like Chesterton, Bailey leans heavily on literary artifice and "style." Too, MR. FORTUNE belongs pretty much to the "intuitive" school of detection, symbolized by Chesterton's little priest, and partakes of the advantages and criticisms of the kind. Both writers are highly mannered and often stretch characterization to the point of caricature. Both, moreover, have the quality of arousing strong partisanship—both pro and con—among their readers. But there are also important differences. A few, at least, of Chesterton's tales reach an "artistic" level to which Bailey does not pretend. By the reverse token, the Bailey *opera* are nearly always better detection per se. For all their stylistic mannerisms, they keep their feet solidly on the ground: in fact, it is difficult to find in modern detection puzzles more elaborately conceived or genuinely mystifying. Bailey has another great asset in his ability to portray certain types of character, particularly children and the pure of heart, with an appealingness and sympathy seldom met with in the form. While this is a little external to the merit of his tales as detection, it is a quality that can not be ignored in analyzing his standing and popularity.

JOSHUA CLUNK, H. C. Bailey's second major detective, whose initial appearance was in *Garstons* (1930; American title: *The Garston Murder Case*), presents a difficult problem in classification. A hymn-singing scoundrel and thoroughgoing hypocrite, he exposes knavery in others only to serve his own dubious ends, though his pious protestations are always otherwise. Now, a villainous detective is something of a contradiction in terms, as critics have not neglected to point out. But popular objection to MR. CLUNK seems to be based less on any such ethical premise than on the fact that the mannerisms with which Bailey has endowed him are a little too fantastic to be quite credible. Whatever the reason, he has never achieved the wide popular success of MR. FORTUNE, though the plots in which he participates are among the most brilliant the author has concocted. Nevertheless, there are a few readers—the present writer among them—who find the scurrilities of CLUNK a rather happy occasional relief from the tricksy affectations of REGGIE. The two characters have had brief meetings in one or two of the Bailey books. Perhaps some day their author will match them in full-dress combat—with no punches pulled!

v

The rise of the feminine author in the field of detective fiction may well serve some future scholar as the subject of a learned thesis. Certainly many a less intriguing and even less "important" theme has been treated for an academic degree. To-day a highly respectable proportion of all detective stories, including many of the finest, are written by women. This was not always so. The first seventy-five or eighty years of the genre produced only a handful of craftswomen who can be mentioned beside their masculine confrères, and even these require qualification. The works of Anna Katharine Green were more significant historically than for their own content. Mary Roberts Rinehart belongs indubitably among the great natural story-tellers, but she is more the narrator of mystery than of pure detection. Baroness Orczy is labeled and classified as the creator of the Scarlet Pimpernel by a generation that never heard of THE OLD MAN IN THE CORNER or LADY MOLLY. Carolyn Wells holds some sort of record for quantity production, yet it cannot be pretended that FLEMING STONE sits in the Detective Valhalla. Whether the change in the nature of the detective story after the Armistice was responsible, or the emancipation of womanhood in general, or both as concurrent and related manifestations of the same social factors, it is yet too early to say. At any rate, it was left for the 1920's to see the development of really distinguished women writers within the full meaning of the act.

First among these, in a chronological sense at least, belongs the name of Agatha Christie, creator of HERCULE POIROT, who was born at Torquay on the Devon coast in the early or middle 1890's. Her father, Frederick Alvah Miller, an American, died when she was a child, and the girl was brought up and educated by her mother, who urged her to write stories at an early age. A neighbor, the author Eden Phillpotts, also lent encouragement. Music was another early interest, but a year in Paris convinced sixteen-year-old Agatha Mary Clarissa Miller that she would never be an opera singer. In 1914, a few months after the outbreak of war, she married a young army officer, Archibald Christie, later a colonel, C.M.G. and D.S.O. When he was ordered to France, Mrs. Christie entered a V.A.D. hospital at Torquay.

"Toward the end of the war," she writes, "I planned a detective story. I had read many detective novels, as I found they were excellent to take one's mind off one's worries. After discussing one with my sister, she said it was almost impossible to find a *good* detective story, where you didn't know who had committed the crime. I said I thought I could write one. She was doubtful about it. Thus spurred on, I wrote *The Mysterious Affair at Styles.*"

This, the first of the POIROT stories, had a difficult time finding a publisher, and it was not until after the Armistice and the birth of Mrs. Christie's only daughter that it appeared in print, in 1920. A modest success, the book encouraged its author to further efforts, which in a little more than two decades have brought her the consistently highest financial rewards believed to have been achieved from book and magazine rights by any writer of detective fiction exclusively. (How the moving pictures can afford to ignore an author of such undoubted audience-appeal remains one of the unsolved and all-too-typical puzzles of the fantastic satrapy called Hollywood.)

Of the impressive list of volumes, mostly about POIROT, that have contributed to this enviable estate, the best known and most widely discussed is the brilliant *Murder of Roger Ackroyd* (1926). At the present late date it is betraying no secret to say that this remarkable story, a tour de force in every sense of the word and one of the true classics of the literature, turns on the ultimate revelation of the narrator as the criminal. This device (or trick, as the reader may prefer) provoked the most violent debate in detective story history. Scarcely had the ink dried on the pages before representatives of one school of thought were crying, "Foul play!" Other readers and critics rallied as ardently to Mrs. Christie's defense, chanting the dictum: "It is the reader's business to suspect *every one*." The question remains unsettled to-day, and the inconclusive argument will probably continue as long as detective stories are read and discussed.

Meanwhile, Mrs. Christie's life had provided events of its own. In 1927 she divorced Colonel Christie. In 1930 she visited Ur in Asia Minor and met Max E. L. Mallowan, who was assisting Sir Leonard Woolley with the archæological excavations there; in September of the year they were married. In normal times Mrs. Christie (as she still calls herself professionally) now spends several months each year in Syria or Iraq with her archæologist husband, dividing her time between writing and supervising the expedition's photography.

Most readers believe that Agatha Christie's great popularity dates from *Roger Ackroyd,* as it clearly deserved to, and chronologically such is the case. But the truth is that this memorable story was primarily a connoisseur's item when it was first published and that Mrs. Christie's introduction to a wider public arrived independently the same year through a bizarre sequence of events that might have come from one of her own novels. As reported by the press in December, 1926, the author vanished from her home without warning. A nation-wide search was instituted; anonymous reports of foul play reached the police; amateur detectives offered assistance and fantastic theories. At length the missing writer was located in a Yorkshire health resort, registered under the name of the woman who subsequently became Colonel Christie's second wife. Physicians pronounced Mrs. Christie a victim of amnesia, and the affair quickly disappeared from the head-lines. The proverbial nine-day sensation was over. But in the meantime two newspapers had begun serializing her stories, reprints of her earlier works sold out of stock, and her name and that of her detective were thenceforth household words.

Happily, POIROT richly merited the attention he received. For when he is at the top of his form few fictional sleuths can surpass the amazing little Belgian—with his waxed mustaches and egg-shaped head, his inflated confidence in the infallibility of his "little grey cells," his murderous attacks on the English language—either for individuality or ingenuity. His methods, as the mention of the seldom-forgotten "cells" implies, are imaginative rather than routine. Not for POIROT the fingerprint or the cigar ash. His picturesque refusal to go HOLMES-like on all fours in pursuit of clues is classic in the literature.

(But his inventor does not scorn to employ one of the tritest of the Conanical devices almost ad nauseam, in the person of Captain Hastings, easily the stupidest of all modern Watsons.) Not quite an arm-chair detective, POIROT nevertheless spurns the aid of science. He is the champion of theory over matter. What this postulate may lack in verisimilitude it gains in dramatic possibilities, which the author knows well how to exploit to advantage.

The only really serious grounds for criticism of the stories, in fact, is Mrs. Christie's too great reliance on, and not always scrupulous use of, the least-likely-person motif. An eminent American detective story author and keen critic of his craft once said to the present writer in private conversation: "I have the utmost admiration for Agatha Christie as a technician. But she never played completely fair with the reader in her life!"

Mrs. Christie occasionally turns her hand, for diversion, presumably, to stories in which other detectives appear; but none of these secondary creations has ever seriously rivaled the mustachioed Belgian. His own investigations, one regrets to report, have begun to reveal now and then symptoms of ennui, so that the publication of "a new Christie" (an event which occurs with semi-annual regularity or oftener) is not always now the item of interest to the discriminating reader that it once was.

Nevertheless, few sleuths have been more rewarding than POIROT at the height of his powers. He still comes closer to symbolizing his profession in the popular mind than any story-book detective since the HOLMES whose methods he professes to deplore—but with whose essential histrionism he has so much in common. The hypercritical may feel that Mrs. Christie sometimes allows her hero to lean too heavily on intuition, and that her own art could be improved by a little greater variety in method and closer attention to the probabilities and the canons of fair play. But none can gainsay that at her frequent best Agatha Christie is easily one of the half-dozen most accomplished and entertaining writers in the modern field.

VI

When Eden Phillpotts gave encouragement and literary advice to his young Devon neighbor, Agatha Miller, in the years before the First World War, he was already a man of middle age and established as one of England's best known novelists, with a good two decades of writing and many of his solid "Dartmoor" novels behind him. But, by a curious coincidence, both the older and the younger writer published their first detective stories within a few months of each other. Whether there was any direct connection between the events, neither author has revealed.

Eden Phillpotts was born in 1862 in India, where his father was a civil servant. He came of Devonshire families on both sides and when schooling age arrived he was sent "home" to Plymouth, where he first made acquaintance with the moorlands and the people whose devoted chronicler he was to become. At seventeen he studied briefly in a London dramatic school, but decided that he lacked the necessary talent for the stage, and entered an insurance office. In the 1890's he began to write and soon was able to devote his full time to literary pursuits, making his home at Torquay and, later, at Exeter. After almost fifty years, during which time he has published more than 150 volumes of prose, verse, and plays, he is still hard at work at his craft in his late seventies: a slender, white-haired man with a mustache and sensitive features. "I do very little except write," he says. "My work has been the consolation and support of a difficult life, and I love it, and can not think of any existence without it."

The first Phillpotts detective story, *The Grey Room* (1921), was published when the author was fifty-nine and was followed by *The Red Redmaynes* a year later. Both are well-written, soundly constructed tales and have been duly praised as such. There seems no longer any doubt that Mr. Phillpotts is also responsible for the workmanlike series of detective novels signed by "Harrington Hext" in the middle 1920's. Perhaps the best of the Hext narratives are *The Thing at Their Heels* (1923) and *Who Killed Cock Robin* (1924). A number of lesser but always competent novels have followed under both names. Although INSPECTORS RINGROSE (Phillpotts) and MIDWINTER (Hext) belong to the company of hardworking police investigators, Mr. Phillpotts is not one of those authors who place their reliance on a single outstanding character; closely woven plot rather than individual detective brilliance is his forte.

Eden Phillpotts finds a brief place on our list chiefly because he brought to the roman policier a name already distinguished in "legitimate" literature, and thus helped importantly to "dignify" the form at a time when it was still held somewhat suspect by the more earnest body of readers. Though he made no startling innovations, his fame and solid technical competence contributed substantially to the prestige of the detective novel in the decade after the Armistice.

VII

No single trend in the English detective story of the 1920's was more significant than its approach to the literary standards of the legitimate novel. And no author illustrates the trend better than Dorothy Sayers (1893-   ), who has been called by some critics the greatest of living writers in the form. Whether or not the reader agrees with this verdict, he can not, unless he is both obtuse and ungrateful, dispute her preëminence as one of the most brilliant and prescient artists the genre has yet produced.

The daughter of a clergyman-schoolmaster, Dorothy Leigh Sayers grew up in the low-lying East-Anglian fen country which she has employed so memorably as the background of *The Nine Tailors*—in the writer's estimation her finest achievement and one of the truly great detective stories of all time. She attended Somerville College, Oxford (recognizable to Sayers students as the women's college of *Gaudy Night*), where she took top honors in medieval literature in 1915 and was one of the first women to receive an Oxford degree. Several years as copywriter in a London advertising agency followed: an experience which was to make fictional reappearance in *Murder Must Advertise*. Compelled by a low salary to live frugally, she entertained herself by writing stories peopled by characters who possessed the affluence she at once lacked and envied. In this manner she created her now famous character, LORD PETER WIMSEY, and his satellites.

The book that began her long "infatuation for her noble hero" (to quote Earle Walbridge) was *Whose Body?*, which appeared in 1923. She had previously published a volume of verse and another of *Catholic Tales*. The LORD PETER of *Whose Body?* was, it must be confessed, only a shadowy outline, a vague, affected caricature of the WIMSEY known to thousands to-day. But the plot was original, the style was articulate and amusing, and the story served to introduce and establish such subsidiary favorites as Bunter, WIMSEY's rather Wodehousian "man" (who also bears a kinship to DR. THORNDYKE's Polton), and Inspector Parker of Scotland Yard (later to become the sleuth's brother-in-law) in an intermittently Watsonian rôle.

A whole shelf of novels has followed, narrating always with great literacy and sometimes with Dickensian characterization, the detective-interrupted saga of the noble WIMSEYS of Duke's Denver. Latterly, a special series has been devoted to the "Biblical seven years" of LORD PETER's courtship of Harriet Vane, detective novelist, begun when he cleared her of a murder charge in *Strong Poison* (1930). Another and highly contrasting Sayers detective, MONTAGUE EGG, wine and spirit salesman extraordinary, has created pleasant diversion for author and readers alike in occasional short stories, but without threatening the supremacy of the erudite nobleman. Mention must also be made, in this brief chronology, of Miss Sayers' single non-WIMSEY detective novel, *The Documents in the Case* (1930). Written with "Robert Eustace," the pseudonymous scientific collaborator of a long line of authors, it is not only a superlative example of the medical detective story, but a graceful tribute in its narrative method to Wilkie Collins' *The Moonstone* (which Miss Sayers justly considers the finest detective story ever written).

In addition to her high status as an original writer, Dorothy Sayers has added other laurels to her brow as the most painstaking and scholarly of detective story anthologists. Her three notable *Omnibuses of Crime* (English title: *Great Short Stories of Detection, Mystery, and Horror*) and their classic introductory essays will be discussed at some length in a later chapter.

One reference, however, to her critical writings will be permissible here, toward the fuller comprehension of her own efforts in the field. In the Introduction to the *Second Omnibus* (1931), she devoted considerable attention to the rather tentative experiments which had been made up to that date toward the amalgamation of the detective story with the legitimate novel, particularly the novel of psychology and character; and concluded by prophesying just such a transfusion as the ultimate salvation of a form fast approaching its limits. This commentary is significant not only as an egregiously accurate forecast of what has actually occurred in the intervening years, but also as an explanation of the later Sayers works.

Even in her early novels strong hints of experimental technique had been observable. (This iconoclasm supplies an interesting paradox in itself, for in all her other views Miss Sayers is a cheerfully unapologetic Tory and traditionalist.) But with *Gaudy Night* (1935), she definitely attempted to achieve a new form. Really the story of

LORD PETER's intensive and finally successful wooing of his Harriet, it introduced a psychological and (mirabile dictu!) murderless mystery, but as a counter-theme rather than as a principal plot. Again, in *Busman's Honeymoon* (1937), frankly sub-titled "a love story with detective interruptions," she told the story of the Vane-WIMSEY nuptials, injecting a considerably inferior (for Sayers) murder problem as complication, in place of the usual domestic contretemps of the honeymoon novel.

These two experiments must, in all fairness, be termed less than completely successful. Some critics, in fact, have been much more outspoken. Writing in the *Saturday Review of Literature* in 1939, John Strachey represented the extreme view when he said, "[Miss Sayers] has now almost ceased to be a first-rate detective writer and has become an exceedingly snobbish popular novelist." A less face-making and more apposite criticism, in the opinion of the present writer (who, incidentally, considers *Gaudy Night* the truer detective story of the two, for all its excess of erudition and lack of a corpse), would be that the author in her frank and laudable experimentation intruded unwittingly on the dangerous no-man's-land which is neither good detection nor good legitimate fiction. Had she gone all the way across to the overtly psychological novel with a crime interest, as did Francis Iles and such of his followers as Richard Hull and Anthony Rolls, on the one hand; or had she confined herself to the accepted detective framework with psychological overtones, as have such later apostles of the "literate school" as Margery Allingham, Nicholas Blake, Michael Innes, and Ngaio Marsh, on the other—the result might have been less upsetting to purists on both sides of the fictional fence. It is only fair to point out, however, that the Allinghams, Blakes, Inneses, and Marshes had the benefit of her researches and mistakes. She was the pioneer in the field, and for all the criticism her laboratory work has evoked, it did much to break down the old tabus which had shackled the form, and thus to make the path easier for others.

Unfortunately, too many readers who announce that they "can't stand Dorothy Sayers" know her work only through these latter books; which, for whatever reasons of publishing promotion or the frequent time-lag between true achievement and mass response, reached far wider audiences than her earlier and solider achievements. (And, by the very fact of attaining the best-seller lists, attracted those still less discriminating readers who absorb *only* best-sellers!) In fairness to themselves and to the author, such readers should investigate her earlier books, all of which are happily in print to-day and for the most part available in bargain-price editions. Let such doubters try *Murder Must Advertise, The Documents in the Case,* and *The Nine Tailors*—and revise their opinions!

Returning briefly to the chronology of Miss Sayers' outward life: the profits from her book and magazine and motion-picture rights have at last brought her the worldly substance and leisure she once envied in others, and in normal years she lives in rural semi-retirement near her girlhood home in East Anglia with her husband, the well-known war correspondent Captain Atherton Fleming, whom she married in 1926. She continues to publish, using her maiden name, but less frequently than formerly. In recent years detection has somewhat given way (temporarily, one hopes) among her interests to experiments in neo-medieval religious drama. But the outbreak of the Hitler War started her on a series of chirky feuilletons known as "The Wimsey Papers," which possibly presage the insouciant investigator's return at a happier tide in the affairs of men.

Despite the presence of some casual similarities, and Miss Sayers' well-known penchant for utilizing real-life material in her fiction, one can not quite credit the belief, held in some quarters, of an autobiographical basis for the Harriet–LORD PETER romance. Of the depth, however, of the author's literary devotion to her titled sleuth —monocle, aristocratic lineaments, esoteric erudition, and all—there is ample documentary proof. Her hero-worship, it is true, frequently borders on preciosity. In the words of more than one reader, she is sometimes too WIMSEYCAL for comfort. But taken all in all her admiration is not misplaced. For only a few of all of fiction's detectives have so brilliantly demonstrated their right to immortality as LORD PETER in his prime.

This does not mean, however, that his creator's technique is always beyond criticism. The later stories, as we have seen, fail by too great experimentation; and a few of the earlier ones embody no less the shortcomings of their own school and era. The great weakness of the British detective story of the 1920's was that, in its reaction against the overly-*physical* writing that had characterized the Romantic period in the literature, it went too far in the opposite direction and approached too closely the static, *mental* style of narrative. The tendency is chiefly evident in the failure of the mystery and suspense elements.

In Miss Sayers' *The Dawson Pedigree,* for example, there is virtually no doubt of the criminal's identity after the middle of the book. Only the *method* employed by the culprit remains to be revealed. That this is accomplished ingeniously only partly abates the reader's disappointment at the premature revelation: for in the perfectly constructed detective story the questions *Who?* and *How?* are answered simultaneously at the dénouement. That story (unless it is an intentional tour de force) which gives away the *Who?* to the reader and confines its puzzle to the *How?* of the crime simply falls short of its avowed goal. In *Suspicious Characters* Miss Sayers does better in maintaining the full puzzle, but the story is so lacking in action and movement that it fails to hold the reader's attention. This is just as fatal as solving the mystery too soon, and is a fault too often apparent in her short stories, at least one of which H. Douglas Thomson has labeled "merely a dramatized cross-word puzzle."

The regrettable feature of this is that no writer to-day can surpass Miss Sayers either in suspense or mystification—when she is of the mind. Nevertheless, most of her faults, whether the occasional underwriting of her early period or the over-elaboration of her later works, are deliberate and on the side of the angels. They arise from her sincere and scholarly devotion to the detective story and represent a knowledgeable effort to improve it. They are honest and frankly experimental mistakes, not slovenly writing.

If the criticisms of the Sayers' canon found in this section have seemed too numerous and minute, let it be said that only a really great writer could deserve or receive them. Dorothy Sayers is one of the fructifying and distinguished names in the form for all time. Her very errors do her honor.

VIII

Of several notable collaborations which have marked the detective story in recent years, none has been more unusual than that of G. D. H. and M. I. Cole, chiefly because of the multiple careers followed by both members of the energetic duo.

George Douglas Howard Cole was born at Ealing in 1889 and was educated at St. Paul's School and Balliol College, Oxford. He is to-day England's outstanding Fabian economist and publicist; the author of more than a score of authoritative books on economic and sociological topics; University Reader in Economics at Oxford; a fellow of University College; and a long time member-of-council of the British Labor Party—not to mention lesser posts and honors far too numerous to record. Margaret Isabel Postgate was born in 1893, the daughter of a professor of Latin at the University of Liverpool, and was educated at Roedean School and Girton College, Cambridge. After teaching at St. Paul's Girls' School she became interested in the Labor movement, with which she has been connected in one capacity or another ever since. She married G. D. H. Cole in 1918, and they have one son and two daughters. Like her husband, she has lectured, written, and published on the subjects of her chief interest, though not so extensively. Together they write detective stories "for recreation"!

The first Cole detective book was *The Brooklyn Mur-*

ders (1923; the title has nothing to do with Brooklyn, New York), which was written, Mr. Cole says, "during an illness, as he had been told not to work, and found the prospect intolerable." It is the only one of the Cole detective stories signed by G. D. H. Cole alone. All the works in the field since that date have carried the names of both husband and wife, and the general understanding is that Mrs. Cole now does the greater part of the actual setting-down, based on outlines supplied by the masculine half of the collaboration. Several detectives have pursued clues through the pages of the Cole *opera*, but the authors are chiefly known for their creation of SUPERINTENDENT WILSON, originally a conscientious Scotland Yarder of the FRENCH school, whose tactical error in catching-out an ex-Home Secretary compelled his retirement to private practice, where, however, he still employs the FRENCH methodology.

The Cole novels are extremely uneven, including some of the best police adventures of the routine school, and some of the most tedious. In general, the earlier books are the more readable. Always slow-paced, they nevertheless contain rewarding detection. In recent years the tales have shown a lamentable tendency in the direction of slovenly construction. Even more sluggish than before, they are further marred by such regrettable minutiæ of carelessness and haste as speeches by unintroduced characters, unannounced changes of scene, and overlooked clues and loose ends. Without doubt the public-minded authors have laudable uses for the pecuniary rewards that their detective novels bring. Nevertheless, one can not help wishing that they would abandon their schedule of two or three books a year (in normal times) in favor of some less taxing method of work that might permit them to approximate their early achievements in the field. At their best, they are a credit to their avocation; at their least, they represent the British police novel at its most British—and dullest.

IX

It can not be pretended, however, that the sin of dullness was any one's exclusive property in the years under our present consideration. In fact, the English detective story in the first two-thirds or so of the 1920's was all too likely to be a pretty solemn affair. To be sure, some notable advances in technique were recorded, a number of fine and outstanding novels and short stories were written, there were flashes of brilliance, and, occasionally, even of humor. But the leading practitioners were in large measure preoccupied with building up the police novel as a separate and recognizable form, distinct from the looser mystery-adventure narrative which had dominated the early decades of the century. In the pursuit of this wholly admirable aim, with consequent emphasis on the factual and routine aspects of the detective profession, it was perhaps only natural that a certain weightiness of treatment should some times result and that the entertainment objective should often be slighted. The arrival on this scene of the ROGER SHERINGHAM novels of Anthony Berkeley (1893-   ) came like a breath of fresh outside air and brought a timely reminder to heavier-handed writers that veritable deduction was not necessarily incompatible with élan and good story-telling.

A graduate of humorous journalism—like E. C. Bentley

before him, whose lineal literary descendant he is—Mr.
Berkeley (in real life Anthony Berkeley Cox) was particularly fitted to deliver this reminder and to restore
the TRENT tradition to its deserved estate. Aside from his
journalistic beginnings, all too little is known of Mr.
Berkeley, who remains singularly reticent about his background and life for so popular an author. Among the few
facts available from random sources: He was the real
founder of the distinguished Detection Club (though he
has modestly refused any office higher than that of Hon-
orary Secretary); he is a delightful and witty correspondent, and one of the few living English writers who really
comprehend the mysteries of American speech; he is
described by Malcolm Johnson, of his American publishers, as one of London's best hosts. In addition it is known
that (in pre-blitz days, at least) he inhabited with
his wife a fine old house in St. John's Wood, and a professional office just off the Strand, where he was listed
as one of two directors of A. B. Cox, Ltd. The nature of
this corporation has not been revealed by any of the
standard London directories. Many readers, however, believe that the remarkable knowledge of obscure legal
procedure he has displayed, notably in *Trial by Error*
with its brilliant murder-trial-in-reverse, betrays a sometime training for the bar. But other works in the canon
equally suggest first-hand acquaintance with journalism,
diplomacy, and politics. In short, not the least intriguing
of the Berkeley mysteries is the author himself.

Asked by the present writer to tell something of his
literary backgrounds and ideas (since his reluctance to
talk about his more personal life is known to be un-
assailable) he has replied from London with characteristic

good nature: "I began by writing sketches for *Punch,* a (so-called) humorous periodical peculiar to this country, but found that detective stories paid better. When I find something that pays better than detective stories I shall write that. . . . ROGER SHERINGHAM is an offensive person, founded on an offensive person I once knew, because in my original innocence I thought it would be amusing to have an offensive detective. Since he has been taken in all seriousness, I have had to tone his offensiveness down and pretend he never was."

Mr. Berkeley-Cox is much too modest on both scores. For all his claim to merely pecuniary motives, few detective stories produced on either side of the water to-day are written with such care or literary skill as those that come from the Berkeley pen; and SHERINGHAM has been justly called by H. Douglas Thomson "a less serious edition of PHILIP TRENT"—no slight tribute in itself.

Several non-detective books had appeared over the signature of A. B. Cox before *The Layton Court Mystery,* published anonymously in 1925, but later acknowledged, introduced SHERINGHAM to the reading public in his author's thirty-second year. Since that date scarcely a season has passed without a welcome Berkeley novel (most, though not all, have carried on the SHERINGHAM saga) to enliven the literary scene with the freshness of situation and portraiture that has become the hall-mark of the author's work. *The Poisoned Chocolates Case* (1929), a notable tour de force with no less than six separate solutions, and a veritable textbook of the literature, must in the present writer's estimation be accorded top place among the Berkeley products. But *The Second Shot* (1930) needs also be given special mention if only for the author's often-quoted and prophetic prefatory remarks, which will bear repetition once more:

> ...I am personally convinced [Berkeley wrote] that the days of the old crime-puzzle pure and simple, relying entirely upon plot and without any added attractions of character, style, or even humor, are in the hands of the auditor; and that the detective story is in the process of developing into the novel with a detective or crime interest, holding its readers less by mathematical than by psychological ties. The puzzle element will no doubt remain, but it will become a puzzle of character rather than a puzzle of time, place, motive, and opportunity.

This is the Berkeley credo, to which the author has stuck admirably. As "Francis Iles" (presumptively) he has gone even farther. Although Mr. Cox freely admits his identity as Anthony Berkeley, he has consistently refused either to confirm or deny publicly the Iles nom de guerre; perhaps because (in the theory of some authorities) the pseudonym may originally have covered a quasi-collaboration. However that may be, publishing and literary circles to-day admit no doubt of Mr. Cox's astute presence behind the nom, in whole or in part.

Strictly speaking, the Iles novels—penetrating psychological studies of murder and horror told from the inside out—are not detective stories; for the element of detection has been subordinated to the fascinating examination of "the events leading up to the crime" as seen and felt by the participants. So great, however, has their influence been on the more "orthodox" type of detective story in recent years that they worthily command our attention here. The idea of the inside-out crime novel was not, per se, particularly new: Mrs. Belloc Lowndes, among others, had achieved a very considerable success with it a decade or more earlier. But the mordant simplicity of the Iles prose added new vitality and breadth and depth to the form—and something else besides. Whereas the Lowndes school dealt with crime in the old, accepted terms of abnormality, the Iles studies invariably point to the killer and say, "There but for the grace of God go I."

It is this convincing insistence on the *normality* of murder that transforms the Iles stories into something apart, which gives them their horrid particular fascination and brings them close to the true "melodrama of the soul." Not many "serious" novelists of the present era, in fact, have produced character studies to compare with Iles' internally terrifying portrait of the murderer in *Before the Fact* (1932), his masterpiece and a work truly deserving the appellations of unique and beyond price.* This book was the second from the Iles pen; a year earlier the author had made his bow with *Malice Aforethought,* a sparkling and original piece, but lacking the frightening overtones of the later effort. A seven-year silence followed *Before the Fact,* broken by *As for the Woman* (1939), a somewhat experimental treatise announced as the first of three projected novels "about murder as the natural outgrowth of character."

The previously mentioned influence of Francis Iles on other writers is evident both within the roman policier proper, in the form of increased emphasis on character, and in the presence of a whole school of followers who have found the "inverted" detective story a rich field. In the latter classification, Richard Hull, Anthony Rolls, and Peter Drax may be mentioned, among many. Some of

---

* Alfred Hitchcock directed a notable motion picture version in 1941.

their books have been very good indeed, but none of them has quite succeeded in equaling the maestro.

Few authors have had a more salutary or vitalizing effect on the detective story than this same A. B. Cox, with his acute perceptiveness, urbanity, humor, literacy, and unfailing taste, whether he is writing as Anthony Berkeley or as Francis Iles. Perhaps because his contributions are usually disguised under a light-hearted style and wear the motley of entertainment—which should be a cause for rejoicing rather than otherwise—his importance in shaping the contemporary crime novel has not been adequately recognized by historians of the genre. More, almost, than any other single writer of his time he has constituted the necessary evolutionary link between the naturalism of E. C. Bentley and its logical result—the "character" detective novel of the 1930's. He perpetuated and elaborated the one form, and introduced the other.

X

Another British author who has carried on the TRENT or "naturalistic" tradition in such competent fashion as to require special mention is Philip MacDonald, whose ANTHONY GETHRYN novels occupy a deservedly high niche in the literature. Like Anthony Berkeley, Mr. Mac-Donald maintains resolute silence concerning his private life. He was presumably born in the early 1890's and is known to be a grandson of the Scottish novelist George MacDonald, best remembered for such juvenile classics as *At the Back of the North Wind*. Philip MacDonald served with a cavalry regiment in Mesopotamia in the First World War, and from this experience came his best known non-detective novel, *Patrol*. Horses are still his greatest interest. He has a score of books to his credit and has "done time" in the Hollywood studios. Several of his lesser works have appeared over pseudonyms: "Oliver Fleming," "Anthony Lawless," "Martin Porlock."

The first GETHRYN story—and still one of the classics of the form—was *The Rasp* (1924). The same lazy humor, smooth characterization, and scrupulous fair play that made this work memorable are found in a long list of subsequent novels. Philip MacDonald is also a subtle past-master of pace and suspense: his *Escape* (1932), a non-GETHRYN novel, achieves an effect of sheer breathlessness attained by few contrivers of melodrama in any form. Often overlooked, it is a volume no dyed-in-the-wool fancier can afford to miss. The same quality of excitement-by-understatement (more than a little comparable to the cinematic technic of Alfred Hitchcock) characterizes *Warrant for X* (1938), which is also something of a tour de force in the circumstance that the criminal is never named and is never viewed alive by the reader—but is, if anything, the more real and menacing for that fact. Most of the MacDonald novels stick more closely to orthodox detective patterns; all of them are well above the average in readability and workmanship. Something less of an innovator than an improver of established techniques, Philip MacDonald nevertheless merits a distinguished place in a history of the modern detective story.

XI

Mention of the Messrs. Berkeley and MacDonald brings inevitably to mind the name of A. A. Milne

(1882-   ), the poet and playwright, who will require no further personal introduction. Mr. Milne has written only one bona fide detective story, *The Red House Mystery* (1922), but this single work did much in its time to keep alive the naturalism of E. C. Bentley until Berkeley and MacDonald arrived on the scene a year or two later. Moreover, light-hearted ANTONY GILLINGHAM anticipated importantly the long line of humorous sleuths, both British and American, who have mingled murder most foul with jollity (not always with the success of the original) in more recent years. The detective story had been treated with some degree of lightness and humor before, but *The Red House Mystery* was the first novel really to go all out for what H. Douglas Thomson has described as the "what fun!" type of crime fiction. Mr. Milne also deserves citations of honor for his successful mystery-detective drama, *The Perfect Alibi* (1928), an ingenious affair in which the audience watched both the commission of the crime and the steps leading up to its detection. The relationship to the "reverse" detective novel is of course obvious.

XII

It has become something of a truism that the authors of the most adventurous tales usually lead the most placid of lives. Edgar Wallace (1874-1932), the most prolific writer of thrillers of modern times, was the exception to the rule. Few professional soldiers-of-fortune, even, have had careers of greater variety or extremes.

Richard Horatio Edgar Wallace was born in Greenwich, England, the illegitimate son of an actress, and was placed with a fish-porter's wife in Billingsgate to be brought up with her ten children as "Dick Freeman." An impudent but engaging child, he sold newspapers, worked for a printing firm, in a shoe shop, on a fishing trawler, and as an errand boy, which gave him his remarkable knowledge of London. His formal education ended at twelve, but he applied himself to his pocket dictionary with good effect. Enlisting as a private in the army, he was sent to South Africa for seven years. There he wrote Kiplingesque poems which won his master's praise, and at his discharge he wangled a post as correspondent with Reuter's, and later, back in England, with the *Daily Mail*. Soon his lively imagination and distaste for routine work involved his employers in expensive libel suits, and he was discharged. Badly in debt (he always lived and gambled beyond his means, in later years on a fantastic scale), he wrote *The Four Just Men* to recoup his fortunes. It became a best-seller, but the profits were eaten up by an ill-advised prize contest and he was no better off than before. However, he had come to the attention of the editors of the popular magazines, and one of them set him to work on the *Sanders of the River* stories, based on his African experiences—and the career of one of the greatest popular entertainers of all time was abruptly launched.

In twenty-seven years Wallace wrote or dictated one hundred and fifty separate books, to say nothing of a score of plays and hundreds of short stories and magazine articles. He had in later years a standing reward of £1,000 to any one who could prove that any of his writing was "ghosted." The reward was never claimed. He once dictated a complete novel between Friday night and

Monday morning, and his most successful stage play was completed in four days. In 1928, when he was earning £50,000 a year, it was said that one out of every four books printed and sold in England, exclusive of Bibles, was an Edgar Wallace! At length the strain began to tell. In 1932 he went to Hollywood to produce a photoplay, and there he died at fifty-seven after a four days' illness. His estate consisted of £150,000 in debts; but in two years' time Edgar Wallace, Ltd., a corporation formed by his heirs, was free of liabilities and paying dividends from accrued royalties on his works. A frank but amusing poseur, with incredible energy for work and play, Edgar Wallace combined great natural talent as a storyteller with an emotional immaturity which drove him to squander his gifts and strength. Edgar Shanks has accurately called him "a lost Dickens."

Of Edgar Wallace's countless thrillers, few but his tales of J. G. REEDER qualify as bona-fide detection, and even the latter require some leniency to come under the rule. MR. REEDER—with his square derby, mutton-chop whiskers, umbrella, and apologetic air, masking relentless courage—is a sure-fire piece of popular character drawing; but his detective triumphs are likely to depend more upon chance than upon deduction. The stories are marred, too, by the haste and carelessness found in most of Wallace's writing. Nevertheless, for entertainment in its broadest sense, they are unsurpassed. MR. REEDER's adventures are found in several books; among the best known in the United States are *Terror Keep* (1927), *The Murder Book of J. G. Reeder* (1929), *Red Aces* (1930), and *Mr. Reeder Returns* (1932).

Edgar Wallace's influence in the popularization of the

detective story was immense and immeasurable—even though it came largely from "the outside."

XIII

These, then, are the authors whom the present writer ventures to consider cardinal in the development—technical and popular—of the British detective story between the First World War and circa 1930. They admittedly constitute only a small numerical fraction of the many excellent craftsmen who flourished during the same years, and occasionally they are not even the "best" of their time and place. For (to repeat a premise from the Foreword) this volume is of necessity less concerned with literary merit per se than with setting forth the history and evolution of the detective romance as a form. Hence, as it was obviously impossible to include *all* authors at length, preferred position has been given to those protagonists whose works, in the writer's opinion, have most significantly *influenced* the progress of the detective story, either in technique or in popularity. This premise has meant in some cases the inclusion of authors of no very great distinction in themselves, and the omission of others whose achievements, judged by purely literary standards, might be considered of a higher order. For example: J. S. Fletcher was, by common consent, a less skilful craftsman than perhaps a score of writers of the same period whose names have not been accorded individual space here. Yet, what one of these more accomplished artists contributed to the detective story even a portion of the impetus it received—mistakenly or no—from Fletcher in the mid-1920's? Much the same thing may be said of

Edgar Wallace, whose vast audience gave him an influence, in popularizing the genre, out of all proportion to the actual merit of his writing.

Nonetheless, the age under discussion was so rich in auctorial competence that common gratitude dictates the mention of at least a few additional names and titles, albeit briefly.

The greatest number will be found, of course, in the field of the straightaway, or conventional, detective story: the routine narrative of crime-and-deduction. Prominent in this classification are the DR. PRIESTLEY novels by "John Rhode" (Major Cecil John Charles Street, 1884-). Under his own name, Major Street is the author of a number of works on international politics. He turned to detective fiction with *The Paddington Mystery* (1925). From one to three of his ursine mathematician's cases have appeared yearly since that date. At their best, they are good examples of the British routine, fair-play school. But too frequently, one regrets to say, they oscillate between impossible melodrama and deadly dullness, with "ciphers in the place of characters," as Nicholas Blake has complained. They have, nevertheless, been influential in the widening popularity of the detective story. . . . The numerous works of R. A. J. Walling (1869-) belong roughly in the same category, with more consistent emphasis, however, on deduction. Mr. Walling is a prominent English journalist and travel-writer. He began writing detective stories, he says, "almost by accident." *That Dinner at Bardolph's* (1928) was his first outstanding success in the field. His later novels, popular on both sides of the Atlantic, have been mainly concerned with the investigations of PHILIP TOLEFREE. The high standard of entertainment set by the early TOLEFREE books has not, unfortunately, always been maintained in the latter ones, which have shown an increasing tendency to become static and lifeless in the development of their plots. . . . The novels of Father Ronald A. Knox (1888-   ), the distinguished Catholic convert and apologist, while achieving a somewhat higher literary plane, suffer from the same general weakness. Although in the past he has made several excursions into the field, Father Knox has contributed nothing for some years now. His stories, as one might expect from knowledge of his brilliant essays, are adroitly contrived and urbanely written, but many readers consider them intellectual exercises rather than fiction. . . . Canon Victor L. Whitechurch (1868-1933) is another outstanding representative of the cloth. In the early years of the century he wrote several impressive semi-detective stories with railroad backgrounds. He returned to the lists in 1927 with *Shot on the Downs* and contributed several other technically competent novels before his death.

CHIEF INSPECTOR WILLIAM DAWSON, in the stories by "Bennet Copplestone" (Frederick Harcourt Kitchin, 1867-1932), is most widely and favorably known through a single short story, "The Butler," taken from *The Diversions of Dawson* (1924), and found in numerous anthologies. Perhaps because of the high expectations aroused by this one tale, the remaining DAWSON adventures are likely to seem clumsy and disappointing. . . . Three writers whose works have much in common, in conventional method and solid British flavor, are "Lynn Brock" (Allister McAllister, 1877-   ) with his COLONEL GORE; "J. J. Connington" (Alfred Walter Stewart, 1880-   ) with his SIR CLINTON DRIFFIELD and THE COUNSELLOR; and

"A. E. Fielding" (revealed surprisingly to be a woman, one Dorothy Feilding) and her INSPECTOR POINTER. Lord Gorell (1884-   ) made a single excellent contribution with his *In the Night* (1917). The quietly pleasant INSPECTOR POOLE stories of "Henry Wade" (Sir Henry Lancelot Aubrey-Fletcher, Bart., 1887-   ), beginning with *The Duke of York's Steps* (1929), lie somewhere between the conventional detective story and the livelier naturalistic method according to the gospel of Bentley and Berkeley. . . . "Anthony Wynne's" (Robert McNair Wilson, 1882-   ) pseudo-psychological DR. EUSTACE HAILEY has achieved a measure of popular success, but the rather heavy melodrama of the body of the works makes unqualified recommendation impossible. . . . Will Scott's humorous DISHER has his share of followers among the connoisseurs. . . . Arthur John Rees (1872-   ) and his COLWIN GREY are not so well known in America as they should be.

Too many excellent authors have written works on the border-line between adventure and bona fide detection for all of them to receive mention here. No wise reader, however, will ignore such deservedly outstanding favorites as the RICHARD HANNAY stories of the late John Buchan (Lord Tweedsmuir, 1875-1940); the BULLDOG DRUMMOND adventures as told by "Sapper" (H. C. McNeile, 1888-1937); the COLONEL GRANBY novels by "Francis Beeding" (John Leslie Palmer and Hilary Aiden St. George Saunders), or the Beeding terror *opera;* Lord Frederic Spencer Hamilton (1856-1928) and his P. J. DAVENANT; the FOX and CLUBFOOT tales of Valentine Williams (1883-   ), as well as Mr. Williams' highly superior closer approaches to detection (unfortunately for our purposes, he remains mostly the writer of mystery —but a top-notcher in his field); the numerous and entertaining narratives from the pen of "Richard Keverne" (C. J. W. Hosken, 1882-   ), of which *The Man in the Red Hat* is a particularly pleasing example; or Bertram Atkey's picaresque SMILER BUNN tales.

Several anticipatory references have been made to the "marriage" of the detective story and the novel of character, destined to be the most significant trend in the genre in the 1930's. One of the earliest works definitely to forecast this fusion was *Enter Sir John* (1928), a novel of theater life built around a murder mystery: a collaboration of two distinguished English "legitimate" novelists, Clemence Dane and Helen Simpson (1897-1940). A sequel which, contrary to the usual rule in such matters, surpassed the original appeared in 1932 under the title *Re-Enter Sir John*. No other SIR JOHN stories are recorded, and Miss Simpson's tragic death in the Nazi air-raids has made irrevocable what can only be called a distinct loss to detective literature.

In ending our consideration of the British detective story for this prolific period—the richest single age in the literature—it may be well to summarize briefly the chief developments of the era. They were three in number: (1) the vast improvement in the "literacy" of the detective story; (2) the new insistence on fidelity and plausibility, as opposed to the old school of melodrama and hokum; and (3) the increased emphasis, particularly toward the end of the period, on character, with the concurrent wane of the story of mechanical plot alone. In all truth, it was "The Golden Age."

CHAPTER VIII

America: 1918-1930

(*The Golden Age*)

I

THERE is no denying that until comparatively recent times the American detective story has consistently lagged behind the English. This was particularly true in the early years of the era under present consideration. The Great Revival of the English detective story began almost immediately after the Armistice in 1918. Its American counterpart did not arrive until the better part of a decade later. This is not to say that *no* good American detective stories were written during the intervening years. There were at least a few; but no important technical advance was made, no spontaneous upsurge of popular interest occurred, until well toward the end of the period.

When the Armistice was signed, Arthur B. Reeve was still enthroned as king of American detective story writers; Anna Katharine Green remained active and influential, though well past her prime; and Mary Roberts Rinehart dominated the romantic side of the picture even more personally than she does to-day. A few, but only a few, new authors had arisen or were on the immediate horizon, and most of these followed established patterns instead of striking out in new directions, as their British confrères were doing in the same years.

The works of Isabel Egenton Ostrander (1885-1924) (who also wrote as "Robert Orr Chipperfield," "David Fox," and "Douglas Grant") are all but forgotten to-day, but in the early 1920's they had a very considerable and not undeserved popularity. Essentially a follower of Anna Katharine Green, Miss Ostrander nevertheless made one important forward step of her own, with her *Ashes to Ashes* (1919), praised by Dorothy Sayers as "an almost unique example of the detective story told from the point of view of the hunted rather than the hunter." In most of her novels, in fact, the careful plot-work will repay the student who can survive the out-dated femininity of her prose.

As far back as 1914, Frederick Irving Anderson (1877-   ), one of the best known "magazine authors" of his generation, had turned his attention to crime with the episodic adventures of *The Infallible Godahl*. A later series of related short stories dealt with the career of *The Notorious Sophie Lang* (memorialized in several cinema incarnations).* Neither of these efforts represented pure detection, but the seed was planted. A character who had appeared in both series was DEPUTY PARR of the New York police. Beginning in 1921, PARR was given a series of his own in *The Saturday Evening Post*. The stories covered a leisurely decade and then were col-

---

* Curiously enough, the book collection of this popular series was published only in London (1925); never in America. A discriminating American bibliophile and newspaperman, Charles Honce of New York —who, incidentally, considers Anderson the finest of living short story writers—says of the heroine of the saga: "Sophie's real life counterpart was a famous New York woman thief. She purchased many copies of the book."

lected in *The Book of Murder* (1930). Because of his small output between permanent covers, Frederick Irving Anderson has escaped the attention of many devotees of the form; yet it is no exaggeration to say that he has shown perhaps the greatest mastery of the American *short* detective story of any writer since Melville Davisson Post, whom he greatly resembles in ingenuity, command of plot, and the carefully integrated backgrounds of his work. Like Post, also, his stories have a quality of timelessness which makes them as readable to-day as when they were written. It can only be regretted that Mr. Anderson has never essayed the detective novel—the detective short story seems unfortunately on the decline, for reasons to be discussed in a later chapter—and that he seems to have retired entirely from the writing field in favor of his Vermont farm. (But the New England locales found in so many of his stories derived from an earlier home in the Massachusetts Berkshires.) These factors have combined to limit the influence and recognition of one of the finest natural American talents of the era.

Another magazine writer who contributed to the genre in this period was Octavus Roy Cohen (1891-   ), best known for his humorous tales of American Negro life. His stories of the private agent JIM HANVEY (white) appeared first in *The Saturday Evening Post* and were collected later in several books. Ponderous, uncouth, but ingratiating JIM HANVEY has entertained a wide circle of readers for many years. Yet it must be confessed that his cases are too often better examples of "slick" magazine formula-fiction than of detection within the purposeful meaning of the act.

Among other authors who enjoyed above-the-average popularity during these years may be mentioned: Ernest M. Poate and his DR. BENTIRON; James Hay, Jr. (1881-1936) and his JEFFERSON HASTINGS; Lee Thayer (1874-), and her PETER CLANCY, who still figures in an investigation or two each annum; and Hulbert Footner and his MADAME STOREY, a favorite of so particular and experienced a reader as Christopher Morley. Mr. Morley's own single mystery, the delightful *Haunted Bookshop* (1919), only sharpens every reader's regret that he has never turned his hand to bona fide detection. Most of the numerous novels of Natalie Sumner Lincoln (1881-1935) belong to the romance-mystery category, but a few qualify as detection for its own sake. Kay Cleaver Strahan's (1888-) early works won considerable favor, despite some particularly atrocious Had-I-But-Knowning; but she seems to have ceased writing almost altogether. Vincent Starrett (1886-) has produced from time to time some ingenious examples of plain and fancy sleuthing, though without endangering his greater eminence in the field as the devoted biographer of SHERLOCK HOLMES; this, after all, is as one would wish it. Ben Ames Williams (1889-) has written excellent tales which escape being detection by only a narrow margin. Another "border-liner" of the era was Arthur Somers Roche (1883-1935), whose works considerably resembled those of Louis Joseph Vance before him. Harvey J. O'Higgins (1876-1929) supplied the form with its only passably believable boy hero to date in his BARNEY COOK stories (based on the actual methods of the Burns agency); while his later DETECTIVE DUFF is equally singular as the only psychoanalytical sleuth of any prominence. A variation of the psychological mode motivates T. S. Stribling's (1881-   ) single and too little known volume of Poggioli tales, *Clues of the Caribbees* (1929). Charles Honce remarks that the concluding story "is positively thunderous; it will knock you right out of your seat."

Special mention must go to Frances Noyes Hart (1890-   ), who "covered" the famous Hall-Mills case and turned the experience (though not the facts) into an unforgettable but unrepeatable tour de force in her *Bellamy Trial* (1927), in which the detective action takes place in a day-by-day account of a murder trial. Her later *Hide in the Dark* (1929) is credited with popularizing the parlor game "Murder" (or vice versa), but was not otherwise important, and she has written nothing new for some years.

II

These authors were all "good" authors, and there were others in the same period who were at least competent. But no one of them (save possibly Frederick Irving Anderson with his quiet excellence and Mrs. Hart with her brilliant solo flight) was doing work to compare with the exciting developments that were taking place in England. The American detective story stood still, exactly where it had been before the War. Suddenly, in 1926, came the long-overdue "break," with the publication of *The Benson Murder Case*, the first of the epochal Philo Vance novels by "S. S. Van Dine" (Willard Huntington Wright, 1888-1939). Overnight, American crime fiction came of age.

Willard Huntington Wright was born at Charlottesville,

Virginia, and was educated at St. Vincent and Pomona Colleges (California), at Harvard, and abroad. A dilettante like his sleuth-hero, he dabbled in art, music, and criticism. In 1907 he became literary critic of the Los Angeles *Times,* escaping the McNamara dynamiting by ten minutes when a splitting headache sent him home just before the explosion. From 1910 to 1914 he held a similar position with *Town Topics,* and from 1912 to 1914 he was editor of *Smart Set,* preceding H. L. Mencken and George Jean Nathan. His first published book, in 1913, was a collaboration with these two, entitled *Europe After 8:15.* Subsequently he was art or literary critic for half a dozen different papers and magazines, and for a period of two years averaged five columns of copy a day including Sundays.

The outbreak of the First World War found him in Paris, writing fourteen hours a day. Two months in a sanitarium followed his return from Europe on the last westward trip of the ill-fated *Lusitania.* In 1916 his only serious novel, *The Man of Promise,* an early piece of realism, was published. Praised by discerning critics, it failed to sell—and a re-issue in 1930, brought out with fanfare after his identity with "Van Dine" had been revealed, suffered the same fate. More years of journalism and editing followed. From early 1923 to the middle of 1926 he was confined to bed with a second and more serious breakdown of health.

Forbidden by his doctors to do any "serious" reading, Wright spent his long convalescence in assembling a library of nearly two thousand volumes of detective fiction and criminology. From this study came not only the VANCE novels but his notable anthology *The Great De-*

tective Stories (1927), issued over his own name, with an analytical introduction which remains one of the finest pieces of detective criticism ever written. Further mention will be made of this work in a later chapter. Convinced from his studies that the highly individual technique of the detective story had suffered from poor execution in America, thereby limiting its field of appeal, he determined to write tales aimed at a higher stratum of the public than had previously been accustomed to read them. (This was exactly the same decision which had been arrived at by the better English writers a few years earlier.) But, as he later explained, "I rather feared ostracism if I boldly switched from esthetics and philologic research to fictional sleuthing, and so I hid behind an old family name [Van Dyne] and the Steam-Ship initials."

He began by preparing three thirty-thousand-word synopses and submitting them to Scribner's, under a pledge of secrecy. They were immediately accepted, and were published in successive years. *The Benson Murder Case,* presumably suggested by the murder of Joseph Bowne Elwell, the New York bridge expert, was for the first few weeks principally a succès d'estime among the chosen few. One must remember that in 1926 in America the pastime was still regarded a little apologetically and cautiously. But gradually the word spread that something unusual had happened in the detective story, and sales began to pick up. The second VANCE investigation, *The "Canary" Murder Case* (another roman à clef, based this time on the "Dot" King murder), magnificently smashed the old tabus into fine smithereens for all time. Serialized in *Scribner's Magazine* prior to book publication, it became a sort of national *cause,* rivaling Floyd Collins, Mah Jong, and King Tut as a popular fad.

The book, published in 1927, broke all modern publishing records for detective fiction and was translated into seven languages. Hollywood's interest was engaged, and each succeeding story was filmed shortly after it appeared in print, with a sizable list of silent and talking screen heroes making VANCE, for a few years, the best known fictional sleuth on the globe. Needless to say, each novel earned Wright more money than all his serious books together, and the picture rights brought him a fortune. Paradoxically, VANCE's vast popularity made it impossible for his creator to stop writing—though he had once declared that no one author "has more than six good detective-novel ideas in his system," and had intended to confine his own output to that number. In all, he wrote twelve; and, as if in proof of his contention, nearly all critics have agreed in pronouncing the last six inferior to the first.

Aside from the brilliant plot-work of the initial novels, two factors contributed principally to the success of the Van Dine books: the great literacy with which they were written, matching the hero's—at first—impressive learning; and a high degree of verisimilitude, so carefully worked out in every detail that in the early years numerous uncritical readers thought the cases had really occurred, while VANCE, District Attorney Markham, Sergeant Heath, and the Watsonian chronicler became the household familiars of thousands of their countrymen. To these attributes of popularity, certain unkind critics have added another: the undeniable aura of pictured ostentation which (say these scoffers) destined the stories for sure success in a decade which measured its own success in terms of yachts or silk shirts, as the case might be.

Whether or not this was the case, it is unfortunately true that the many superlative qualities of the novels were accompanied by a heavy pretentiousness and lack of humor which became increasingly obtrusive as tastes changed. PHILO VANCE "dates" to-day much as Calvin Coolidge and Jimmy Walker symbolize a past which seems many years dead. (Van Dine's one embarrassing attempt to cope with change—his next-to-last book, *The Gracie Allen Murder Case*—is most charitably forgotten.) Likewise, VANCE's very erudition began to grow thin and wearisome as the series progressed. In the early tales it had served a legitimate function in the plots and had contributed causatively to the solutions. In the later novels it was too often introduced in large and gratuitous chunks, without essential relationship to the criminal problem under consideration. In such circumstances, even its "snob appeal" * eventually faltered, and it became faintly ludicrous, almost a burlesque of itself.... Another strength-turned-to-weakness was Van Dine's repetition of his "formula." Gilbert Seldes once went so far as to say he could detect the murderer early in a VANCE novel, because he always entered the story on the same page!

At any rate, much of VANCE's popularity had evaporated, rather unjustly on the whole, before Wright died of thrombosis in 1939, at the age of fifty-one. Obituary accounts invariably commented on the author's resem-

* That curious synthetic quality which (for example) elevates a *How to Read a Book* to best-sellerdom, while the true bibliophilic delights and graces of the Newtons, Pearsons, Morleys, and Starretts are tasted only by the far too limited few.

blance to his hero. Like VANCE, he was something of an exotic and a poseur. He lived in a penthouse, favored costly clothes and food, excelled in several fields of collecting, and wore a beard (which VANCE did not). Ernest Boyd called him the most interesting and attractive *un-likable* man he had ever known. He was in many ways an enigmatic and frustrated character, a man who could pathetically "pad" his *Who's Who* autobiography with titles of erudite works that had never actually appeared in print. There is no doubt that he resented VANCE'S success, even while surrounded with the luxuries that his "serious" works could never have brought him, and this fact is very probably the explanation for the sharp falling-off in the quality of the later books.

But whatever Willard Huntington Wright, the disappointed critic of the arts and unsuccessful realistic novelist, thought on the matter, "S. S. Van Dine" should have died content. In a few short years he had become the best known American writer of the detective story since Poe; he had rejuvenated and re-established the genre in his native land; and his name and that of his sleuth will endure—for all their joint pretentious faults—among the immortals of the literature.

III

For all his wide and undeniable influence and achievements, "S. S. Van Dine" was essentially a developer, an adapter and polisher of other men's techniques, rather than a true innovator. In this, though scarcely otherwise, his position was not unlike that of Conan Doyle a generation earlier. By contrast, his almost immediate chronological follower, Dashiell Hammett, acknowledged founder of the realistic or "hard-boiled" division of detective writing, must be called a *creator* of the first rank, deserving to sit with such diverse comrades-at-arms as E. C. Bentley, Francis Iles, and the small handful of others who brought something really new to their chosen field of effort. Van Dine's PHILO VANCE novels—to continue the comparison—were epochal in the sense that they raised the detective story to a new peak of excellence and popularity in the land of its birth; they were American in the narrow sense that their milieu and subject matter were American; yet in method and style they departed no whit from the well established English tradition. On the other hand, Hammett's lean, dynamic, unsentimental narratives created a definitely *American style,* quite separate and distinct from the accepted English pattern. (So separate and so distinct, in fact, that to this day certain short-sighted formalists refuse to admit they are detective stories at all! But with such narrow parochialism the truly eclectic student can have no traffic.) In no slight degree the circumstances of this achievement arose from Hammett's own career, on which he has drawn copiously for material and inspiration.

Samuel Dashiell Hammett was born on the Eastern Shore of Maryland in 1894. At the age of thirteen he left Baltimore Polytechnic Institute to work successively as a newsboy, freight clerk, railroad laborer, messenger, stevedore, advertising manager, and, for eight years, as an operative of the Pinkerton private detective agency. It was this last experience, of course, which principally gave him the backgrounds and many of the characters for his stories, if not the actual plots. In his own career he won his first promotion by successfully pursuing a man who had absconded with a Ferris wheel, and among the cases on which he worked were those of "Nicky" Arnstein and "Fatty" Arbuckle. During the First World War he was a sergeant in the ambulance corps and contracted the tuberculosis which was later to compel his retirement from professional detection and turn him to writing for a livelihood.

Hammett had been writing for the pulp market (he is the most notable of the numerous "alumni" of *Black Mask*) and reviewing detective fiction for the New York *Post* for some time before he published his first novel, in 1929. It was called *Red Harvest* and was a loosely constructed blood-and-thunder yarn with more gangster-ism than detection, even of the Hammett definition, in it. *The Dain Curse,* published the same year, showed a sub-stantial improvement and crystallization of his talent and technique. He reached his zenith (and one of the all-time high points in the detective story) with *The Maltese Falcon* (1930). This novel holds the unusual distinction of being the only contemporary detective story to date to be included in the carefully selected Modern Library series. *The Glass Key* (1931), ranked by most critics as only below *The Maltese Falcon* (though it is Hammett's own first choice among his books), was a worthy suc-cessor. But *The Thin Man* (1932), the most popular of his works, paradoxically marked (in the opinion of the initiated) a distinct softening of the author's talents. A film version with William Powell and Myrna Loy in the leading rôles was sensationally successful and has been followed by a number of cinematic sequels with the same actors. The affluence which the series has brought Hammett is probably the reason that he has produced no published work in many years. Nevertheless, *The Thin Man,* while his least typical and least important contribution, is not without significance on its own account, as one of the first works to bring humor, and of a distinctly native brand, to the detective story in this country.

Because of their startling originality, the Hammett novels virtually defy exegesis even to-day—though their external pattern is by now all too familiar by process of over-much imitation. As straightaway detective stories they can hold their own with the best. They are also character studies of close to top rank in their own right, and are penetrating if often shocking novels of manners as well. They established new standards for realism in the genre. Yet they are as sharply stylized and deliberately artificial as Restoration Comedy, and have been called an inverted form of romanticism. They were commercial in inception; but they miss being Literature, if at all, by the narrowest of margins.

The *Bookman's* comment in 1932 that "it is doubtful if even Ernest Hemingway has written more effective dialogue" may seem a trifle over-enthusiastic to-day, but only a little. And Hammett's talents in this direction are, if anything, exceeded by his ability to delineate character by sharp, frugal, telling strokes admirably suited to the form. He is at his best in depicting his central figures, invariably private inquiry agents (drawn from life, he has intimated): brutal, grasping, lecherous "heels"; each, however, with his own hard and distinct code of Hemingwayesque courage and fatalism and a twisted sort of personal integrity incomprehensible to conventional minds. His secondary characters are not always realized with equal care, but some of them (as the tormented baby-faced gunman of *The Maltese Falcon* or the gorilla, Jeff, in *The Glass Key*) give new and unforgettable inflections to the word "sinister."

The action of the novels is machine-gun paced and so violent that, in the first two books particularly, it occasionally defeats its purpose by exhausting the reader's receptive and reactive capacities. Some of the incidents, also, by the extremity of their sadism, tend to stand out too strongly from the main thread of the story and thus to imperil the unity and balance of the novel as a whole: too often they are merely stunts in realistic narration and definitely impede the progress of the plots in which they occur. (This is no moralistic objection, but a statement of the recognized fact that artistic excesses bring their own retribution.) The prose, except for the few such moments of intemperance, is economical, astringent, and muscular, while the Hammett vocabulary, as might be expected, is consistently and quite properly for the *mores* depicted blunt and outspoken. In fact, *The Thin Man's* lively success in the bookstores is commonly ascribed in publishing circles to the inclusion of a single usage seldom seen in polite print. But it would be an error and an injustice to dismiss Dashiell Hammett's novels as merely salacious or sensational—even though their author wrote with a keen eye to the box-office and a not-too-reluctant use of some of the more dubious tricks of the trade. For the tremendous impact and virility he achieved transcend the means employed.

Dashiell Hammett is currently in Hollywood, writing for the moving pictures, for which in the past he has expressed no high regard. He is married and has two daughters. He does most of his writing at night and sometimes works on a scenario as long as thirty-six hours at a stretch. With his slender six feet in height, crest of prematurely gray hair, small, dapper mustache, and poker-features, he might serve as the physical model for one of his own detectives. As enigmatic in many ways as his fictional heroes, he has surprised his associates in recent years by the indubitable sincerity of his interests in social and political movements of a Left-wing nature. No great admirer of his own detective stories, he hopes eventually to sever his moving picture connections and write "straight" plays and novels. There is no doubt of his ability to do so if he chooses, but many of his well-wishers will hope that he may find the time and inclination for at least an occasional book in the *Maltese Falcon* and *Glass Key* tradition. But should he never write another detective story, it is already safe to say that no other author of modern times—certainly no other American—has so basically changed and influenced the form.

Like all originators, Dashiell Hammett has suffered at the hands of his imitators. But the circumstance does not and should not obscure what he has done to give the American detective story a nationality of its own.

IV

It is perhaps a mistake to insist on too-minute classifications and categories within any literary frame. For example: it would be possible, if one chose, to contend that a mating of the more successful elements of the contrasting Van Dine and Hammett schools was inevitable in the

American detective story. The point could be quite readily proved by the accurately titled "adventures in deduction" of and about ELLERY QUEEN (who functions both as author and as sleuth). Less pretentious than the Van Dine *opera* but agreeably livelier, lacking the startling impact but also the mannerisms of the Hammett novels, the Queen tales are nevertheless entirely American in their idiom, and could be easily cited as an example of the successful blending of the two methods. The only obstacle to so delightfully pat a theory is the purely evidential one that the first Queen novel was "work in progress" well before the earliest Hammett efforts appeared in print. This does not alter the fact, however, that, by accident if not by design, or perhaps as the result of independent developmental trends, the Queen stories *do* fall somewhere between the two styles, where they represent some of the most competent writing that has been done on this side of the water in the field of the deductive tale contrived for purely entertainment purposes.

"Ellery Queen" (as author) is a pseudonym covering the identity of two young Americans who are also cousins, Frederic Dannay and Manfred B. Lee. Both were born in Brooklyn in 1905. Lee attended New York University, where he had his own orchestra (he still plays the violin); Dannay did not attend college, but by the age of twenty-four was art director of a New York advertising agency. Lee was writing publicity and advertising for a motion picture company. Both seemed destined for conventional business careers when they chanced to read an announcement of a detective story prize contest. In a light-hearted moment they entered the contest, and to their great surprise won it, only to see the magazine sponsoring the competition cease publication. But a book-publishing house became interested, and with the publication of *The Roman Hat Mystery* (1929), one of the most successful collaborations in contemporary writing was launched. Since then, to quote *News-Week,* "ELLERY QUEEN has been uncovering murders and untangling mysteries with such suavity and sophistication that he has become one of the most popular fictional sleuths extant."

For some years elaborate precautions were taken to conceal the identity of "Queen," who appeared at autographing parties and literary teas wearing a black mask, and likewise of "Barnaby Ross," the name under which Messrs. Dannay and Lee created their second and by no means negligible sleuth, DRURY LANE, an ex-Shakespearean actor. At one time the cousins undertook a lecture tour, engaging in a series of joint debates as "Queen" and "Ross": not even the lecture management knew their double-dual-identity! But the harmless make-believe is now abandoned, and the DRURY LANE novels are currently being reissued under the Queen nom, though it is doubtful if the retired tragedian will ever attain the prominence or popularity of his younger confrère—known familiarly to his affable creators as The Great Man. For ELLERY QUEEN is to-day deservedly one of the two or three best known names in American detective fiction, while the invariably workmanlike stories with which he is associated have recently attracted the attention of new and vastly wider audiences through radio and moving pictures. (There is even, it is reliably reported, soon to be an "Ellery Queen, Jr.," who may conceivably remove the hoodoo that has always hovered over boy detectives.)

The collaborating cousins regard their writing as essentially a business, for all that they derive more fun from their livelihood than perhaps any other writers in the game. Each cousin works on a regular schedule at his home, with occasional meetings together in a purposely barren office on Fifth Avenue, which they maintain chiefly as a mailing address, and where the only suggestion of their trade is a small bullet-proof window (but that was left behind by a former tenant, a jeweler). They interrupt their routine occasionally for trips to Hollywood. Lee is married, has two daughters, lives in the city, and collects stamps as a hobby. Dannay is also married, has two small sons, and lives in suburban Great Neck, where he possesses one of the finest collections of short detective stories extant. In 1940 he narrowly escaped death in a traffic accident, but recovered after many weeks in a hospital. It is his ambition someday to edit *the* definitive detective story anthology, an objective which all who know his enthusiasm, analytical ability, and literally astounding knowledge of the field cordially hope may be fulfilled. In *Challenge to the Reader*, Dannay and Lee together produced a highly novel and entertaining anthology which will be discussed in a later chapter of this volume.

Asked to state what they believe to be the cardinal quality that has brought the QUEEN stories their wide reputation and success, the authors modestly speak of the "absolutely logical" fair-play method of deduction, which, indeed, has been the sign-mark of their work from the beginning. But there is more than this. Although the Messrs. "Queen" frankly and necessarily regard their output as a means of livelihood, they have brought to the detective story a respect and integrity which—combined with their unflagging zest—accounts largely for the high level they have consistently maintained. Unlike other writers who have wearied of the game and too often endeavor to substitute mere cleverness or sensationalism for hard work, the "Queens" have never failed to give their multitude of followers honest merchandise. If the stories have a flaw it is the occasional tendency to too-great intricacy, but even this occurs so rarely as to be negligible.

For the great part, the Queen tales are as adroit a blending of the intellectual and dramatic aspects of the genre, of meticulous plot-work, lively narration, easy, unforced humor, and entertaining personae, as can be found in the modern detective novel. They represent the deductive romance at its present-day skilful best.

v

Every now and then writers of fiction create characters who strike so universal a note of humanity that they transcend the narratives in which they appear. Dickens frequently did this. So did Mark Twain. So, in the particular field of our consideration, did Conan Doyle. And so did Earl Derr Biggers with his patient, aphoristic Chinese-Hawaiian-American, Charlie Chan, who has probably inspired more genuine personal affection in his readers than any other sleuth in recent years.

Earl Derr Biggers was born in Warren, Ohio, in 1884, attended Harvard, and as his first job undertook to conduct a humorous column for the Boston *Traveler* in 1907. (A good example of his kindly wit was his comment on this experience in later years. Writing a humorous column in Boston—he said—was a good deal like making faces in church; it offended a lot of nice people, and it wasn't much fun.) Occasional dramatic criticism for the *Traveler* gave him an interest in the theater and he had an early play produced in 1912, with small luck. But a mystery novel published the next year, *Seven Keys to Bald-pate,* was hugely successful and led to an even more profitable dramatization by George M. Cohan which had a classic career on Broadway, with Cohan in the leading rôle, and on tour, in stock, and in the moving pictures over the better part of a generation.

For the next decade Biggers devoted himself chiefly to the theater and to magazine fiction, and it was not until 1925 that Charlie Chan made his bow in *The House Without a Key.* (Biggers had a predilection—rather confusing to his readers—for titles using the word "key.") All the Chan novels were serialized in *The Saturday Evening Post* before book publication. There is no Chan short story, to the perennial regret of anthologists. Charlie was not drawn from real life, his author said, although one Chang Apana of the Honolulu police force believed otherwise. "Sinister and wicked Chinese are old stuff," Biggers once explained, "but an amiable Chinese on the side of law and order had never been used." And he added, "If I understand Charlie Chan correctly, he has an idea that if you understand a man's character you can nearly predict what he is apt to do in any set of circumstances."

This pleasantly sound premise, however, must not lead the reader to expect psychological brilliance in the Chan adventures. Rather (like the author himself) they are clean, humorous, unpretentious, more than a little romantic, and—it must be confessed—just a shade mechanical and old-fashioned by modern plot standards. This absence of any novel or startling departure, in fact, is probably the reason that the first CHAN story created no such popular or critical stir as the first PHILO VANCE case (which, in point of strict chronology, it preceded by a good year). CHARLIE'S fame was of slower growth than the more scintillant PHILO'S, and it was not until two or three of his adventures had appeared that he struck full stride.

Once started, however, he has been difficult to stop. The stories have been translated into ten different languages; almost a score of CHARLIE CHAN moving pictures have appeared, although the original stories were long since exhausted; J. P. Marquand's later Japanese sleuth, MR. MOTO, who is also cinematically popular, seems more than generically indebted; and CHARLIE has also figured in numerous radio scripts and, currently, even in a newspaper comic-strip. One must believe that Biggers (who died of heart disease at his Pasadena, California, home at fifty-eight in 1933) would scarcely be pleased with some of the posthumous transformations his originally simple and dignified character has undergone at the hands of others. Biggers himself was short, round, and dark, with twinkling eyes and a friendly manner. He was a skilled and genial craftsman who knew his audience and his métier. Nevertheless, his detective stories are remembered less for themselves than for the wise, smiling, pudgy little Chinese they introduced. Conventional as the narratives often were, CHARLIE CHAN'S personal popularity played a part in the Renaissance of the American detective story that can not be ignored.

*   *   *

This brings to a close our consideration of the detective story in the 1920's. The difference between the British and American product during the period was chiefly temporal. The American detective story simply required longer than the English to pass a given point, until the last years of the decade, when its pace of development was belatedly accelerated. Otherwise, the evolutionary pattern of the two was much the same. Both became more literate and more convincing; both attracted new and more intelligent classes of readers; both produced their share of "great names." And, with the 1930's on the horizon, both stood on the edge of a quantitative and qualitative upsurge that had never been dreamed of, and in which there was to be little distinction of nationality.

CHAPTER IX

England: 1930-

(*The Moderns*)

So far the most fascinating attempt made to renovate the detective story consists in assigning a more important rôle to psychology.—DENIS MARION

IF the output of the detective story in the 1920's was a torrent in comparison with what had gone before, that of the 1930's was a veritable flood. Exact numerical statistics are difficult to come by, for a number of mechanical and classificatory reasons of no interest here. But a helpful indication of the growth of the genre may be gained from a study of that important bibliographical aid, the *Book Review Digest*. In 1914, the year of the outbreak of the First World War, this publication included reviews of only twelve books of a mystery-detective nature (the two classifications being lumped together). For the year 1925, the mid-point of the post-War decade, ninety-seven such volumes were listed. And in 1939, the year that saw the start of the Second World War, the number was 217! (In all cases, the number which find their way into this medium are somewhat less than the total output: for some of the lesser efforts fail to receive sufficient reviews to qualify for inclusion.) These figures are necessarily incomplete, but there is every reason to suppose that they are relative and representative. In fact, the full gain of the "pure" detective story during these years was even greater than the bare numbers indicate, for the proportion of detection to mystery also advanced greatly in the quarter-century. Of the volumes classified as mystery-detection in 1914, scarcely more than a third could qualify as bona fide sleuthing; by 1939 the amount of acceptable detection in the total was well upward of seventy-five per cent.

This overwhelming increase in production has been accompanied by a scarcely less substantial improvement in quality, on both sides of the water. The average detective yarn before the Armistice was likely, with a few notable exceptions, to be a pretty poor thing in a literary sense. The 1920's marked the introduction of many first-class writing talents, especially in the upper brackets, and especially in England. (American progress, as we have seen, was consistently slower.) But to-day even the most routine detective story that is not at least as creditably composed as the comparable work of non-detective entertainment is the rare exception.

Because of the tremendous numerical advance—and, as well, because the progress of the detective story during the period has been marked somewhat less by brilliant individual leadership than by all-around improvement—the method of detailed discussion by authors followed up to this point will be a little subordinated in this and the following chapter to consideration by groups, or movements. In this fashion it is hoped to mention, if only briefly, a greater number of names than would otherwise be possible; while according the leaders a little more space than the followers, though less than in previous sections.

Even such an approach, of course, will not permit giving the attention which could be desired to *all* good authors. The writer can only express his regret if (as is only too certain) his choices do not coincide with those of each reader. In the absence of a Gallup Poll on the subject, the responsibility of selection is not one that can be shirked, and, for all effort toward objectivity, personal preference must often be the governing factor.

I

In striking contrast to the numerous phases of detective story composition which saw their greatest flowering in Britain in the 1920's, the years which have followed, while witnessing the intensification and refinement of earlier methods, have been distinguished by only one really significant technical departure of their own. This is the novel of detection-cum-character, to which several preliminary references have already been made. In this form, sometimes called because of the enhanced stylization which is its inevitable concomitant the "literary" detective novel, the British specialists again showed their heels for some years to their American brethren in the craft.

We still have to-day, in both lands, a few stories dependent on the poison-that-leaves-no-trace; or the intricate (and usually unconvincing) mechanical murder-device; or the locked room; or the iron-clad alibi. But such forced fashions in crime are waning, and current emphasis tends to be on simpler, more plausible puzzles, relying on a higher order of narration for their success. Thus the seed planted by Wilkie Collins and nurtured by

Bentley, Berkeley, and Sayers, has been brought to full flower by Margery Allingham, Michael Innes, Nicholas Blake, Ngaio Marsh, and a host of others. The critics are not lacking who will declare, with some justice, that at least a few of these writers have exceeded the bounds of the detective story, and, for all their praiseworthy intentions, have taken something away from the form as well as added to it. Nevertheless—whatever their faults—these are our true Moderns, whom we shall now examine in some detail.

*   *   *

Margery Allingham (1904-   ) was born in London, into a family of publishers and "blood" writers. Soon after her birth, her family moved to Norman Essex and she grew up in a little village close to her present home at Tolleshunt d'Arcy.* She began to write at seven and published her first novel, a successful swashbuckling adventure tale, at the incredible age of sixteen. After a term of studying dramatic art, with the intention of becoming a playwright, she married Philip Youngman Carter, an artist of her own age, in 1927. The Carters live to-day in a Queen Anne country house, where plump, dark-haired Margery Allingham divides her time between writing and village and household activities. She calls herself "a domesticated person with democratic principles and very few unorthodox convictions. I have no particular ax to grind and I belong to no rigid school of thought but am content to hold with the poet that the proper study of mankind is man." She enjoys horses, dogs, and gardening; Shake-

---

* By what seems more than a coincidence, a character in one of the novels of a fellow-craftsman, Francis Gérard, is named Lord Allingham, with a seat known as Tolleshunt!

speare, Sterne, and the elder Dumas are the authors she names as most influential in her life; of Americans, she admires Don Marquis.

It was in the year following her marriage that Miss Allingham published the first of her stories featuring mild, bespectacled, engaging ALBERT CAMPION. The CAMPION books fall into two distinct periods—those written before and those written after 1934. The early novels are likely to disappoint readers who have become Allingham fans in recent years, for, while lively and pleasant enough, they follow the picaresque tradition of the author's inheritance and previous writing, to the virtual exclusion of the unpretentious cerebral detection which is the distinct forte of the later CAMPION. *Death of a Ghost* (1934) was the work which signified the turning-point, as Miss Allingham herself disclosed in a preface to the volume; and discriminating readers were suddenly aware that the promise of the Naturalists of the previous decade had come into full bloom.

It is scarcely too much to say, in fact, that had any one of the later CAMPION books been able to appear singly and without the detective label, critics and public alike might have accepted it as an unusually subtle and exciting "legitimate" novel. For the Allingham-CAMPION "method" is an admirable blend of good story-telling, delicate, yet sharp, delineation of character, and puzzles that hinge primarily on mental rather than physical means—the whole presented in the fluid prose of a thoroughly adept and sophisticated craftsman.

In addition to her superior characterization and narration, Miss Allingham has a virtually unique ability to combine detectivism with pentrating comment, less of a political than a social nature, on the contemporary scene.

(This is *not* recommended to beginning writers of the detective story!) In *Death of a Ghost* the world of art felt her scalpel. In *Flowers for the Judge* (1936) she sent CAMPION behind the scenes of a London publishing house. *The Fashion in Shrouds* (1938) investigated decadent Mayfair. Her 1941 novel, *Traitor's Purse*—a breathtaking tale of espionage and treachery in which CAMPION battles not only his country's enemies but an attack of amnesia—paid timely and devastating tribute to the dictatorship mentality.

In *Black Plumes* (1940) Miss Allingham made her only attempt to this date to dispense with her amiable hero, substituting a professional policeman, the canny Scot INSPECTOR BRIDIE. Had the book appeared over some other name, it would doubtless have been hailed as a significant and promising achievement. But it only caused the established Allingham public to demand CAMPION's return the more avidly.

Occasionally even this able and versatile author commits the error (previously sanctioned by Dorothy Sayers) of becoming a little too profound and precious for her medium and audience; but not often. Her works have maintained so remarkably high and uniform a level of excellence that few could disagree when John Strachey (writing in the *Saturday Review of Literature* in 1939) named her as one of three "white hopes" of the British detective story; Michael Innes and Nicholas Blake being, in his opinion, the others.

* * *

"Michael Innes" (1906-   ) was born "just outside Edinburgh and almost within the shadow of the centenary

monument to the author of *Waverley.*" His full and real
name is John Innes Mackintosh Stewart and he is the
son of a Scottish scholar. As a boy he attended Edinburgh
Academy, of which Scott was the founder and Robert
Louis Stevenson a pupil for a time. The headmaster once
told him (as a form of rebuke) that someday he might
write a *Kidnapped* or *Treasure Island*! These books and
similar romances were Stewart's boyhood favorites, but
to-day he considers Homer, Dante, and Shakespeare "the
world's most satisfactory writers."

At Oriel College, Oxford, he won a first class in English
in 1928 and the Matthew Arnold Memorial Prize the
following year. His first published work was an edition
(in his own name) for Francis Meynell and the None-
such Press of Florio's *Montaigne;* this in turn landed him
his first job, as a lecturer in the University of Leeds. A
fellow-lodger was a young feminine medical student,
whom he later married. Though they now have three small
sons, Mrs. Stewart (a qualified physician) still finds time
for infant welfare work. After five years at Leeds, Stewart
was invited to become professor of English at Adelaide
University, where he resides to-day. On the long voyage
to Australia he wrote his first detective story. His later
ones have been penned between six and eight o'clock in
the morning: "for nine months of the year the climate is
just right for this sort of authorship," he writes from
Adelaide.

Photographs of "Michael Innes" show a pleasant, bespectacled, thirty-ish young Scot, not unlike one's mental
picture of Margery Allingham's ALBERT CAMPION. He
says of his own detective stories: "I would describe some
of them as on the frontier between the detective story

and the fantasy; they have a somewhat 'literary' flavor but their values remain those of melodrama and not of fiction proper." This is a fairly accurate self-estimate, but many admirers will object that it is overly-modest as regards at least two of the Innes novels, *Hamlet, Revenge!* (1937) and *Lament for a Maker* (1938)—of which more later.

The first book of the series, introducing C.I.D. In-SPECTOR JOHN APPLEBY—university bred and surely the most avid spotter of literary quotations and allusions among professional sleuths—was *Seven Suspects* (1936). Laid in an English university, it poked a good deal of sly fun at academic foibles and pretensions, and in between whiles, and amid a veritable haze of classicism, unrolled a mystery of fantastic conception. Too complex to be really good detective literature, it nevertheless showed rich promise, which was abundantly realized in *Hamlet, Revenge!*, a mystery adroitly woven into a high-grade amateur-professional performance of the play in an important English country house.

The publication of the third Innes novel, *Lament for a Maker,* marked not only his most mature achievement, but also one of the vividly outstanding detective novels of the generation—a work to be re-read and savored. As the title (taken from Dunbar's poem) might indicate, the scene is the author's native Scotland, and so lovingly and handsomely is the stage set that one suspects the tale must have been composed in a season of nostalgia. The narrative method of *Lament for a Maker* is an almost literal paraphrase of *The Moonstone*: perhaps an acknowledgment of Innes' obvious discipleship. As for characters, story, and style—only an actual reading can convey the overtones and flavor of this richly tapestried work. On the purely mechanical score of structure, objection must be made to the author's reliance on some rather astonishing coincidences; but these will soon be forgotten in the joy of discovery, the unexpected and delightful recapture of the Wilkie Collins mood and abundance in modern dress.

Unhappily, the more recent Innes works (to the date of this writing) have fallen considerably short of his early achievements. To put it bluntly, the author seems too well content to rest on his laurels. In *Hamlet, Revenge!* and *Lament for a Maker* his erudition served a legitimate function; in his later novels he has too often stooped to merely show-offish quotation-spouting. (One recalls the similar degeneration of the PHILO VANCE tales—and hopes that the parallel will not be continued!) All this is not to say, however, that the later Innes novels fail to entertain and amuse, for they do both, but only that the author's public has come to expect superlative performances from him and is dissatisfied with anything less. There is cheerful promise in the fact that Michael Innes is one of the youngest of first-rank detective-story writers. Sooner or later he will almost certainly return to the mood of his best work. To aid him, he has one of the finest natural talents operating in the genre to-day.*

* * *

"Nicholas Blake" is the pseudonym of Cecil Day Lewis (1904-   ), who is even better known under his own name

---

* As if in answer to the implicit plea, Mr. Innes obliged in 1941 with *The Secret Vanguard,* a thrilling piece of adventure-detection concerning a Nazi plot in the Scottish highlands, told in the finest RICHARD HANNAY tradition of high romance.

as one of the ranking younger British poets. He was born
in Ireland, the only son of a clergyman. His mother, who
died when he was four, was a descendant of Oliver Gold-
smith and wrote unpublished poetry. Young Day Lewis
began writing verse at six. He attended Sherborne School
and Wadham College, Oxford, on scholarships. At the
university he was co-editor of the magazine *Oxford
Poetry,* and he has ever since been associated with the
group of "younger poets" led by his friends W. H. Auden
and Stephen Spender. In 1928 Day Lewis married the
daughter of a master at Sherborne; they have two sons.

From the year of his marriage until 1935 he taught in
several institutions to support his growing family. This,
however, did not give him the leisure he desired for his
poetry, and he turned to writing detective stories under
the "Blake" nom de guerre for the frank purpose of sup-
plementing his income. The attempt was so successful
financially that he was soon able to give up teaching altogether. While, regarding the quality of his detective
fiction, John Strachey has dared to say: "He writes even
better when he is, presumably, pot-boiling as Nicholas
Blake than when he is 'giving himself to literature' as
Day Lewis." Also, as Blake, he has been a leading and
highly discriminating reviewer of detective fiction, chiefly
for *The Spectator*—a journal whose political views are far
removed from his Leftist bent as Day Lewis.

His first detective novel, *A Question of Proof* (1935),
had, like Michael Innes' maiden effort, a scholastic background. But Nicholas Blake is less insistently "erudite"
than Innes, as he is likely to be less pretentious in his
writing than Margery Allingham sometimes allows herself
to become. Nevertheless his NIGEL STRANGEWAYS belongs

to the same school of studied casualness and insouciance as ALBERT CAMPION and JOHN APPLEBY, and Blake is as insistent as his colleagues on character as the chief determinant of his solutions. His detection, too, is always meticulous and soundly reasoned, if not always predominant.

In fact, in *The Beast Must Die* (1938), undoubtedly his magnum opus to the present date, he largely subordinated the detectival element to a gripping internal study of murder that deserves to stand with the best of Francis Iles. If the rationale of this truly epochal novel is perhaps too complex to be entirely convincing, the fault will be readily forgiven, for the best of the chapters achieve a level of sheer mental suspense that has seldom been surpassed. In *The Smiler With a Knife* (1939), a departure of quite different nature, he turned his back completely on conventional detection to write an unabashed intrigue-adventure yarn in the tradition of John Buchan's HANNAY series, converting STRANGEWAYS' wife, Georgia, into what Miriam Allen deFord calls "a sort of female Superman." (The allusion is to the American comic-strip character, *not* Shaw's or Nietzsche's.) His other works are more orthodox, in external pattern at least.

Until the Hitler War, Day Lewis and his family lived in a cottage on the Devonshire coast. He enjoys walking, sailing, and shooting (hence he has been called "the poet with a gun"). Tall, with a shock of dark hair and a deeply lined face, he looked to one interviewer like "a young farmer or aeroplane mechanic—strong, almost tough"; but his voice retains an Irish softness. He says that he enjoys writing detective stories, which he considers a harmless release of an innate spring of cruelty present in every one.

This unusual interpretation is typical of "Nicholas Blake's" refreshingly original approach to the genre. He belongs definitely to the Character group of detective novelists, but he senses more than most of his fellows the dangers of being too "highbrow" in an essentially entertainment form. In contrast to the melodramatic intellectualism of some of his colleagues, his books are honest *though* intellectual melodramas. He is one of the rare writers who manage to bring high literacy and thrills together under one cover, without pretense on the one hand or condescension on the other. By any criterion, he is a major figure and force in the modern detective story.

*   *   *

Ngaio Marsh (1899-   ) was born, according to her own account, at Christchurch, New Zealand, "of what the Victorians used to call poor but genteel parentage." Her father was descended from an ancient English family which has been traced back to the piratical de Mariscos, Lords of Lundy. Her maternal grandfather was an early colonizer of New Zealand, and her own given name (pronounced approximately "ny-o") is the Maori name for a native flowering tree. She was educated in New Zealand, at St. Margaret's College, and for five years attended the art school of Canterbury University College.

From an early age she had intended to make painting her career, but she also had ambitions as a playwright. Having completed "a terrible romantic drama," she "had the temerity to show it to Mr. Alan Wilkie, the Shakespearean actor-manager. He rejected the play, but offered to take me into his company, so I became a touring actress and stuck to it for two years." In 1928 she went to London and was a partner in a prosperous house-decorating business for four years. When she was called back to New Zealand for family reasons in 1932 she left with an agent the typescript of her first novel, *A Man Lay Dead.* "I had written it to amuse myself during odd hours and was astonished when I learned it was accepted for publication."

During the next five years she stayed in New Zealand and wrote five more detective stories. In 1937 she returned briefly to England, toured the Continent, and went back to New Zealand, where she lives to-day at Christchurch with her father. She is unmarried, continues her interest in the theater by acting as producer for a local repertory company, and has "a mania for travel." She has written many travel articles and also short stories and verse in addition to her detective novels. Her first American publication, *Artists in Crime,* was really her sixth effort in the field. All her later books have appeared simultaneously on both sides of the Atlantic, and her earlier novels (including some of her best work) are very sensibly being gradually "caught up" by American publishers.

The central figure of her stories is INSPECTOR RODERICK ALLEYN, a sort of modified (but not consciously imitative) edition of LORD PETER WIMSEY. Though he is a hard-working, untitled professional, his mother is Lady Alleyn, and doors are frequently opened to him through family "connections" which would probably remain closed to sleuths of less gentle birth. Otherwise, the tales are faithfully naturalistic, rather than romantic.

Miss Marsh's personal backgrounds of art and the

theater have served her well in fiction, and not only as thematic material. It is doubtful if any other practitioner of the form to-day writes with so vivid a talent for picturization, so accurate a grasp of "timing," or so infallible a sense of dramatic situation. Many of the scenes in her novels could be transported bodily to the stage or screen without the mediation of the dramatist or scenarist. (The wonder is that they have not been!)

Sometimes, it must be admitted, this sense-of-the-theater is almost her undoing: if the stories have a major weakness, it is her tendency at times to substitute dialogue for action. Occasionally, too, her fondness for her native "Down Under" vernacular, amusing enough in small doses, leads her dialogue to become somewhat unintelligible to the untutored reader, while now and again her depiction of polite society smacks a little of preciosity. But on the whole her novels are agreeably free of pretentiousness and affectation. One senses in Miss Marsh a level-headed refusal to regard herself—or others—either too seriously or too negligibly.

As might be expected from her other talents, her power of characterization is also excellent; but somehow she is essentially more the novelist of manners than of character, and in this respect she lies a little closer to the current American school than to the English. (This frequent affinity between Americans and British Colonials has been marked in many other connections.) Her solutions, too, are more likely to depend on routine police methods than on the brilliant psychological revelations of the "character" writers at their most intense. Undeniably the British and American schools of detective fiction are drawing constantly closer together. At the date of the present writing no single author more succinctly symbolizes this synthesizing process than New Zealand-born Ngaio Marsh, who has so happily combined the best features of both shores.

If the Detective Story of the Future should happen to resemble the intelligent and diverting products that have thus far come from her pen, there will be little cause for lamentation in any quarter!

*   *   *

A lighter or at least lightened tone has been increasingly apparent in recent years among many of the newer English writers. An outstanding example is Georgette Heyer (1902-   ), whose *Merely Murder* (1935) and subsequent novels have added a new and harder veneer to the English humorous detective story as largely conceived by A. A. Milne a decade earlier. Her work, however, has been somewhat uneven. Also in a generally amusing vein are the invariably delightful NICHOLAS SLADE stories by R. C. Woodthorpe. Lady Harriette Russell Campbell's (1883-   ) SIMON BRADE is another competent sleuth illustrating this trend, though the average reader will want to skip the chapters in which he communes with his microscopic bricks. Gladys Mitchell (1901-   ), who also writes as "Stephen Hockaby," has created an entertaining character in her MRS. BRADLEY, of the highly colored garments and the macaw-screech, if some of her psychological discussions are not quite fathomable. All out farce is the stock in trade of "Caryl Brahms" (Doris Caroline Abrams, 1901-   ) and S. J. Simon, better known as serious writers on the ballet, who have outrageously travestied the world they know best in *A Bullet in the*

Ballet (1938) and later scandalously funny works. Among other new-comers of especial promise in the field of the lighter, if not necessarily facetious, division of the character novel may be mentioned—of many—Harriet Rutland, Eileen Helen Clements, Anita Boutell, Dorothy Bowers, and Anne Hocking.

II

Closely paralleling the evolution of the detective novel of character in the years since 1930 has been the accelerated growth of the "inverted" or "events-leading-up-to-the-crime" type of story, which was known to earlier generations chiefly through the works of Mrs. Belloc Lowndes and Francis Iles. If we apply the most rigid definition of the term "detective story," most of these efforts will fail to qualify for our consideration in this volume. Nevertheless, they have had an influence on the detective novel proper out of all proportion to their number. They find their chief audience, moreover, in the most critical type of detective-story reader—the reader who would instantly reject such other border-line approaches as intrigue or secret service or mystery-adventure. Therefore, though they are not *quite* within our field, we can not ignore them entirely.

Of several competent and stimulating English writers who have flourished in this department since Iles showed the way, perhaps the best and best-known is "Richard Hull" (Richard Henry Sampson, 1896-), whose *The Murder of My Aunt* (1935) remains a classic of its kind, an intellectual shocker par excellence. Sampson was born in London and was educated at Rugby. His mother's name

was Hull; hence his pseudonym, which he freely acknowl-
edges. Intended for Trinity College, Cambridge, he obtained instead a commission on his eighteenth birthday
and served in France for the duration of the First World
War. Demobilized, he was articled to a firm of chartered
accountants and later went into practice for himself.

"It can't be said," he writes, "that he was ever a very
successful accountant, and in 1935 he began to think that
he would be more interested in writing. The decision to
do so and to concentrate mainly on a particular type of
detective fiction was made after reading Francis Iles'
Malice Aforethought." The Hull novels, indeed, are for
the most part closer in spirit to this lighter and more
stylized of the Iles' studies in murder than to his later
somber and penetrating *Before the Fact.* Yet they have a
peculiarly acid "bite" to them that is quite original and
often raises them to a level above purely escapist literature. Some one has characterized them as "brilliantly
vicious," and in truth they expose the appalling capacity
of the human mind for self-delusion as mordantly, at
times, as anything from the pen of Hull's avowed master.
They are all written, "for preference," in the first person.
To one of his most despicable villain-narrators, in fact,
the author has given the name Richard Henry Sampson—
a singularly effective method of underlining the "but for
the grace of God" quality!

Mr. Hull-Sampson further comments on himself and
his writing: "In fiction, he specializes in unpleasant characters because he says there is more to say about them
and that he finds them more amusing. In life, he pleads
a kind heart as a set-off to an occasional flash of temper
and an endless flow of conversation. For many years he

has lived almost entirely in a London club [he is un-married], qualifying, as he says, as the club bore. He is convinced that his photograph would be detrimental to his sales." Of Hull's eight books to the date of this writing, only half have appeared in America.

Among other practitioners of the "inverted" form may be mentioned (of several): "Anthony Rolls" (Colwyn Edward Vulliamy, 1886-   ), whose *Clerical Error* (English title: *The Vicar's Experiments*, 1932) is regarded by some readers as a small masterpiece and by others as merely dull and imitative; "Peter Drax" (E. E. Addis), who has written quietly effective fictional studies of the London underworld and step-by-step police procedure; Ethel Lina White, whose *The Wheel Spins* (1936) was made by Alfred Hitchcock into the incomparable film, *The Lady Vanishes;* Alice Campbell (1887-   ), whose works resemble a good deal those of Mrs. Lowndes; "Joseph Shearing," with "his" fictional reconstructions of famous crimes; F. Tennyson Jesse's SOLANGE stories; Graham Greene (1904-   ) and his psychological "entertainments"; perhaps J. Russell Warren (1886-   ); and certainly Raymond Postgate (1896-   ), G. D. H. Cole's brother-in-law and occasional collaborator in the field of economics, whose *Verdict of Twelve* (1940), a tour de force interpreting a murder trial in terms of the jurors' past histories and backgrounds, aroused unusual interest for a first essay. Mention must also be made of Rubie Constance Ashby's (1899-   ) *He Arrived at Dusk* (1933), an unrepeatable blending of the ghost story and legitimate detection; one of the few of its kind. Constance Rutherford should also, perhaps, be included in this category. Her work is little known in America, but Alexander

Woollcott has named her *The Forgotten Terror* (1938) in a list of "best mysteries" for the White House library.

Such works (let it be said again) may not always test out as "pure" detection, but they have had, and happily continue to exercise, a needed and vitalizing influence on the roman policier of more conventional mode and pattern.

III

It is perhaps inevitable that any evolutionary study of a literary form must give most of its attention to the innovators and experimentalists. The very number of the conventionalists, if nothing else, precludes admitting them to the same detailed consideration, enjoyable as their works may be. Occasionally, however, a writer appears, who, utilizing only conventional and accepted techniques, nevertheless raises those techniques to so high a level of excellence that he stands out above his fellows and merits special mention. Such an author in the field of the detective story is John Dickson Carr (1905?-), who also writes as "Carter Dickson." Though he qualifies as an English writer by residence and subject matter, John Dickson Carr is by nativity an American. He was born at Uniontown, Pennsylvania, the son of Wooda N. Carr, later a United States Congressman, and at the time of this writing Postmaster of Uniontown.

"At the age of eight," John Dickson Carr writes, "I was hauled off to Washington. While my father thundered in Congress, I stood on a table in the members' anteroom, pinwheeled by a God-awful collar, and recited Hamlet's Soliloquy to certain gentlemen named Thomas Heflin and Pat Harrison and Claude Kitchin and others whom I have apparently since inspired along that line." Inasmuch as the elder Carr served in Congress from 1913 to 1915, this statement would seem to place the year of the author's birth—which he has never directly revealed—at about 1905. His other activities in the nation's capital, Carr adds, included asking Woodrow Wilson what his name was, sitting on Uncle Joe Cannon's lap listening to ghost stories, and learning the rudiments of crap-shooting from the legislative page boys. Among his earliest heroes were Sherlock Holmes, D'Artagnan, and the Wizard of Oz, and at fourteen he was writing for an unnamed newspaper. Also unnamed are his schools and colleges, with the exception of Hill School, which he mentions "with pride because it is the only institution from which I wasn't fired. My college career—or shall I say careers—turned out with more notoriety than fame. Harmless matters, such as staging fake murders with a dummy. . . ." Another academic stumbling-block was mathematics, which he still calls with characteristic vividness "that last refuge of the half-wit." He was intended for the law, but scholastic difficulties plus the call of journalism frustrated his family's designs.

Sometime in the late 1920's he went abroad, traveling and living in England and on the Continent. "I wrote a novel: an historical romance with lots of Gadzookses and sword-play. Somewhat later I wrote *It Walks by Night* [1930]. I think it's pretty terrible, but I hope it's entertaining—to me the one unforgivable sin is being dull. The characters split bottles, heads and infinitives with equal zest. It is melodramatic, like birth and death and love and all honest, fundamental things. And, thank heaven, it is not 'significant.' But if it gives the nervous reader a bad night or the puzzle-connoisseur a headache, I shall be satisfied."

This quotation and the ones preceding will already have given the reader a working-idea of John Dickson Carr's animated and picturesque style, which has made his thirty-odd books since *It Walks by Night* among the liveliest and most readable examples of detective fiction to-day. They have been praised by the best critics for such varied qualities as a unique sense of the macabre, and a three-dimensional quality "with plenty of connective tissue." They also read, as another reviewer has said, as if the author had a lot of fun writing them.

The first few novels were laid in France, with BEN-COLIN of the Paris police as the detective-hero. They were reasonably successful, but the author's fullest popularity did not arrive until John Dickson Carr created DR. GIDEON FELL; and "Carter Dickson" (né "Carr Dickson") invented his SIR HENRY MERRIVALE, better known as "H.M." or "The Old Man"—the present writer's admitted favorite among contemporary fictional sleuths. Either character, one can not resist remarking, would be more recognizable in a stud poker game in Washington, D. C., than in the purlieus of Adelphi Terrace or Whitehall. But the British public, so suspicious of undisguised Yankees, has been hocused (to use one of Carr's favorite words) into taking them both to its heart. It is, in fact, an amusing paradox that although John Dickson Carr is proudly accepted and classified as an English author, and is a member, now Secretary, of the English Detection Club (where his sponsors were Dorothy Sayers and Anthony Berkeley), his robust, racy idiom, salty characters, and unfailing gusto of style—in short, the factors that make his work what it is—stamp it as purely American for all his European backdrops.

The technical position of Mr. Carr-Dickson in the British detective story is very similar to that of the Messrs. Ellery Queen in the native American product. Both are avowedly "entertainment" writers, presenting sound puzzles in the guise of swift-moving fiction, with characters by no means profoundly drawn but nevertheless colorful and adequate to the day. Carr has one important additional asset (present also, it should be said, but to a lesser extent, in the Queen novels). His forte has been and remains the rational crime problem costumed as an eerie tale of the seemingly supernatural. Were not his explanations so meticulously complete and realistic, this would be a chargeable error under the canon. As it is, his method represents perhaps the most consistently satisfactory combination to date of the "shudder tale" with bona fide sleuthing.

Even in those of his stories which do not fully depend on this device, he excels—as does Queen on the other side of the Atlantic—in bizarre, fantastic statements of the case (e. g., the opening chapters of *The Arabian Nights Murder*), which are capable of later and logical explication. But also like Queen, he has the fault that his processes are sometimes too intricate, his devices too far-fetched, to carry entire conviction, regardless of their careful logic: May Lamberton Becker has referred to his "almost over-ingenious exercises." This is the only major flaw in the Carr *opera;* if there are others, they remain to be discovered.

Carr resides today in England with his wife, a native of Bristol, and their small daughter, Julia. Photographs disclose a dark, mustached pipe-smoker, whose thinning hair gives him the appearance of a somewhat older man than he presumptively is. With his wife he visited the United States in 1939, just before the outbreak of war. The return voyage to England in a blacked-out ship gave him the background for the effective Dickson novel, *Nine—And Death Makes Ten* (1940).

In another similarity to the Queens, Carr created, in pre-war days, a highly successful series of "wireless" detective episodes for the British Broadcasting Corporation. He apparently regards "Carter Dickson" as merely a pseudonym-of-convenience (his works under the two names are issued by separate publishers) and he has never made any effort to conceal the identity behind the second nom. DR. FELL and SIR HENRY MERRIVALE, in fact, are so closely akin that at moments it is almost impossible to distinguish them (while a later character, COLONEL MARCH, is also cut from the same bolt); and some of the author's too infrequent short stories have appeared in various anthologies under interchangeable signatures.

In truth, the only personal mystery surrounding Mr. Carr-Dickson is how a single writer can produce so many stories so consistently high in quality. Under either of his names he has been an incomparable boon to the English "straight" detective story.*

*   *   *

Of the scores—nay, literally hundreds—of English authors who have turned out competent-or-better detective fiction of a more or less straightaway variety in recent years, space will permit only the bare cataloguing of a hand-

* In the Spring of 1941 Carr wrote his American publishers a letter describing the fortunes of his family in the blitzkrieg. Apart from its

ful of names and sleuths as typical: Sir Basil Thomson
(1861-1939; ex-Scotland Yard) and his sometimes too-me-
thodical CONSTABLE RICHARDSON (but not his ill-advised
MR. PEPPER parodies); Christopher Bush (1885-) and
LUDOVIC TRAVERS; John Alexander Ferguson (1873-)
and his likable Scotsman, FRANCIS MACNAB; Miles Burton (1903-) with INSPECTOR ARNOLD and DESMOND
MERRION; "Milward Kennedy" (M. R. K. Burge,
1894-) and INSPECTOR CORNFORD, among several
sleuths; Ernest Robertson Punshon (1872-), whose
SERGEANT BOBBY OWEN has never had the following in
America that he seems to command in his native land
(though Alexander Woollcott included *Proof Counter
Proof* on his "White House" list); Elspeth Huxley and
her African VACHELL; Patricia Wentworth and INSPEC-
TOR LAMB; "Bruce Graeme" (1900-) and Leo Bruce
who follow a rather determinedly humorous vein that
seems somewhat related, with, respectively, SERGEANT
BEEF and PIERRE ALAIN; John Bentley and Peter Chey-
ney whose DICK MARLOW (Bentley) and SLIM CALLAG-
HAN and LEMMY CAUTION (Cheyney) work hard to prove

personal interest, it qualifies as at least a small footnote on recent history
and will bear repeating, in part, here. In September 1940, the letter
reveals, the Carrs' house in London was demolished with nearly all their
furniture. Mrs. Carr and the remaining furniture went to her parents'
home in Bristol while Carr moved to the Savage Club, "having to leave
there when a bomb sliced off the back of it. Then, running out of
houses, I went down and joined Clarice at Bristol. The blitz hit Bristol.
A bomb landed across the street, removing from our house windows,
doors, and roof. The only reason why more damage was not done was
because of a small shed or pavilion which took the main blast. This
contained what was left of our furniture, salvaged from our London
house. Jerry's score was complete. I can imagine the triumphant German
airman hurrying back to Goering and saying: 'Ich habe busted der resten
den furniture von Carr!' and Goering swelling under his medals and
saying, 'Gut! Sie wilst der iron cross getten! Heil Hitler!' "

themselves the British equivalent of NICK CHARLES and
SAM SPADE; and perhaps such prolific and industrious
practitioners as Cecil Freeman Gregg (1898-), Colonel
Walter S. Masterman, Francis Durham Grierson
(1888-), "E. C. R. Lorac" (1894-), and Leonard
Reginald Gribble (1908-).

IV

On the border-line between detection and related
fields, in this era, belong such authors as Leslie Charteris
(1907-) and his picaresque SIMON TEMPLAR ("THE
SAINT"); Gerard Fairlie (1899-), who continues the
"Sapper" tradition; Nigel Morland (1905-), whose improbable but frequently entertaining MRS. PYM recalls a
little too insistently the Edgar Wallace style; Francis
Gérard, another self-appointed heir to the Wallace mantle
(query: are Gérard and Fairlie the same writer?); Sidney
Horler (1888-) for out-and-out shockers; Jefferson
Farjeon (1883-) in the romantic vein; and Anthony
Morton with his Rafflesque BLUE MASK stories. Every
reader will have his own favorites, ad infinitum; these
are but a few of the more recurrent and prominent who
happen to come to mind.

One writer in this category, however, must receive individual attention. Eric Ambler (1909-) has not only
given the spy-and-intrigue story new life in its own right
in recent years; he has brought it close to a legitimate
marriage with detection. "Streamlined" is an over-worked
word, but that is virtually what Ambler has done for the
intrigue novel, replacing its stereotyped clichés and slinky
females in black velvet with skillful plotwork and char-

acterization and believable human beings. Furthermore, though there is ample physical action, cerebration is for once as important as shooting, and the two are blended together with neatness and credibility. *Background for Danger* (1937) was the first Ambler novel to be published in the United States (his first English publication occurred a year earlier), but it was not until the memorable *Coffin for Dimitrios* (1939) that he really came into his own with the discriminating readers who are now his devoted clientele. It is a little too early yet to calculate the full influence of the new lease-on-life he has offered the secret service novel, but the signs are not lacking that it will be extensive. The mood of subtle understatement which he established seems already to have found an echo in such superior works as the Manning Coles' *Drink to Yesterday* and *Toast to Tomorrow* and David Keith's *A Matter of Iodine,* as well as in the sudden interest of so many of the erstwhile orthodox English fictional sleuths in espionage. If Ambler's own work is still a little (but only a little) removed from bona fide detection, it is not too much to think that he has opened up a fresh avenue of development for the form proper, in much the same fashion that Frances Iles a few years ago showed new pathways in another direction. Though he is still a young man in his early thirties, Eric Ambler has already enjoyed a varied and colorful career. He is reported to be serving in his country's armed forces at the time of the present writing.

CHAPTER X

America: 1930-

(*The Moderns*)

I

THE chief technical advance made by the English detective novel since 1930 has been its trend toward amalgamation with the "legitimate" novel of character and
psychology. It can not be said that there has been an
American movement of equal strength in the same direction, though both character and psychology are currently
receiving more attention than they did in previous years.
One or two of Dashiell Hammett's novels will qualify,
and amply; but Hammett himself has not followed them
up, and his imitators have contented themselves mainly
with copying his more obvious mannerisms.

Rather, the American detective story has revealed a
tendency to blend itself with the novel of manners: meaning usually the comedy of manners. This tendency has
followed two principal lines of expression: (1) the
"straight" police tale lightened, humanized, and often
stylized in much the same manner as that in which Ngaio
Marsh performed these services for the English detective
novel; and (2) the aforesaid imitations, in various degrees, of the Hammett method. Often, of course, the two
lines overlap. Brief attention will be given to a few ex-

ponents of each. If the consideration accorded many of the individual authors is even less detailed than in the chapter immediately preceding, it must be understood that the number of writers to be touched on is even greater, and that their "evolutionary" significance—quite apart from the entertainment value of their works— is less pronounced.

*   *   *

In the movement toward what may be loosely termed the "liberalization" of the straightaway or routine American detective story, Rex Stout (1886-   ) stands in the forefront. Indiana-born, he was educated in Kansas, joined the Navy, and had a dozen different "careers" before he "retired" in 1927, at the age of forty, and went to Paris to write a psychological novel. (Whether he acquired his famous beard at this time does not appear, though it seems likely.) This novel and three later ones in similar vein were respectfully received by the critics but did not by any means approach the best-seller lists. The "economic disillusionment" of the 1930's was, Stout says, the underlying cause of his turn to detective fiction.

His first work in this field, *Fer-de-Lance,* was published in 1934, introducing crabbed, elephantine NERO WOLFE, whose two great loves are beer and orchids, and his paint-fresh assistant, the narrator of the stories, Archie Goodwin—the one example in history (in this writer's opinion) of a Watson who steals the play from his HOLMES, and a first-rate HOLMES to boot. Rex Stout brought to the detective story not only its keenest wit, but also exceptional literary talent, a fact sometimes missed by readers who overlook the bland art that gives

Archie's picturesque slang and breezy narration their appeal. It is this skill, rather than any technical innovation, which has given him his high station in the form.

Whether or not he succeeds in his declared ambition to write "one of the two or three best mystery stories in the world," Rex Stout has already produced several of the most intelligent and entertaining works of his time. His plots, detection, and narration are of the highest order. He has created several detective characters, all told, but none to rival seriously the popularity of WOLFE and his Archie.

*   *   *

The novel of manners in general fiction is frequently accompanied by a purposely pointed mode of narration, usually taking the form of mild tongue-in-cheek irony. It is no great surprise to find the same sort of stylization beginning to appear in the detective novel of manners. Particularly pleasant examples of this type of story-telling are found in "David Frome's" accounts of the rabbity little Welshman MR. PINKERTON, who blinks and gulps his apologetic way through sundry adventures in the protective wake of his burly friend INSPECTOR BULL.

"David Frome" is the pseudonym of an American woman, Mrs. Zenith (Jones) Brown (1898-   ), whose very different works under her alternative pen-name, "Leslie Ford" will be discussed in a later section. The daughter of an Episcopal clergyman, she was born in California and educated in the state of Washington, but lives today in Maryland, the home of her family for many generations. In 1918 she married Ford K. Brown, and when he sailed to study in England a few years later, preparatory to his present position on the faculty of St. John's College (Maryland), she went along and absorbed the British scene and idiom so authentically that few readers identified the resulting "Frome" stories as the work of an American woman, until Mrs. Brown herself voluntarily revealed the secret.

The early PINKERTON tales (the first was *The Hammersmith Murders,* published in 1930) were laid in London. In later novels he and BULL have taken their readers on a sort of murder-travelogue of provincial Great Britain, much as "Leslie Ford's" characters are currently conducting a Cook's Tour of crime in America. In this fashion Mrs. Brown profitably combines a passion for travel with the practice of her craft. The detection in the "Frome" stories is about evenly divided between PINKERTON (first named "David," but now generally known as "Evan") and BULL, though the former has become the chief and sympathetic actor. The wistful Welshman, it must be admitted, usually blunders rather than thinks his way into his solutions; but somehow this sort of thing is less objectionable in the stylized detective story (perhaps by the very nature of the form) than in the straightaway crime narrative. At any rate, the puzzles are always mystifying and MR. PINKERTON himself is one of the most delightful, if sometimes exasperating, of contemporary sleuths.

*   *   *

The development of the stylized detective story has also led, logically enough, to experiments in the closely connected humorous forms of farce and extravaganza. Two recent authors who have quite notably succeeded in this apparently simple but really difficult field are, albeit in quite different milieus, "Alice Tilton" with her hilarious LEONIDAS WITHERALL (or BILL SHAKESPEARE) novels, and Elliot Paul (1891-) with his Rabelaisian HOMER EVANS murder mysteries.

Her publishers have not officially announced that "Alice Tilton" is really Phoebe Atwood Taylor (1909-), author of the capable adventures in straightaway detection of ASEY MAYO, the shrewd Cape Codder. But readers of Ellery Queen's *Mystery League* magazine a few years back will remember with pleasure the serialization of the first WITHERALL story, *over the Taylor signature*. Oddly enough, also, this tale has appeared in book form in England, signed "Alice Tilton" and somewhat incredibly titled *Beginning With a Bash* (1937); but for some unfathomable reason it has never been published in America—an oversight which, one trusts, Miss "Tilton's" publishers may soon see fit to remedy. *The Cut Direct* (1938), really the second story in the series, was the book which marked WITHERALL's American début.

Elliot Paul is, of course, the versatile, lusty, bearded ex-Montparnassian, war correspondent, boogie-woogie artist, would-be lighthouse-keeper, and distinguished author of *Life and Death in a Spanish Town* as well as of many serious works of criticism. (The less said of his writing as "Brett Rutledge," the kinder!) His first HOMER EVANS story was *The Mysterious Mickey Finn* (1939).

Two more widely disparate authors than "Alice Tilton"

and Elliot Paul can scarcely be imagined; they have been selected purposely to typify here, jointly, the "new humor" in the American detective story, for the very reason that they represent such different facets of the same development.

Among others who have pleasantly blended laughter and deduction may be mentioned Frances and Richard Lockridge with their tales of MR. and MRS. NORTH and LIEUTENANT WEIGAND; Timothy Fuller and his JUPITER JONES; and Elizabeth Dean's EMMA MARSH and HANK FAIRBANKS adventures. The wonder is not that there are so few competent names to be listed, but—after the fashion of Dr. Johnson's dog—that there are any at all; for mixing murder and merriment is a much more serious business than it might seem, requiring a sure eye and a steady hand. The slightest error of judgment is enough to turn the whole mixture sour, as a plethora of cachinnatory "quickies" (which shall for charitable reasons remain nameless) in the last few years has demonstrated. At best, the completely humorous detective story can never become a major development; but in competent hands, and kept within bounds, it is capable of remaining a pleasant, occasional dietary variation.

*   *   *

Humor is also a distinguishing mark of the second major department of the American novel of manners-cum-detection—the school of the Hammett followers—but with an important difference. Where the Tiltons and the Pauls have made the effort, at least, to achieve humor of situation and character, the members of the Hammett group are more likely to rely on the humor of dialogue:

the justly famous American wise crack. Some species of hard-boiledness is also a prerequisite for membership in this school, but this is becoming increasingly a matter of external conformance only. A few of the chief representatives—in greater or lesser degree—include: Jonathan Latimer and his BILL CRANE; A. A. Fair with his BERTHA COOL and DONALD LAM; Frank Gruber and his JOHNNY FLETCHER and SIMON LASH; "Geoffrey Homes" (Daniel Mainwaring, 1902-) and his ROBIN BISHOP and HUMPHREY CAMPBELL; "Kurt Steel" (Rudolf Kagey, 1904-) and HANK HYER; Cleve F. Adams and REX McBRIDE; William Du Bois and JACK JORDAN; George Harmon Coxe (1901-) and KENT MURDOCK; Brett Halliday and MICHAEL SHAYNE; and the tough-guy novels (with or without recurrent characters) of Raoul Whitfield, Whitman Chambers (1896-), Raymond Chandler, and perhaps a good half-hundred others. Many of these are more than mere imitators, to give them their due. But it is doubtful if any of them would have written exactly as he has, had not Hammett come first. The mode, as has already been suggested, seems to be receding today. As the years pass it will probably tend more and more (as such forms usually do) to lose its separate identity, while its more effective characteristics, such as pace, action, naturalness, will be picked up and utilized by fashioners of the routine police novel. This will be all to the good, for it must be confessed that in its pristine form the hard-boiled tale of detection—once so vigorous and refreshing—is beginning to become just a little tedious from too much repetition of its rather limited themes.

II

One of the unexplained mysteries of present-day detective literature is the continuing gulf between women writers in Britain and America—particularly in an era when the two nationalities and literatures have otherwise drawn steadily closer together. English women detective story writers have been found, from the beginning, in the vanguard of the most inventive and imaginative minds practising the form. Their American sisters, on the other hand, with relatively few exceptions, have stuck stubbornly and on the whole rather dully to the stereotyped formula of romanticized mystery-detection established by Mary Roberts Rinehart in the early 1900's. It is obvious that the romanticized form is much less technically exacting than the police novel proper, and is thus better suited to the "domestic" author. But why should such a consideration operate more strongly in one country than in another? One suspects that the greater dominance exercised over all fiction in America by the magazine editors—particularly of the powerful and convention-bound women's journals, which have no true English counterpart—has had a good deal to do with the matter; but that is a problem that can scarcely be examined here. The quarrel between the literary market-place and even the most limited sort of originality is too old and too ever-present to be disposed of summarily: save, perhaps, to remark that experience has repeatedly shown how much less conservative, how much more receptive, are readers of all classes than the cautious editors who presumably interpret their tastes.

Whatever the cause, the fact remains that the large

proportion of American women writers approaching the genre still elect to follow the Rinehart tradition, to some degree at least. For this reason they may be considered as a more or less homogeneous group.

At the top, or certainly close to it, of the authors in this group, we must place the name of Mignon G. Eberhart (1899-), whose NURSE SARAH KEATE, SUSAN DARE, and LANCE O'LEARY stories are not only among the most popular but also exemplify many of the best characteristics of the Rinehart School. In recent years Mrs. Eberhart has achieved something of a blend of the conventional American-feminine method with a type of tale slightly reminiscent of some of Mrs. Belloc Lowndes' psychological studies of murder. Another prime favorite in the women's magazine field is "Leslie Ford," whose alter ego is "David Frome" (see previous section of this chapter). Her COLONEL PRIMROSE and GRACE LATHAM novels can scarcely rival "Frome's" PINKERTON tales, but they are competent in their kind and entertainingly narrated—although some readers insist that the author selects her culprits by the "eeney-meeney-miney-mo" method. Dorothy Cameron Disney, an open and avowed Rinehart disciple, scored with her *Death in the Back Seat* (1936) and has continued in the same vein since. At least one reader, however, would thank her to drop her "Had-I-But-Known" digressions and fortuitous interruptions. She writes far too well to need the assistance of such obvious and outworn hokum. Charlotte Murray Russell with her Tish-like spinster, JANE AMANDA EDWARDS; Constance and Gwenyth Little; Anita Blackmon (1893-); Margaret N. Armstrong (1867-); Clarissa Fairchild Cushman; and Medora Field (1898-) are some other names that come to mind. These represent the "better element" in the School. Concerning some of those remaining, it is perhaps kindest to remain silent.

*   *   *

One author, however, must be given special and individual mention here for the new lease on life she has given the tottering old formula—the first substantial "transfusion" it has received in a good quarter-century or more. She is Minnesota-born Mabel (Hodnefield) Seeley. Superficially, she seems to follow the Rinehart pattern. She relies on first-person narration. She employs the double-crime plot, a present and an antecedent crime, which is so often the basis of this type of tale. She indulges in more "ifs" and premonitory shudders than she has any need to. And her stories represent distinctly the feminine point of view.

But it is a feminine point of view new to the mode, a modern and more naturalistic approach. Her backgrounds are neither chattily cozy nor impossibly Gothic (the twin evils of most of the sorority), but almost religiously faithful to her native mid-western America. It is not the least of her achievements that she has dared to use, and with striking effectiveness, the most commonplace of settings: a drab Minnesota lake resort, a grain elevator, a cheap rooming-house. Akin to this restraint is her ability to create breath-taking moods of suspense and fear, not by the old, whipped-up underscoring and "purple-patchery," but by a technique of brooding understatement not unlike the cinematic methods of Alfred Hitchcock, whom, indeed, she resembles in many ways, despite such obvious dissimilarities as nationality, gender, and artistic medium.

Mrs. Seeley lives in Minneapolis, where her husband is an instructor in one of the high schools. It is said that she learned her craft in a free writing course (she was without previous experience) conducted by the Minneapolis Public Library. Her first manuscript was not only accepted by the Crime Club, but was made one of its monthly "selections"; it was *The Listening House* (1938), which had a St. Paul locale. Her third novel, *The Whispering Cup* (1940), was sold to Hollywood at a substantial price.

There is every reason to expect many more fine novels from Mabel Seeley's pen. With a little luck, and by continuing the hard labor she has already demonstrated herself capable of, she is in a position to do much for the form. If there is to be a White Hope who will pilot the American-feminine detective story out of the doldrums of its own formula-bound monotony, Mabel Seeley, as these lines are written, seems the logical candidate for the job!

III

The largest numerical field in the American as in the British detective story during these years has been, inevitably, the routine or straightaway police novel (whether the hero be professional or amateur) of the purely entertainment school. King of the "time-killers" among American writers today, at least if sales are a criterion, is Erle Stanley Gardner (1889-   ) with his frenetic PERRY MASON and DOUGLAS SELBY stories. There is at least a little of Hammett in the Gardner method, but there is more of the author's own background of years spent in writing for the "pulps." With no pretensions to literary style, but with a solid understanding of "action" fiction, the Gardner yarns are a sure two-hour cure for anybody's boredom. (Some readers believe that the prolific Mr. Gardner is also A. A. Fair.) Only slightly less popular than the Gardner novels, according to the sales figures again, are the straight police stories of Rufus King (1893-   ), starring Lieutenant Valcour and serving their purpose in pleasingly workmanlike fashion. A good deal of competent entertainment of the routine sort has come from the joint pens of Richard W. Webb and Hugh C. Wheeler who collaborate under three pseudonyms, as "Q. Patrick," "Patrick Quentin," and "Jonathan Stagge." Their best work has been as "Quentin," whose *Puzzle for Fools* (1936) and *Puzzle for Players* (1938) come close to qualifying for inclusion in the "manners" classification. Stuart Palmer's Hildegarde Withers and Oscar Piper have been too long absent in recent seasons while their creator (it is understood) toils in the Hollywood vineyards. "Diplomat" (John Franklin Carter, 1899-   ; also known as "Jay Franklin," the columnist) has apparently abandoned the form after some excellent work. "George Bagby's" Inspector Schmidt has been steadily advancing toward the upper brackets; rumor says that this author also appears between covers as Aaron Marc Stein. Other "candidates" for "promotion," all of whom have loyal backing among the reading electorate, might include "Christopher Hale's" (Mrs. Frances Loyer Ross, 1895-   ) Bill French; Frederick C. Davis' (1902-   ) Cyrus Hatch; Clifford Knight's Huntoon Rogers; Darwin and Hildegarde Teilhet's Baron Von Kaz; "John Stephen Strange's" (Mrs. Dorothy Stockbridge Tillett, 1896-   ) Barney Gantt; George Dyer's (1903-   ) Cata-

LYST CLUB; Cedric Worth's (1900-   ) PAXTON SEVREL; Hulbert Footner's (1879-   ) AMOS LEE MAPPIN; Clyde B. Clason's THEOCRITUS WESTBOROUGH: A. B. Cunningham's SHERIFF JESS RODEN; George Worthing Yates' LORD BROGHVILLE and HAZLITT WOAR; "Anthony Abbot's" (Fulton Oursler, 1893-   ) THATCHER COLT; Milton Propper's TOMMY RANKIN; Cortland Fitzsimmons' ETHEL THOMAS; George Robert Dean's ANTHONY HUNTER (of a number); Craig Rice's JAKE JUSTUS and HELENE BRAND, who are somewhat easier to take than most of their brothers and sisters of the "wacky" school; Hugh Austin's PETER QUINT; and the several sleuths invented by William Anthony Parker White (1911-   ), who writes both as "Anthony Boucher" and "H. H. Holmes." (And some scores of other favorites whose unavoidable omission because of space limitations will doubtless be irately brought to the writer's attention as soon as this volume appears!)

*   *   *

Not *all* American women writers have followed the Rinehart procession. Several have contributed excellent detection of the straightaway variety, among whom may be mentioned: Helen Reilly (sister of the encyclopedic John Kieran) whose INSPECTOR MCKEE stories are among the most convincing that have been composed on the premise of actual police procedure; Phoebe Atwood Taylor (1909-   ) and her delightful Cape Cod sleuth, ASEY MAYO; Kathleen Moore Knight with her ELISHA MACOMBER, whose resemblance to MAYO has not diminished his popularity; Inez Oellrichs and her quietly rewarding MATT WINTERS; Harriette Ashbrook (1898-   )

and her all-American SPIKE TRACY; "March Evermay" and her INSPECTOR GLOVER; Elizabeth Daly and her GAMADGE; and Helen McCloy and her credible psychiatrist, BASIL WILLING. (As well as several authors included in other sections.)

IV

A peculiarly American sub-division of the routine police novel has been the occupational or vocational story— the detective narrative with a specialized background. Dorothy Sayers did something of the sort in England with her *Murder Must Advertise* and *The Nine Tailors,* it is true; but the practice does not seem to have been taken up by many of her countrymen. This development may have had its origin in the works of S. S. Van Dine, none of which was considered complete without its erudite explanation by PHILO VANCE of some esoteric branch of knowledge. Current examples might include: the excellent and prodigal MERLINI novels (magic) of Clayton Rawson; the INSPECTOR BONDURANT stories (medical) of "James G. Edwards" (James William MacQueen); *Fast Company* (1938) by "Marco Page" (Harry Kurnitz), and *Cancelled in Red* (1939) by "Hugh Pentecost" (Judson Phillips?), which, respectively, exposed the rare book and philatelic "rackets" (each won the Dodd, Mead "Red Badge" prize in its year); the sporting specialties of Cortland Fitzsimmons (when he is not writing about ETHEL THOMAS); the BILL PARMELEE stories (cardsharping) by Percival Wilde (1887-); the novels of "Sue MacVeigh," whose husband ANDY combines detection with railway engineering; and the charming and medically authentic JEFFREY and ANNE MCNEILL stories by Theodora DuBois. In addition to these, a considerable number of authors mentioned in other classifications have made some use of the method.

When properly employed, the specialized background can be a pleasant variation and a restorer of jaded plots and situations. It is at its best when crime and solution can be conclusively correlated with it (the perfect example, of course, is Dorothy Sayers' *The Nine Tailors*). It is at its worst when it degenerates into mere didacticism, unrelated to the plot. Fortunately, the latter situation is already beginning to disappear.

v

As in all the eras we have investigated, such related types of fiction as mystery-adventure, intrigue, secret service, criminal romance, and the like have continued cheerfully on their way—and some people who should know better (though fewer than in the past) persist in confusing them with bona fide detection. There is some excuse for this confusion in the fact that these stories often masquerade as detective novels and do contain some modicum of sleuthing to give the claim color. Thus, detectival elements are present to a greater or lesser extent in the international adventures of CAPTAIN HUGH NORTH as chronicled by Van Wyck Mason (1897-   ) (who also writes sometimes as "Geoffrey Coffin"); in the MR. MOTO stories of J. P. Marquand (1893-   ); in Alexander Laing's (1903-   ) tales of his DR. SCARLETT; in the stories of James Warner Bellah (1899-   ); and of the indeterminate Harry Stephen Keeler (1890-   ).

One hesitates to extend the list further when limitations of space have already excluded so many writers whose product comes more legitimately within the scope of this book, but at least a line or two must be found for such "unclassifiables" (who, nevertheless, have influenced the detective story proper) as Cora Jarrett, Elisabeth Sanxay Holding (1889-   ), Dorothy Hughes (1904-   ), William Sloane, Harrison R. Steeves (1881-   ), Percival Wilde, Cornell Woolrich, and David Keith—whose general position as writers of crime tours de force is in some degree comparable to the Lowndes-Iles-Hull school in England.

CHAPTER XI

The Rules of the Game

(A Reader Looks at Writers)

> The crime was at once intriguing and bizarre, effi-
> cient and theatrical.
>
> · · ·
>
> Pentreith's books are the best in their kind;
> pleasantly fantastic but pleasantly closely-reasoned.
> I fancy you must take quite a professional interest
> in the pleasantly fantastic, pleasantly closely-
> reasoned death of Dr. Umpleby.—MICHAEL INNES,
> *Seven Suspects*

BEGINNING with Poe, many of the greatest writers of
the detective story have been moved, by what complex
and diverse considerations one may only guess, to belittle
their own craft. "Where," asked Poe, with unconvincing
because unwonted modesty, "is the ingenuity of unraveling a web which you yourself have woven for the
express purpose of unraveling? The reader is made to
confound the ingenuity of [the detective] with that of
the writer of the story." That the very achievement of
such an effect is in itself high art, no one of course was
better aware than proud Israfel. Robert Louis Stevenson, who dabbled a little in the form, undoubtedly had
his tongue likewise in his cheek when he said: "It is the
difficulty of the police romance that the reader is always

a person of such vastly greater ingenuity than the writer."
The net result, however, of this sort of ingratiating but
essentially false humility has been to convince much of
the public that the execution of the detective story is
child's play, something that may be accomplished almost
at will by any one who wishes to take the required
time.

Nothing could be more distant from the truth—as hundreds of would-be writers have learned to their sorrow.
If all the trained men and women of letters, even, who
have failed in casual attempts to dash off police novels
in odd and pot-boiling moments could be laid end to end,
they would extend approximately from Great Russell
Street to Fourth Avenue. For no other form of literary
endeavor requires a more particularized talent. The
ability to write well is no handicap—in fact is becoming
more and more of the essence. But other qualities of
mind and pen are vastly more important. To paraphrase
Poe, the writer of the really superior detective story must
be both "poet *and* mathematician" if he is to achieve the
exactly proper blends of imagination and reason, bafflement and analysis, deception and logic, clockwork and
showmanship, to satisfy an audience as informed, critical,
and downright finical as any in literature. An audience
which insists more forcefully than almost any other that
if the thing is worth doing at all it is worth doing properly
and well. The unfortunate wretch who foolishly supposes
that the crime novel may be constructed on the principles
of the cross-word puzzle is as quickly annihilated by such
an audience as, on the opposite side, the mere romancer
who commits the unpardonable sin of letting crass coincidence extricate his characters from their predicaments.

In the years since the police novel came of age—and it is happily no longer necessary to defend a form of literature which numbers among its devotees so many international leaders of intellectual, professional, and public life *
—several valuable and often amusing compilations of rules have been laid down for its conduct. The late Willard Huntington Wright, whose identity with "S. S. Van Dine" every one now knows, Father Ronald Knox, Dorothy Sayers, the late E. M. Wrong of Oxford, the London Detection Club, and a number of lesser lights on both sides of the water have issued learned and sometimes brilliant pronouncements in this vein. All these obiter dicta are well worth the attention of the student and the would-be author. Like a holier decalogue, however, they may be condensed into two main requirements: (1) The detective story must play fair. (2) The detective story must be readable. On these two commandments depend the several considerations of technique and ethics which will follow.

But first, a qualification and explanation of the initial commandment. To say that the detective story must play fair means much more to-day than the obvious necessity

* At this date there can be no useful point in promulgating another mere list of names of The Great, from Abraham Lincoln forward, who have found surcease and solace in the pages of the detective romance. But it is somehow curiously touching, on picking up the collected letters of the second Oliver Wendell Holmes and Sir Frederick Pollock, to discover the revered American jurist writing his English friend, at ninety-two, that he has found it necessary to "sweeten" the reading of some particularly tortuous work of philosophy by dipping again into the pages of *The Moonstone* and the Baker Street saga! On another occasion Holmes wrote Pollock that his great devotion to detective stories had compelled him to "ration" his consumption of them. Of course, in no one else could such a devotion be more seemly—for was not Holmes born in the year of the "Rue Morgue," and did not his own father give name to the world's greatest sleuth?

of laying all the clues before the reader. It means, as well, that no evidence shall be made known to the reader which remains unknown to the detective (except in intentional tours de force); that false clues are automatically forbidden; that fortuity and coincidence are outlawed as beneath the dignity of the self-respecting craftsman; that all determinative action must proceed directly and causatively from the central theme of crime-and-pursuit; and that no extraneous factors (such as stupidity or "forgetting") shall be allowed to divert or prolong the plot in any essential manner.

Similarly, the·commandment of readability means not only ordinary literary competence, but that the detective novel must avoid becoming a static and immobile puzzle, on the one hand, and that it must forswear the meretricious aid of hokum, on the other. The former fault, as every intelligent reader knows, is one of which the English tale is most often guilty; the latter, the gleaming particular sin of the American story, particularly the American-feminine variety. It was G. K. Chesterton, if memory does not fail, who declared somewhere that there is more difference between a good and bad detective story than between a good and bad epic—as it was also G. K. C. who hazarded the statement that the police novel, properly executed, is the only form of popular literature "in which is expressed some sense of the poetry of modern life."

The whole question of the Rules of the Game (the relation of reader and writer) is so closely bound up with the problem of the author's own craftsmanship that it is difficult to know where the one leaves off and the other begins. Presumably there will be no objection to considering their several and frequently over-lapping phases in the same general discussion. Both problems, however, will be approached here primarily from the point of view of the average friendly reader, rather than of the practising technician.

Is there such a thing as an "average" reader of detective stories? Perhaps not, for if the devotees of this type of fiction have a single common denominator, it is their insistent and outspoken individualism. As Professor Harrison R. Steeves has remarked, they are "profoundly varied." Yet certain roughly inclusive groupings do exist. There is, for example, the Soporific Reader, who takes his detection—so to speak—Lying Down; who asks only that the problem be undisturbing and the writing swift. At the opposite pole we find the Puzzle Hound, the reader who regards the police novel as an active challenge to his intellect rather than as passive recreation. In only one essential respect do these opposing groups meet, and that is in their mutual distrust and dislike of innovation or any "literary" quality in their reading. Fortunately for whatever future the detective story may possess, a third and vastly larger group lies somewhere between the two extremes. The Eclectic Reader (to adopt a term which once had quite a different connotation) is bound by no fixed prejudices. He can enjoy Conan Doyle, Dashiell Hammett, and Margery Allingham on successive evenings. He welcomes good writing and honest experimentation as warmly as he rejects mere faddism, sensationalism, or pretence. If a certain lack of modesty may be permitted, he will now present his views in greater detail.

Structure and Sources

Structurally speaking, the first thing to know about the detective story is that it is conceived not forward and developmentally as are most types of fiction, but *backward*. Each tale, whether novel or short story, is conceived solution-foremost in the author's mind, around a definite central or controlling idea. The controlling idea may be a unique crime method; an original way of concealing the culprit, as in Agatha Christie's arguable *Roger Ackroyd*; perhaps a point of law turned to the criminal's or sleuth's advantage; an untried departure in detective technique; or virtually any combination or variation of established formulas. Such focal points may derive from a number of sources: usually the author's own fertile brain, implemented as it may be by some external stimulus. A few writers even confess that they find their best ideas in planning imaginary murders of people they don't like! The first detective story, Poe's "Murders in the Rue Morgue," very probably grew out of a news item about an escaped orang-outang; and many a thumping police romance since has taken its origin from some obscure newspaper paragraph—not necessarily of criminal nature itself.

This is as good a place as any to remark that the influence of real crime on the fictional variety is much slighter and less direct than is generally realized, for the principal reason that the two are quite different entities. The truth is that most real-life crime is duller, less ingenious, less dramatic, lacking in what Poe called "the pungent contradiction of the general idea," as compared with fictional felony; while the few exceptions to the rule are, paradoxically, usually *too* improbable to make good fiction. Too, real-life detection attains its results more often than not by means of undramatic, routine investigation, confession, "information received," or pure chance —none of which is suited to the police romance. (A related absence of art and artifice probably explains the failure of attempts to popularize non-fiction "puzzle books" with a crime theme.) This is not to say that detective story writers never make use of real crime and detection as source material, but only that the relationship is nearly always suggestive rather than directly imitative.

The Need for Unity

Once the motivating theme is arrived at, the next and infinitely more difficult step is making the story fit the crime. For the tyro confronted with this problem, no better single guiding principle can be laid down than Willard Huntington Wright's dictum that the detective tale must at all times possess "unity of mood." Which, of course, is only another way of saying that characters, crime, style, dialogue, setting, the person of the detective, in fact all the structural minutiae, must be kept sternly and prayerfully "in key."

The Detective

In any detective story worth the name, at once the most important and most difficult integer is the sleuth. The evolution of the fictional detective has been both a curious and a significant one. DUPIN, of course, set the fashion in eccentricity, and SHERLOCK HOLMES raised it to high art. For many years an investigator without a complete and assorted set of idiosyncrasies was unthinkable, and in the hands of the inept the style soon degenerated into mere caricature. At length, inevitable reaction set in, and for another interlude most writers were at pains to emphasize how utterly commonplace were their detectives. This, too, had its drawbacks—sometimes the reader took the author's declaration at face value and stopped reading forthwith! Eventually a sort of compromise was worked out. Thus modern fictional bloodhounds are individual without being fantastic, and the affectations they do possess are carefully balanced by other factors: we accept NERO WOLFE's mannerisms, for instance, because we see them through Archie Goodwin's irreverent eyes. The safest rule for the novice, however, is to keep contrived eccentricity at the minimum, remembering that ordinary humanity is never dull if perceived and described with sufficient care.

In all fairness, women and boys do not make satisfactory principal detectives. Some examples of each class may be produced to counter this argument, but by and large to assign either to full-fledged criminal pursuit is a violation of the probabilities if not the strict possibilities. They may, and often do, figure as important and attractive assistants. The beginner, at least, will do well to confine them to such rôles.

Under all circumstances, a single principal sleuth is advisable, else the reader's essential identification of himself with the pursuer is likely to falter.

Whether the detective-in-chief shall be professional or amateur should depend largely on the writer's experience and background and access to information. Obviously, the police sleuth is the more plausible, but requires much greater technical knowledge. (Even the writer who employs an amateur hero, however, should study at least the standard textbooks of police procedure to avoid committing embarrassing blunders.) Another drawback of the professional policeman is his tendency, inseparable from routine, to be a little on the dull side. The amateur, on the other hand, is inherently livelier and offers much wider latitude to the author, but has become increasingly unconvincing in a mechanized and departmentalized civilization. To resolve this two-horned dilemma, several reasonably successful combinations have been devised, uniting the advantages of the respective methods while avoiding their pitfalls. Among them may be mentioned: the "gentleman policeman" (such as Ngaio Marsh's RODERICK ALLEYN or the Lockridges' LIEUTENANT WEIGAND) who is brought logically onto the scene in official capacity, but because of his social charm functions with some of the freedom and insouciance of the amateur; the semi-pro or consulting specialist (as REGGIE FORTUNE or ELLERY QUEEN) who has the backing of Scotland Yard or Centre Street, yet remains free from professional routine; the retired professional (as EX-SUPERINTENDENT WILSON); or, in quite different vein, the non-police or agency operative in the style made popular by Dashiell Hammett.

The ambitious author will find it an advantage, if he can withstand the personal boredom, to follow a single character throughout his tales. Not only is a great deal of preliminary structure eliminated because it remains standing between books; readers become devoted to familiar sleuths (indeed, know their names better than those of the authors in many cases) with consequent material benefit to their creator. An illustration of this has been furnished recently by the publishers of the MR. PINKER-TON stories by "David Frome." For several years the tales appeared under titles in which the sleuth's name appeared. Finally a book was issued in which the PINKER-TON name was omitted from the title—and sales showed an immediate drop. There is no stronger merchandising asset than habit. Use it!

The characterization of the sleuth is an item of the utmost importance. We have already seen that elaborate eccentricity is to be avoided. But the detective is in distinct need of a personality, and in a form so compressed as the police novel has necessarily become, the careful selection of significant details can not be overemphasized. The Régie cigarette, the Duesenberg automobile, a "pretty taste in wines and incunabula," a hothouse of orchids— all may seem chance details to the reader; actually, in the hands of an astute author, they replace whole chapters of description in a Scott or a Hardy.

In this connection, it is difficult to understand why so many contemporary authors neglect to give their sleuths full names and characters. "Inspector Doakes" indeed! How can a man have a face who hasn't a name? We readers want to know our heroes' names, first, last, and middle initial if any; we want to know where they live, what they wear and smoke, even what—though we mustn't be told too often—they eat for breakfast. The indifference of some writers to such matters is particularly incomprehensible, because the rewards of making a character the reader's familiar are obviously out of all proportion to the slight effort required. Moreover, the absence of such elementary details is a virtual confession of the author's lack of interest in his character. How, then, can he expect his audience to be interested?

Watson or Not?

As every detective tale was once expected to offer an Eccentric Sleuth, so too was it required to have its Watson. But styles have changed here, too. To-day the Watson method of narration, despite its patent advantages to the author, is pretty much frowned upon in the better writing circles, unless handled with great care and well disguised: partly because of its triteness, partly, perhaps, because it is a little *too* easy. The objective third-person approach, while more difficult technically, seems clearly to be better suited, logically and aesthetically, to a genus of literature in which the analytical mode is so greatly of the essence. Furthermore, it does not offer the temptation to over-writing that seems to assail many authors when they are confronted with the pronoun "I."

A word of caution to the beginner: if you *must* have a Watson, make him (or her) brash, whimsical, sceptical, critical, tart, sour; in short, anything *except* the worshipful friend of yore. The day of the fidus Achates has been definitely ended by over-use, and failure to realize the fact is only to run foul of strong reader and editorial prejudice.

Viewpoint

Concerning the problem of viewpoint in a wider sense, the safest rule for the novice is to select one approach and stick to it. A finished literary artist may, perhaps, employ a shifting viewpoint to advantage and without loss of unity; but in the hands of lesser fry nothing is more irritating than the story seen now through the detective's eyes, now through the observation of one or more of the characters, and again from the "omnipotent" angle. Used singly, these approaches are equally valid. Combinations of them are not advisable for the tyro and are filled with traps for the unwary, more so in this type of fiction than any other.

The Crime

In a purely theoretical sense, it may be possible to have detection without crime; but such experimentation is only for the definitely established author, and even then it is seldom satisfactory. The beginner should take no such chances. Similarly, murder has come to be the accepted theme of the detective novel, for reasons too numerous and obvious to require attention. A Wilkie Collins may be able to hold our interest in lesser crime throughout a full book, but there are few Collinses writing to-day. Slighter offenses, moreover, tend to deprive the writer of the Motive string to his technical bow, leaving him only Means and Opportunity for his serenade. The motives of murder are manifold; the motive of theft—save in the unusual case—is, self-evidently, theft. . . . The writer who is overtaken by an unusual idea involving a crime of lesser degree than homicide, or that even rarer avis, a really unique crimeless puzzle, will do well to employ it in a short story. To attempt to use it as the main theme of a full-length novel is almost certainly to risk months of hard work for a rejection slip.

Many critics and readers have a strong prejudice against mass, or multiple, murder, and this is certainly an objection for the tyro to keep in mind. To be strictly fair, however, a distinction should be drawn between additional killings dragged in to pad out the story or extricate the author from a difficult situation; and, on the other hand, the deliberate series of murders which is the criminal's objective or to which he is logically driven to cover his tracks as the sleuth closes in. There can be no legitimate objection to the latter situation; the former, however, is an unblushing confession of technical inadequacy and can not be condemned too strongly. Nevertheless, the wise writer will restrict his homicides to three or four at the most, if only for the reason that undue repetition of any theme is poor art and brings its own penalty in loss of interest on the part of the reader. Instances will doubtless be cited where a greater number of killings has been used without payment of this penalty. But these will usually be found to be intentional tours de force, of the nature of John Rhode's *Murders in Praed Street* or Philip MacDonald's *Mystery of the Dead Police*.

Specific methods, motives, and mechanics of murder will be discussed a little later in the section entitled "Devices."

The Title

The best advice to the author faced with the selection of a title is not to worry about it. Some lucky writers arrive at their titles before they write their books; others achieve them in the silent watches of the night. But it is safe to say that any author who turns out a 60,000 to 80,000 word opus will have thought of a number of satisfactory possibilities before his manuscript is completed. Certain elementary rules must be obeyed, of course, such as the requirement that the title must be in key with the nature of the book. Likewise, it is well not to strain too much for effect. Most of the too-bright titles perpetrated by authors and publishers in recent years have demonstrably failed to increase sales, and as a consequence the vogue for such forced absurdities as *Death Dunks a Doughnut* or *The Corpse With the Artificial Umbilicus* is happily beginning to wane. In any event, it is helpful to study the type of title in current favor, with special attention to the better works and authors. Imitation of mediocrity is seldom beneficial.

The Plot

Plot is something that can never be taught; it must be learned. Such rules as have been formulated for its construction will be found in any good manual of fiction writing, and, in general, will apply to the detective story. In addition, the writer of this type of literature must keep in mind at all times the necessity of avoiding the use of coincidence, of making certain that every major episode subsequent to the opening crime proceeds directly and causatively from the duel between sleuth and criminal. Minor unrelated incidents may be introduced occasionally to divert or to relieve tension, but they must never be allowed to interfere with the progress of the main plot.

"Had-I-But-Known"

It is a safe guess that no single practice among present-day soi-disant detective story writers has aroused such

MR. MILQUETOAST MEETS MURDER

(From the New York *Herald Tribune*, December 15, 1940.
By special permission of H. T. Webster.)

concentrated distaste among so many readers as the style of plot-work and narration which has come to be recognized—in Ogden Nash's telling phrase—as the "Had-I-But-Known" school of writing. The allusion will be obvious to any intelligent reader. By it is meant the type of story which is artificially stalled and prolonged by coincidence and happenstance; by characters performing senseless acts and upsetting the sleuth's carefully laid plans, or getting bashed over the head (never sufficiently hard!) and "forgetting" to tell about it, or neglecting to report or investigate the most obvious clues until it is "too late"—while the narrator (invariably first-person and feminine) chants in the fashion of a Greek chorus equipped with faultless if slightly dilatory logic: "If we had only known what was going to happen, we might have prevented it!"

The beginner to-day will do well to avoid this style. Not only is it phony writing; its day of doom is clearly in sight. Increasingly it is the subject of published ridicule and satire, and the words that are spoken of it in rental libraries and private homes are not fit subject for print. In time, news of this steadily growing opposition will penetrate even the cloistered sancta of the editors, and when it does it will bode ill for the unfortunate author who can not write without the aid of such meretricious crutches.*

* Subsequent to the penning of these lines, the Columbia University Press has released through its weekly bulletin, *The Pleasures of Publishing,* April 14, 1941, the results of a diverting but nonetheless valuable survey of the detective story predilections of several hundred habitual readers of the form. Among the questions asked, the participants in the questionnaire were polled on their "pet dislikes." By "a large vote of guilty," according to the compilers, third place on this list of aversions went to the Had-I-But-Known school of writing. (First place was voted

Emotion and Drama

The question of emotion presents a particularly difficult choice for the budding author who wants to stay within the detective framework. On the one hand, the detective story must have *some* element of drama and excitement if it is to satisfy its theme and readers. On the other, it is one of the unwritten rules that fortuitous personal peril must never be allowed to supersede detection as the integral motif. Such a fine balance is not easy of achievement. A familiar attempt to circumvent the dilemma is the tale in which the central character is forced to turn detective either to clear himself of accusation or to escape the machinations of the criminal. But in nine cases out of ten such an essential reversal of the rôles of pursuer and pursued is likely to result in better melodrama than detection. Even such memorable adventures in breathless-

to "too much love and romance," which few readers need be told is one of the cardinal sins of the H.I.B.K. sorority; second place to "poor writing" generally; and fourth to the hard-boiled school, "but mostly on the basis of too much of a good thing.") While in the voting on *preferred* types of writing, the H.I.B.K. mode placed a poor last among all forms! Likewise, among the comments attached by many of the voters to their ballots, numerous unchivalrous aspersions were cast on such moth-eaten H.I.B.K. devices and trappings as "nosy spinsters," "women who gum up the plot," "super-feminine stories," and "heroines who wander around attics alone." Lest mere misogyny among the voters be suspected, the conductors of the poll point out that almost as many women readers as men replied to the questionnaire, and that the first two authors in point of popularity were women (both English, however): Dorothy Sayers and Agatha Christie. In the several "favorite" classifications on which opinion was sought—such as favorite author, favorite detective, favorite novel, etc.—not a single one of the supposedly popular H.I.B.K. authors reached the first ten! Granting that this poll may represent a rather specialized cross-section of the detection-reading public, it will nevertheless afford little aid or comfort to H.I.B.K.-minded authors or editors; but rather should serve as a valuable indication of the direction the wind is blowing to-day.

ness as John Buchan's RICHARD HANNAY stories and Philip MacDonald's *Escape* can not quite elude this character. The method should therefore be regarded with extreme caution by the beginner who wishes to establish a reputation in legitimate detection rather than "the blood." (If he does not care, that is something else again, outside the scope of the present discussion; but he must make his choice—he can not have both.) A sounder and safer procedure, on the whole, is to retain the detective in the orthodox position of pursuer and to create drama out of the criminal's attempt to escape the encircling net of justice. Scores of superior and exciting stories have been built on exactly this premise, barren as it may appear in the unadorned statement. A little intensive study of the better authors will reveal some of the specific methods employed.

The Puzzle Element

The antithesis of excessive emotion and drama, of course, is to have too little—and this is equally perilous. We have heard far too much in some circles about the detective story as a "game" between author and reader. This is certainly true insofar as it means that the writer must not cheat or unfairly hoodwink his audience. But carried to an extreme, this conception of the genre as primarily a competitive contest tends to deprive it of literary entity and relegate it to the realm of mechanical puzzles, to its eventual stagnation. As Philip Van Doren Stern has accurately remarked: "Were the detective story *only* a puzzle, there would be no need to make it a book." Such a tendency was alarmingly observable in the British detective story in the mid-1920's, but has since happily given way to a large extent, even in England, to more liberal conceptions. For to-day, it seems safe to say, more readers come to the detective novel to pursue crime *with* the author and his sleuth than to challenge them to a duel of wits; to escape the woes of a cruelly competitive world in the forgetful bliss of the purely vicarious chase, rather than to invent new competitions.

Generalizations are dangerous, but if it were possible to build up statistically a really "typical" detective story reader, it is a good wager that this hypothetical individual would reveal himself as more the "introvert" than the "extrovert," more the onlooker than the inveterate game-ster. Christopher Morley, that devoted and discerning de-tectophile, came close to the core of the matter when he remarked in the mellow person of his John Mistletoe on "the narcotic value of the detective story." And from the other side of the ocean H. Douglas Thomson has stated his considered judgment that "the puzzle can be over-done, and it is fatal to deprive it of its trappings."

All of which is simply to say that writers should never forget the necessity of the detective story to be dynamic, not static; to move continually *forward;* to entertain as well as perplex. There is more than a grain of truth in B. J. R. Stolper's humorous "recipe" for the tasty police novel:

> $\frac{1}{2}$ Sherlock Holmes
> $\frac{1}{4}$ P. G. Wodehouse
> $\frac{1}{8}$ sheer adventure
> $\frac{1}{8}$ anything you know best *

---

* *Scholastic,* October 22, 1938.

With the addition of only one other ingredient—a liberal portion of salt—this is a formula well adapted to the beginner's needs.

Background and Setting

Approaching the problem of background and setting, a dependable rule is to select something the author knows well. There are virtually no limitations, save that the *less* exotic the scenes, the better they will serve the essential interest of verisimilitude. Chesterton remarked somewhere that the detective story is at its best when it "stays at home"—or words to that general effect. (There are many who regret that G.K.C. did not follow his own precepts more closely!) But, on the opposite hand, the setting should not be *too* drab or commonplace or sordid: the confirmed addict does not come to the detective story in search of Dostoevsky. Most successful are those backdrops known to the average reader, yet "touched up" by artful brushwork; for it is the "semblance of reality" which is desired, rather than reality itself.

As Carolyn Wells has said, the detective story must *seem* real in the same sense that fairy tales *seem* real to children; while Marjorie Nicolson demands that it be "photographically real though never realistic." For this reason one ventures to differ with Willard Huntington Wright's pronouncement of a few years ago in favor of elaborate floor-plans and diagrams. The well-plotted tale to-day will avoid the involutions which make such adjuncts of mere criminology necessary. A sizable group of readers, in fact, flatly refuses to read novels in which such charts are found, maintaining with some cause that their presence confesses either to lack of descriptive skill on the author's part or to a plot too complex to be entertaining. (Maps, for some reason, are received more tolerantly.) A variation of this objection would seem to account for the short life of several attempts at picturized detective stories: such embellishments only quarrel with the mental image the audience has formed.

In setting, as in all other departments of the genre, the author must be on constant guard against triteness. Several standard backdrops have been so overworked that a faint odor of the bogus has begun to exude from them: among them, weird old mansions and castles, or for that matter anything partaking of the Gothic mode. Such trappings have long since been relegated to the less critical mode of mystery, and even there they have lost much of the power they once possessed to astonish and excite. In slightly different vein, the country estate and its inevitable accompaniment, the week-end party, are due for a rest. A little intelligent reading will warn the beginner of other scenes-of-action which have grown wearisome through too frequent repetition.

We have spoken in an earlier paragraph of the curious failure of many writers to equip their sleuths with full names and recognizable traits. Equally hard to comprehend is the predilection of other authors for artificial settings—when *real* streets, buildings, neighborhoods, even trains and tram-cars, add so greatly to the believability, nay, the fascination, of narratives particularly dependent on verisimilitude for their success. It is not essential that the audience should be personally familiar with the settings for them to produce this effect. Thousands of readers who have never visited New York believe implicitly in the better Philo Vance cases, if for no other reason than that the topographical details are as readily recognizable as this morning's newspaper. And millions who have never seen London can picture Baker Street as vividly as their own homes.

Some day, perhaps, an inquisitive statistician will enumerate the number of police novels which use these two cities as their scenes. Apart from the circumstance that they are the residence of many of the practitioners and readers, there is a solid reason for their predominance: their world-wide familiarity to all peoples through picture, song, and story—as the saying goes. Since the coming of the moving picture, particularly, there is scarcely a reader who can not readily visualize at least the general appearance and topography of both metropolises.

This is not to suggest that the writer who lives in, say, Nebraska, should attempt to lay his story in the purlieus of Manhattan. He will do far better to stick to the Nebraska he knows. R. C. Woodthorpe, one of the most competent of contemporary English detection writers, once placed an amusing conceit in the mouth of one of his characters, whom he induced to declare that if he ever attempted a police novel he would steal the plot of *Hamlet* and translate it into modern dress: laying the whole action in some quiet suburb, with the players' scene to be staged by the village dramatic society and the ghost of Hamlet's father to appear at a spiritualistic séance. One would hesitate to say how many times portions of this idea have already been put into successful effect. Certainly, one of the finest of recent detective stories, Selwyn Jepson's *Keep Murder Quiet* (1941), bears a discernible plot-resemblance to the immortal legend of the Melancholy Dane, converted into modern terms. (An almost exactly opposite application of the reconstruction-motif is found in Victor Luhrs' *The Longbow Murder*, laid in the days of Richard the Lion Hearted, with the dauntless monarch himself functioning as chief sleuth. But such stunts, however diverting, can never become a major development in the literature.)

To those who fail to see the possibilities in near-at-hand, commonplace, homely settings, it should be necessary to point only to the works of that startling American newcomer, Mabel Seeley. If further examples are needed, there has even been a successful *Murder in a Nunnery* (by Eric Shepherd, 1940), a slight but pleasant effort which was a monthly choice of the Catholic Book Club. . . . One wonders, incidentally, if the day may not arrive when one of the major non-sectarian book societies will have the courage to name a superior detective novel as its principal selection. Assuredly there have been less notable choices than a *Benson Murder Case*, a *Nine Tailors*, a *Roger Ackroyd*, a *Before the Fact*, a *Maltese Falcon*—out of many—would have been. The naming some years ago of Dorothy Sayers' anthological *Omnibus of Crime* was exemplary—but scarcely the same thing.*

Characters and Characterization

Like so many of the other conventions, treatment of character in the detective novel has undergone consider-

---

* Just as this volume is sent to press, word comes that one of the important book societies has at last conferred the begged-for boon on its subscribers.

able change in recent years. Formerly there existed something of an unwritten law that the personae, apart from the central sleuth, should be purposely "played down." To do otherwise, it was argued, would distract attention from the integral problem (this was in the days when the "puzzle" aspect of the detective story was receiving its greatest support); and for whole decades shadowy, faceless stencils floated in and out of a multitude of murder chambers, leaving little trace of their passing in the mind of the reader. Whatever merit this fashion may have had began to decline as the police novel, even in its more routine concepts, slowly turned from mechanical crime toward something approaching the psychological. This does not mean that every writer should attempt the all out character novel of detection—for it is given to only a few to write with the penetration of a Francis Iles or a Margery Allingham—but the beginner will do well to set as his goal at least the standards of contemporary magazine fiction of the better class. The old days of cardboard heroes and hissing villains have gone with the gaslight, and nothing will so quickly doom the novice's chances of acceptance by reputable publishers as failure to comprehend the circumstance.

Admittedly, not all characters can be drawn with the same amount of detail as is devoted to the central sleuth in a form as compressed as the modern detective story. (How often the contemporary writer must envy Wilkie Collins and his three-deckers!) But they must be made clearly recognizable in outline—just as a clever caricaturist or shadowgraph artist can identify his subjects in a few strokes. This situation requires even greater care in the selection of significant detail than does delineation of the detective. Contrast, too, is of the greatest importance: in physical appearance, in traits of speech and behavior, in age, particularly in name. If any two names convey the slightest similarity, either to the eye or the ear, confusion of the characters is almost sure to result. Recurrent references to the contrasting traits should be employed to help the reader (and the author!) keep the characters sharply in mind.

As in the case of the sleuth himself, full names should be given to all the principal figures. An excellent device is the printed cast of characters, with an identifying phrase for each, published in the front of the book for the reader's convenience. Both S. S. Van Dine and Ellery Queen—among several—have used this with high effectiveness. Such a list or table will also be highly useful to the author during the actual writing.

Inasmuch as the culprit is concealed among the characters in the modern detective novel, the temptation to the novice is to hide him by the very multitude of personae. But this device is likely to backfire; the author will quickly find that he has weakened the effectiveness of the tale and increased and complicated his own structural problems. In general, eight or ten principal characters should be the limit; with the number of actual suspects held to five or six. Incidental actors, in the form of servants, medical examiners, police sergeants, etc., may be added to taste and within reason.

Some critics hold that there should always be a secondary hero or heroine, in addition to the sleuth, to engage the reader's sympathy. This is on the whole a sound principle, though it may be obviated by certain unusual plots and circumstances.

Style

In style, again, the developments of recent years have belied even so astute a critic as Willard Huntington Wright, who declared in 1927 that style had no more excuse in the detective story than in the cross-word puzzle. It is necessary to cite no more than Mr. Wright's own best novels, written as "S.S. Van Dine," to disprove this thesis. Perhaps, however, his premise may be qualified, in the light of later custom, to read that too great *pretentiousness* of style is still as fatal to the detective novel as is any other distracting element. (Oddly enough, it is mainly this fault which makes the later Van Dine novels so distinctly inferior to the earlier ones.)

But if there is no room for over-writing in the form, there is always a place, indeed, a clamoring necessity, for those indefinable qualities of statement that have ever distinguished good fiction of all sorts from bad. Whatever else the detective story may or may not do to-day, it definitely must not be—to borrow a term from another glossary—"corny," either in style or device.

The Devices of Detection

A respectable book might be written on the devices of the detective story alone. Seeking a single guide-post in a wilderness of detail, we can do no better than to prescribe simplicity as the chief desideratum. A prime reason for the failure of many excellent and ingenious plots is their very involution and excessive elaborateness. In general, it may be said that the detective novel which requires a long and detailed explanatory chapter at the end has failed in its purpose. A few valedictory remarks by the detective are always permissible, to explain the thought processes by which he arrived at his conclusion. But in the really well constructed story, the "denunciation" should of itself answer all the determinative questions ("how") and show, besides, why *only* the culprit ("who"), out of all the characters, can be guilty. (A plague, in passing, on all stuffy tales in which the criminal's sole qualification is his least-likelihood!) If the dénouement has been sufficiently prepared, and if no evidence has been withheld from the reader, relatively few additional paragraphs will be required for the detective to tell us what he observed and deduced that we did not as we followed him down the path.

A good secondary rule might be to require of all prospective writers of detective fiction a thorough course of critical reading in their chosen subject: S.S. Van Dine read more than 2,000 stories before he tried to write one! Only in this way may all the pitfalls of the overworked and hackneyed be successfully skirted.

It is in the matter of evidence, of course, that most of the dangers and clichés lurk. In her still helpful manual, *The Technique of the Mystery Story,* Carolyn Wells more than a decade ago made an amusing catalogue of evidential devices which were taboo even then, including "gravity clues," "shredded evidence," and similar means and methods outlawed either because of over-use or because of far-fetchedness. One of the illuminating differences, incidentally, which will strike the reader who compares to-day's detective story with that of a quarter-century ago is the prevalence of material clues in the older form and the predominance of what may be called "behavioristic" evidence in the new. (For a particularly blithe modern travesty on the old-fashioned "dropped clue," see the episode of the lost pipe which HILDEGARDE WITHERS pursues relentlessly through the pages of Stuart Palmer's *The Red Stallion*.) This is not to imply that physical evidence no longer has a legitimate function; only that if it is to whet the jaded appetite of to-day's reader it must be served up with piquant sauces. The best single example, perhaps, of the modern method of handling the material clue is Philip MacDonald's brilliantly simple *Rasp*. Still other instances particularly suited to the beginner's study are the radio adventures (even more than the book appearances) of ELLERY QUEEN.

Some random *do's* and *don'ts* for the beginner concerning device and general technique:

Avoid the Locked Room puzzle. Only a genius can invest it with novelty or interest to-day.

Eschew footprints, tobacco ash, and ballistics. Don't expect your reader to be excited by fingerprints, either!

Use plenty of conversation but only a minimum of description, save where it serves a definite rather than a decorative purpose. Atmosphere is important; but convey it economically, suggestively.

Disguise, of course, went out with the bustle.

Love, once barred from the premises, is permissible in moderation to-day (indeed, is essential for the women's-magazine market) but it must not be allowed to interrupt or divert the directional flow of crime-and-detection any more than any other incidental factor.

The least-likely-person theme, in the old sense, is stale stuff. Give the reader cause to suspect every one, including the culprit, but *apparently* clear him in the early stages.

An infinite number of variations on this formula can be—and constantly are—worked out.

A related rule proclaims that the criminal must be some one who has appeared throughout the story. Father Knox adds the further qualification that the culprit "must not be any one whose thoughts the reader has been permitted to follow": a justifiable if lock-the-stable-door rule obviously inspired by *Roger Ackroyd*—and at the same time an argument for the "constant" viewpoint in narration.

Make your crime method, whatever else it may be, "practically demonstrable." To this dictum one is tempted to add a remonstrance against all methods of killing so complex, so dependent on the exact juxtaposition of a multitude of factors and persons, that they have about the same chance of success as a hole-in-one in golf—yet which always come off to perfection! A century ago Edgar Allan Poe warned against mistaking "what is only complex for what is profound," and the admonition still holds true. Remember that plausibility is your best friend!

Don't introduce a "trick" murder device unless you are certain that it is both original and plausible. The ice-bullet, the ice-dagger, and similar "sells" so popular a decade ago are to-day as archaic as the Florentine paper-cutter of an earlier era. The same objection applies to mechanical alibis of the nature of the phonograph to simulate conversation, doors unlocked from the inside by Rube Goldberg-ish contraptions, and similar over-ingenious inventions. Even the skill of a John Dickson Carr can not quite carry off such far-fetched contrivances to-day, and the unknown beginner will only handicap his chances by attempting them.... An additional weakness of the mechanical mode is its requirement of some special knowledge or aptitude on the part of the perpetrator, thereby narrowing the field of suspects—for the rules of fair-play demand that the reader be duly informed of all such special abilities.

The better fictional homicides to-day are accomplished —like those in real life—by shooting, strangling, stabbing, pushing (off cliffs and buildings and into water), bashing, and poisoning; not necessarily in the order named.

Poison is an increasingly popular modern murder weapon, concurrent with the intensified emphasis on psychology and character in the detective story. In all psychology there is no more fascinating study than the warped mentality of the poisoner. But beware, young author, of unusual poisons requiring expert medical knowledge, and *never, never* succumb to that trade-mark of the hopeless hack, the poison-that-leaves-no-trace! Choose an ordinary poison, not too difficult to obtain, and make your puzzle out of the mentality of the murderer, or the circumstances of administering, or both.

Like unto the method, the motive of the crime must be strictly plausible. It must also be adequate. Murder, as some one may have remarked before, is a serious business, for all the nonchalance with which the detective story customarily treats it. No mean or trivial motive—frequently as these occur in real life—will satisfy the artistic verities of the fictional form. Avarice is acceptable, if on a sufficiently large scale, but is somewhat difficult to conceal for the reason that the person who gains by the death of another is usually quite readily discoverable. For this reason many writers have come to employ financial gain only as a subsidiary or false-suspicion motive. Revenge, jealousy, ambition, passion, are all motives which seem somehow more suited to the nature of the crime, at least in its fictive guise. In connection, again, with the new emphasis on psychology and character, numerous writers are finding fear-of-exposure at once a most convincing motive and one capable of wide variation. It also lends itself to combination with virtually all the other motives.

But so much emphasis on the criminal phases of the subject must not lead the would-be writer to forget (as too often happens) that the crime in a detective story is only the means to an end, which is—detection. All too many originally intriguing crime-plots have turned out to be weak sisters in the bookstores solely because the authors failed to match their starting ideas with equally brilliant deduction. Concerning this aspect, little general advice can be offered aside from Poe's twin and initial dicta: that whenever all the impossibilities have been eliminated, that which remains, however improbable, will be the truth; and that the more outré the crime in appearance, the easier the solution. (And the demand by modern readers that the solution must be brought about by the detective's reasoning and actions—never by chance or coincidence.) As for specific methods and styles of deduction, the beginner can only be advised to read, read, and read again until he is thoroughly saturated with his subject.

A few more Pearls of Wisdom and we shall be finished:

Let your readers and characters become acquainted before the killings set in. To be introduced to a corpse is not an exhilarating or even interesting experience. A few unpleasant traits distributed among the victims-to-be will prevent the intrusion of undue grief when the homicides begin.

Forget your social and political prejudices; or, if you can't, at least express them obliquely and with caution. The detective story may be a novel of manners, even a novel of character; but it can not, without losing its essential form, become a novel of ideas.

Shun the "master-mind" criminal—as trite as he is implausible in fiction. To be sure, "crime syndicates" exist in real life (some even control entire continents!) but they are pursued and brought to bay by *mass* methods, not by lone-wolf sleuths. The unities of fictional detection demand a single principal criminal and a single principal detective. Both should be believable human beings, of superior and closely matched intelligence.

The supernatural in a detective story may be "evoked only to be dispelled," to quote Dorothy Sayers. All incidents and circumstances must have physical explanations, and *all* must be explained.

Try to close your case without recourse to legal procedure. Not only do the legal aspects of crime offer the most difficult technical problems and pitfalls for the novice—the excessive craze for court-room plays, novels, and motion pictures in recent years has, temporarily at least, worn out the dramatic possibilities of even the coroner's inquest. Many of the better contemporary writers have resorted to reporting all such proceedings (when inescapable) off-stage, while creating a diversion on the actual scene.

Avoid as you would the plague long lists and tabulations of clues and evidence. There is no quicker way to antagonize friends and lose readers. If a résumé seems unavoidable, handle it conversationally. Better still, start an argument among your characters and introduce your rehashing in the disguise of debate. . . . Leave railway and other time-tables to Freeman Wills Crofts.

Similarly, a transcript of evidence is not fiction. Don't seat your detective at a table and parade the witnesses before him. Move him around, mix evidence with events —or else you will have a Yawning Reader on your hands. (British writers please note!)

Trace the insidious false clue to its lair and eliminate it—remembering that by this term is meant the clue that has no explicable connection with the crime. The false clue should not be confused with the legitimate clue which the writer, by exercise of his skill, persuades his audience to *misinterpret,* and which is quite within the rules of the game. The distinction is a delicate and deceptive but highly important one, and should be watched carefully by the author who wishes to avoid giving offense.

The list might be continued indefinitely to include a whole host of minor rules, such as the familiar prohibitions against secret passages, sinister Orientals, twin brothers from Australia, concealment of information, intuitional solutions, unmotivated confession, and similar matters. But these are largely canons of good taste and as such are easily acquirable by all readers and writers of average perception and discrimination. It has therefore been the purpose of the present discussion less to set forth such specific statutes than to attempt to establish some of the larger principles from which they derive.

The Physical Boundaries

A word must be said somewhere about the physical limitations of the detective story manuscript. These are determined chiefly by certain commercial considerations, which will be more fully examined in the next chapter. But it may be said briefly here that the beginner who submits a detective novel longer than, say, 80,000 words, is courting almost certain rejection. The established author, with an assured volume of sales, or whose books might conceivably fetch a higher retail price, is of course in a more favorable and flexible position.

Some detective novels total no more than 40,000 or 50,000 words in length. But such an extreme of abbreviation is scarcely to be recommended, either. A book that does not fill at least an evening of the reader's time is likely to leave him with the resentful feeling that he has somehow been cheated of his due—and his rental fee.

If an author is interested in attempting short-story selling in the magazine field, he should begin by careful study of editorial needs and lengths. These vary so greatly with the individual periodical that no attempt will be made to elaborate on them here.

Some General Considerations

English writers have had one inestimable advantage denied to their American brethren, in the existence of the highly honorable company of the Detection Club, of London. Numbering in its membership the most eminent names in the field in England, this association has for some years functioned as a virtual Academy of the genre, acting as an arbiter and oracle of auctorial ethics and taste and constituting a goal and reward for ambitious newcomers. (An interesting historical account of the Club and its activities will be found in the 1940 anthology,

Line-Up, edited by John Rhode.) No banding together of accredited American craftsmen along similar lines seems thus far to have been contemplated. But the very thought opens up stimulating possibilities. For instance, should such an association some day be formed and should the London club's stringent "Hippocratic Oath" be adopted (in which each author is required faithfully to forswear "mumbo-jumbo and jiggery-pokery"), certain of Uncle Sam's best-selling nephews and nieces would be automatically barred from membership—unless they changed their ways! It is not too much to say that such a prospect could be borne with equanimity by many readers.

*   *   *

One serious word in conclusion. The detective story, while admittedly a form of escape literature and unlikely ever to become anything else, has nevertheless made a respectable place for itself in contemporary letters. This position was not won without a struggle, in which, it must be conceded, English authorship has to date played a considerably more important rôle than has American. But, as these lines are written, it seems only too likely that the future of the detective story (as, perhaps, of all literature) will rest in non-European hands for at least the next few years. Thus the very survival of the genre in a troubled world (assuming this, as we do, to be desirable) may depend on the clarity and completeness of American understanding of the basic principles responsible for the present eminence of the detective story and necessary for its continuance. Regrettably, such a realization is not held as widely as could be desired. In the absence of pronouncements by better qualified authorities, the attempt will be made here, as briefly and simply as possible, to remedy the difficulty with a final summarizing statement:

Stripped of its decorations and embellishments, the detective story is at bottom one thing only: a conflict of wits between criminal and sleuth, in which the detective is traditionally victorious by out-thinking his adversary. Each important plot incident, every structural step of the story, must be the perfect and logical consequence and result of this central conflict of crime and pursuit, just as each move in a chess game determines and is determined by a counter-move. The formula is capable of infinite variation, as is chess. It may be adorned and disguised in almost any fashion the author chooses, whether gaudy or sober. But in basic structure it must never vary by so much as a hairsbreadth from absolute logicality. Beside this one simple rule, all other rules pale to relative unimportance. This *is* the detective story.

Conversely, the one completely unforgivable sin in the detective story is the substitution, at any point, of accident, chance, or coincidence for logical deduction. If this uncomfortable shoe may seem to fit certain dainty American feet—well, let it be put on, and high time too!

CHAPTER XII

The Murder Market

I

CLOSELY akin to the popular delusion mentioned in the preceding chapter that the construction of the detective story is child's play, is an equally unfounded general belief that the form is a literary gold mine, with financial rewards to the author out of all proportion to the amount of labor involved. This misconception may be ascribed not only to the common underestimation of the technical equipment required of the writer, but, as well, to a number of widely published articles and discussions in recent years about what has been facetiously called the "murder market." Crime and police stories—we are told—are read by such-and-such an astounding number of readers yearly; their gross sales are estimated at so many millions of dollars; this and that author have made fortunes and retired to lives of sybaritic ease.

All these things are true in degree, yet they do not mean that the *average* detective story author, even if he be reasonably successful, enjoys more than a moderate annual income or that he works less hours per year at his craft than a shop clerk or a bricklayer. It will be the purpose of the present chapter to elaborate on this proposition.

Publishers are notoriously chary of revealing specific

auditors' accounts of any save their biggest successes—
and the detective story, as we shall shortly see, seldom
achieves that classification. Nevertheless, enough representatives of the profession have spoken guardedly from
time to time on the subject of detective fiction sales so
that out of their several statements a few commercial
generalizations may be pieced together.

In the course of an American publishing year (we can
not speak for England, but the general relationships are
presumably similar in normal times) approximately 300
novels appear which, by some exercise of leniency, may
be classified as "crime literature." This output represents
a good one-fourth of all new fiction published, estimated
at 1,200 titles in the normal twelvemonth. The average
sale of the ordinary crime novel—as nearly as may be
gauged from the cautious statements of the publishers—
lies somewhere between 1,500 and 2,000 copies. Best-
sellers are rare. Even the most successful books of the Big
Name authors seldom pass 15,000 copies. For example:
Dorothy Sayers' *Murder Must Advertise,* published in
her writing prime and easily one of her two or three
finest books, was lucky to reach 9,000 copies in its original
American edition. (Though a subsequently acquired
"woman's magazine" audience lifted her later, and sadly
inferior, *Busman's Honeymoon* to 20,000 copies.) "S. S.
Van Dine's" sales, the greatest ever achieved by an
American detective story writer, are said to have *averaged* only 30,000 copies per title. But even these are
exceptions. An entire year may pass in which no crime
story tops the 10,000 mark.

Yet—by an odd paradox which seems inseparable from
the modern crime novel—there is a continuing and steady

demand by publishers for such tales. For, if they seldom break sales records, neither do they produce many costly failures. This is largely true because of the fixed and stable nature of the ultimate market—at once the contemporary detective story's greatest strength and weakness in a commercial sense.

From sixty to eighty-five per cent, it is variously estimated, of all copies printed are sold to rental and public libraries. No single library of either class, perhaps, purchases *every* story published; but it is clear that enough of them regularly buy several hundred new volumes a year (including duplicates) to guarantee any established publisher, issuing a reasonably well executed crime tale, against actual loss. Conversely, needless to say, this easy availability of crime novels through libraries exercises a rigidly limiting influence on sales direct to readers.

Accurate statistics are admittedly hard to come by. But for the reader who is content with round figures it is possible to make a few generalizations. Accepting for the moment an annual output of 300 new crime titles and an average sale of, say, 2,000 copies (which is probably too high), it will quickly be seen that a maximum of 600,000 new copies are *sold* in the United States yearly. At a retail price of two dollars per copy, this means a gross of a little more than a million dollars, not allowing for trade and other discounts. To this must be added the sales of a completely indeterminable number of reprint editions, retailing at from twenty-five cents to one dollar a copy. Even so, the total—while "a tidy sum," as Franklin P. Adams might say—is still far below certain rather vague published estimates of $5,000,000 turnover annually.

Perhaps if the income from rentals, magazine sales and serializations, and moving-picture rights is included, the $5,000,000 all-over figure may not be far from the mark.

If it is difficult to get at the annual sales of crime literature, it is even harder to gauge the number of readers with any accuracy. This much may be said: every crime novel, no matter how undistinguished, which is placed on the shelves of a rental or public library reaches a vastly greater number of readers *per copy* than any save the very top-notch successes in "legitimate" fiction or non-fiction. So avid and omnivorous is the mystery clientele, in fact, that rental libraries frequently report as many as fifty readers per copy before discarding; and public libraries as high as one hundred readers, with rebinding. On this basis one American publisher has recently estimated in the *Publishers' Weekly* that every new mystery published is read by not less than 15,000 readers. Multiply this by our figure of 300 new titles a year, and you have a total not far from 5,000,000 readers. How many of these are "repeaters" may only be hazarded; but it is surely not unreasonable to assume that a good million Americans may be numbered as more or less regular devotees of detective fiction in book form.*

In short, the detective story holds the anomalous distinction of being one of the most widely read and steadily consumed of all modern varieties of literature—while its *sales* are usually negligible!

---

* If this figure may seem small, let the reader remember that even *Gone With the Wind,* the most phenomenal of all modern fiction successes, has been read by *less than one-thirtieth* of the population of great, literate America! Chronic overestimation of book sales and circulation is an essential part of what the Messrs. Mencken and Nathan once labeled The American Credo.

II

What does this mean to the individual author? What it all adds up to is that detective story writing—so widely regarded as an occupation at once easy, remunerative, and glamorous—is really as difficult and unrewarding a vocation as could be selected by the young man or woman with a pen; save for the chosen few.

To express the problem concretely: the average royalty to a beginning author on a two-dollar detective novel is seldom more than twenty cents a copy. Should the writer have the exceptional fortune to achieve a 2,500-copy sale at his first attempt, this means an optimum return of $500. A customary advance is $250, which some publishers pay on acceptance of the manuscript, others at publication. From three to six months is likely to intervene between acceptance and publication. And from six to eight months after publication (depending on the time of year and the individual publisher's custom) the "artist" receives his final $250—or less! Unless a reprint edition follows (at a greatly reduced royalty) this marks the end of the author's returns; for the sales-life of the ordinary mystery seldom exceeds two months, and even its rental-life rarely goes beyond six months. So standardized have all these figures become, and so small is the likelihood that they will vary, that some publishers are understood to offer a flat $400 or $500 for this type of fiction, to be paid in full on acceptance. It is claimed, moreover, that such sums more frequently exceed the usual percentage royalty than otherwise, as well as eliminating the long wait; but the beginner will do well to seek professional advice on the point.

A little further simple arithmetic will show what this means to the author who is entirely dependent on book sales of his detective fiction for his income. If he turns out one $500 novel a year, he is earning by his pen just less than $10 a week. Two such books a year are needed to approach a weekly salary of $20; four to reach a rough equivalent of $40 in the Saturday envelope; and so forth.

In the attainment of the quantity output which thus becomes almost inescapable, the brevity of the modern detective story offers a little help: for some "full-length" crime novels are no longer than 40,000 words. But it is scarcely necessary to mention that the basic plot construction of a 40,000-word novel is only less elaborate, not less intrinsically difficult, than of a 100,000-word novel; in fact, many writers find compression a more serious problem than expansion. Collaboration, of course, offers certain productive advantages, but these would seem to be almost completely offset in most cases by the necessity of dividing the already slim rewards.

Under all these circumstances it is little wonder that so many detective stories are the product of: (a) those who have other means of regular livelihood and who write either to supplement their incomes or for sheer love of the game; or (b) of poor, hard-driven devils, modern Gaboriaus often using several pseudonyms, whose natural talents are largely thwarted by the deliberate necessity of overproduction. This situation is not particularly the "fault" of any persons or system—for nobody is *compelled* to write detective stories for a living, and no publisher can be accused of "exploitation" on a 2,500-copy sale! But it is a harsh fact that should be thoroughly understood by those novices who conceive of crime-fiction writing as an easy road to fame and fortune.

An interesting suggestion recently advanced by an experienced editor is that the author should receive a small royalty on *rentals*. Considering the peculiar status of the detective story as we have just examined it, there is both justice and merit in this suggestion, though it is difficult to see at this time how any sufficiently accurate and inexpensive system of collections could be devised.

It may be asserted, of course, that the situation of the detective story writer in modern life does not differ appreciably from that of any other literary practitioner, and that some of these other servants of the pen have higher purposes to serve, which makes the pittance of their rewards the more deplorable. This is at least partly true. Yet there are alternative avenues open to many of these other writers which are virtually closed to-day to the builders of crime literature exclusively—for all its supposedly less exacting standards. Many "serious" writers manage to support their solider endeavors by turning their talents to occasional short magazine fiction, with its substantial compensation to the successful. But this outlet is only theoretically possible for the fashioner of detective stories, for two chief reasons, the one technical, the other commercial. On the technical side, the gradual exhaustion of possible mechanical novelty (almost the only detective theme which will succeed within the increasingly rigid limits of to-day's short story) has brought the brief police tale, with a few exceptions, close to extinction. Why, the author asks himself, should he waste a painstakingly conceived crime method on a short story, when only a little more labor will turn it into an acceptable full-length effort? Even so, he might be willing to make the gamble, save for the reluctance of most present-day "slick" magazine editors to accept anything in the detective story line, short *or* long, unless it is backed by a superlatively Big Name. The tendency is by no means limited to the detection field, but happens to be more stringently applied there. Whether in any case it is quite the "good business" it is supposed to be one ventures to doubt, considering the high rate of magazine mortality. But this is aside from our point.

An auxiliary field open to some beginners, who possess or can develop the requisite style and necessary facility, is that of the "pulp" magazines, which indeed have served as a training school for some of the leading talents in the American field to-day and are agreeably free of the snob-appeal which motivates so many of their more pretentious contemporaries. Nor are the rewards of this market, to those who can serve its needs, to be scorned. In a recent article in *Publishers' Weekly*, Frank Gruber, one of the most able and entertaining "graduates" of the school, made the interesting revelation that an identical novel had brought him a considerably higher monetary return in fees for pulp serialization than in the royalties received from book publication. But the chief drawback to the pulp market is that it limits itself to-day almost entirely to stories of the hard-boiled or at least medium-boiled genres. Furthermore, its more substantial rewards are reserved for the ultra-prolific. Mr. Gruber, for example, discloses that he wrote the novel previously mentioned (and, it may be said, a good one) in the elapsed time of fifteen days. Unfortunately, there are many writers of equally professional stature who simply can not approximate any such physical output, nor for that matter write in the hard-boiled or medium-boiled medium demanded, by the pulp editors, at all. This is neither to their discredit nor particularly to the credit of those who can—it is a plain commercial fact which should be faced candidly. The novice who finds that he falls within this classification may as well dismiss the thought of pulp-sales from his mind at once.

Recently some of the more venturesome "slick" magazine editors have been experimenting with novelette-length condensations ("one-shots" as they are called in the trade) not only by well-known authors but occasionally by promising beginners. But at best these can absorb only a handful of stories a year.

By and large it must be said that the novice has only a limited chance of augmenting his income by magazine sales.* Query: why does not some astute publisher establish a magazine aimed *directly* at book-readers of detective stories, giving them the authors and quality to which they are accustomed? The suggestion is offered gratis.

All these things being true, why do some hundreds of writers each year (not counting unpublished aspirants) continue to follow the detective story as a presumably gainful occupation? Possibly, one guesses, because of reasons of personal temperament: the freedom from business and professional routine and the like that make a

---

* The beginner who wishes to explore this possibility, however, will find useful hints in *How to Write For a Living* by T. M. White (New York, Reynal & Hitchcock, 1939), an excellent practical manual with an especially helpful chapter on crime-fiction markets.

small, uncertain, but independent income seem desirable to many individuals—just as the absence of security would be perfectly unbearable to others. In numerous cases, certainly, the writer is sustained by the will-of-the-wisp hope of some day "hitting the jackpot" of the high-priced serial field or the gold mines of Hollywood. But such instances are all too few, and it must be said in honesty that they require a high degree of luck as well as of merit. In a few cases, even, the body of evidence suggests that *only* the former factor has been present.

The beginning author should also be warned somewhere against the practices of a few publishers who, unhappily, thrive on the inexperience of novices. No hard-and-fast rule can be laid down, but in general it may be said that the beginner who can not place his novel with any one of the established publishing houses had better put it away and start again. It will do neither his pocketbook nor his reputation any permanent good to have traffic with those who offer him greatly reduced terms—or, even worse, ask him to defray any portion of the publishing expense. Even in dealing with reputable publishers, most novices will find it worth their while to be represented by some one of the recognized literary agents. The agent's small commission will be repaid many-fold in mistakes and pitfalls avoided, as well as assuring the widest possible market and most favorable terms for the author's work. Obviously no lists of publishers or agents can be given here, but the beginner who has taken the trouble to familiarize himself with the better writers' magazines and manuals (and if he has not, his approach is considerably less than intelligent and professional) will know to whom he can apply for advice.

III

No discussion of the commercial aspects of the detective story will be complete without mention of the Crime Club movement in England and America. Of the details of the English organization one knows little, save that, uniquely, it operates as a department of William Collins and Sons, a firm known almost entirely for some generations for its leadership in the field of religious publishing. The American colophon was created as a subsidiary of Doubleday, Doran, Inc., and has functioned successfully for better than a dozen years, publishing four selected titles a month, forty-eight in a year. With a number of the best authors scattered under contract among other publishers, it must be obvious that not all the annual forty-eight books will be of equal excellence; nor is it surprising that they sometimes transcend the bounds of the police novel—which is entirely the publisher's right under the trade-mark selected. What would seem more important is that the Crime Club movement has provided a hearing for many new authors who might not otherwise have been published, including some of the best and most original talents in the field to-day. . . . To those exacting readers who may object that what is needed is not more but better detective stories, the best answer, perhaps, is the vast improvement in the quality of the form during the exact years that it has been increasing quantitatively.

One other American publishing house has done so much to elevate the standards of the native detective story that it also deserves special mention. The imprint of Dodd, Mead and Company has come to be a virtual guaranty to many readers, and the justly famous "8 points" observed in selecting the company's "Red Badge" novels are so excellent that they have become a sort of Baedeker for beginners. A request addressed to Dodd, Mead and Company, 432 Fourth Avenue, New York, will bring a copy to any applicant.

At least half a dozen other American firms have done outstanding if more limited work along the same lines; space does not permit a complete catalogue, but every discriminating reader will know the imprints that are meant. On the other side of the picture, about the same number of other publishers (equally recognizable by the enlightened) must share the blame for the thoroughly bad books: the hackneyed romances of coincidence, the synthetic shockers, the forced, unfunny "quickies," that are the curse of the detective story in this country to-day. To such publishers is respectfully suggested a little quiet meditation on the ancient fable of the goose and the golden egg! On the whole, however, editorial standards in the book houses have not only kept pace with the improvement in detective story quality in recent years, but have had much to do with its occurrence.

But even the most careful publishers in an editorial sense sometimes fall prey to another sin: the failure to classify, advertise, and promote their output to its greatest advantage. One of the most pointed criticisms of publishing practice in this respect has been voiced by a member of the profession himself, Mr. Clarence B. Boutell of the Putnam firm:

> The publisher . . . is at fault for the fate of many stories. Instead of some sort of classification, he labels all stories in the field alike. He presents thrillers as detective stories, and psychological stories and horror and intrigue all in the same manner.

Actually, they have only one thing in common—heightened suspense—while they may appeal to very different tastes. . . . It is somewhat naïve to-day to contend that the [mere] inclusion of a detective in the cast of a thriller makes the thriller per se a detective story.*

Such facts should be pretty obvious, but it is surprising how many publishers fail to realize them. Certainly, a little time spent in understanding the predilections and prejudices of the several classes of detective story readers, and a little further time devoted to bringing each tale to the attention of its most likely audience, will repay substantial dividends.

But to return to the main topic of this chapter: the commercial aspects of the craft as they apply to the individual writer. The soundest practical advice which can be given to the would-be author of detective stories is to hold firmly to whatever routine method of livelihood he may have and to regard his fiction as avocational only —at least until he learns definitely what sort of income it can be counted on to bring him.

* *Publishers' Weekly*, April 15, 1939.

CHAPTER XIII

Friends and Foes

(*The Critical Literature*)

The literature of crime detection is of recent
growth because the historical conditions on which
it depends are modern.—F. W. CHANDLER, *The
Literature of Roguery*

I

To BE strictly accurate, the foregoing quotation was written with reference to detective fiction itself. But the same
remark might have been made with equal pertinence and
even greater force of the *critical* literature of the subject,
which has been still slower to develop. Despite the age
of the genre and the honorable estate it had achieved,
comparatively little worth-while objective comment, aside
from a few sporadic and tentative magazine articles, appeared in print before the early 1920's. And even then
most writing on the topic was confined to repeating the
startling thesis that really respectable and intelligent
people (presidents and potentates, it was said with bated
breath!) could read and enjoy detective stories.

By the middle of the decade, however, really important
criticism began to emerge. Three of what are still the
finest dissertations on the subject appeared in the space

of as many years. In England, in 1926, the late E. M. Wrong of Oxford penned his memorable introduction to the first Oxford Press anthology of *Crime and Detection*, which after the passage of years remains the most succinct of all statements of detective story principles. In 1927, in America, Willard Huntington Wright (not then revealed as "S. S. Van Dine") introduced his collection *The Great Detective Stories* with a much more elaborate and comprehensive essay, predominantly in the historical mood. In 1928 Dorothy Sayers mounted the same pulpit, again an introduction to an anthology, in this case her *Great Short Stories of Detection, Mystery, and Horror*—known in America as the first *Omnibus of Crime*—to propound what is still the most brilliant critical analysis of the medium and its practitioners. Her preliminary remarks to the *Second Series* (1931) are no less valuable, if briefer and supplementary in nature.

The year 1931 also saw the publication, in England only, of the first full-length study of the police novel in the language, H. Douglas Thomson's valuable but mistitled *Masters of Mystery*. Carrying into print some of the earmarks of the doctoral thesis, and characterized on the whole by a rather scholastic and theoretical approach, *Masters of Mystery* is nevertheless an original, suavely written, and well documented study which must stand close to first place in the student's or collector's library. The chief weakness of the volume lies in its American section; but here Mr. Thomson must be largely absolved, for his book was composed before the full effect of the American Renaissance of the late twenties and early thirties had time to be felt abroad. (One can not help wondering, however, if he has subsequently revised his egregiously mistaken analysis and estimate of Dashiell Hammett.)

In France, critical interest in the detective novel has at all times exceeded original achievement. Several studies of varying length and pretension have appeared (none, to the present writer's knowledge, in translation), of which the longest and most important must, anomalously, be dismissed as mostly beyond our ken. It is Régis Messac's *Le "Detective Novel" et l'Influence de la Pensée Scientifique,* a stout and promisingly titled volume which, however, ends its consideration of the subject with 1900! Entire chapters are devoted to the treatment of crime in ancient fiction, and to such writers as Dumas, Balzac, and Fenimore Cooper. Considered as a whole, the Messac work stands forth as the most complete and elaborate demonstration extant of the hieratic fallacy of mistaking analysis for detection, of confusing the detective story proper with its merely spiritual precursors. The few of M. Messac's chapters, however, which deal with bona fide detective fiction are full of rewarding penetration and insight. (But the critic Abel Chevalley quarrels with Messac's insistence on what his title calls "scientific thought," maintaining: "I am not at all sure that M. Messac's idea of science is scientific!")

François Fosca's *Histoire et Technique du Roman Policier* discloses a much more contemporary and lively approach, but is mostly derivative and contributes little thought or matter that is really original.

Carolyn Wells' *The Technique of the Mystery Story* still occupies top position among the "how-to-do-it" manuals in America, despite its age and a sòmewhat desultory and repetitive treatment of the subject. . . . If he can obtain a copy, the beginning writer will find many practical suggestions and a somewhat more modern attack in Basil Hogarth's *Writing Thrillers for Profit,* even though it is published only in England and is written in terms of the British market. Incidentally, the title of this work illustrates a difference in nomenclature which has puzzled many American readers. In America, the term "thriller" is usually employed to indicate the sensational crime story, as distinguished from the police novel proper. In England, on the other hand, it has come increasingly to mean the bona fide detective story. When the English wish to signify the sensational novel they say "shocker."

In quite different vein, John Carter's chapter on detective fiction in *New Paths in Book-Collecting* (also published as a separate pamphlet), while primarily concerned with a specialized phase of the topic, must not be overlooked for its keen critical implications.

*   *   *

These, then, are the major prophets and the law. In addition, the serious student and even the random reader may frequently wish to know where to find a number of important essays and articles about the police novel which remain buried in magazine files or in books of a collective nature: as, for example, R. Austin Freeman's celebrated but elusive manifesto on "The Art of the Detective Story," Van Dine's twenty rules, Father Knox's ten, and so on. The bibliography which concludes this chapter has been prepared in the hope of making some of the more representative of these writings more readily available than they have been in the past.

It is plain of course that any such listing must be lim-

ited to definite and topical essays, articles, and chapters;
no attempt has been made to discover or bring out merely
incidental or casual references. For the most part the
writings listed will be found to treat of the subject in its
more general aspects, rather than of individual authors,
though occasional exceptions have been made for particularly outstanding individual criticism, such as Brander
Matthews' essay on Poe, Valentine Williams' on Gaboriau,
and Vincent Starrett's *Private Life of Sherlock Holmes*
with its valuable appended bibliography of Sherlockiana
(and occasionally Sherlockivia!). Only those introduc-
tions and prefaces to larger works have been included
which have seemed to make some definite contribution to
critical literature. Not all the writings listed, by any
means, are favorable to the subject: attacks as well as
eulogies will be found.

At least a few of the pronouncements will reward the
seeker with gratuitous chuckles—as the London
Academy's flat declaration in 1905 that "from henceforth
he [the detective of fiction] retires to limbo with the
dodo"! Still others of the articles and essays abound with
intended humor, as—to mention but two out of many—
Robert J. Casey's "Oh, England! Full of Sin," and Marjorie Nicolson's "The Professor and the Detective," the
latter masking a flanking attack on both pedantry and
modern literature that comes dangerously close to being
Higher Criticism.

It will be noted that the earliest general commentary on
detective fiction which the writer has been able to turn
up through the ordinary channels of bibliography carries
the date of 1883: an article entitled, simply and adequately, "Detectives," in the London *Saturday Review*

for May 5th of that year. Surely, the topic must have received previous attention in the public prints. (A large number of earlier references may readily be found, of course, to *real-life* detection, but they manifestly will not do.) The day will perhaps arrive when scholarship will incline its august attention to the subject and a really definitive bibliography be assembled. The list which follows here must be understood to be no more than the suggestive beginning of such a work. Doubtless a vast amount of fugitive material remains to be uncovered.

*   *   *

But before leaving this discussion, at least a brief word must be devoted to the increasing excellence of detective story reviewing on both sides of the water. A few years ago Dorothy Sayers complained, with justice, of the editorial practice of "lumping together" basically unrelated types of fiction under a generic title, and of the curious disregard of reviewers for the specialized and highly divergent tastes of readers. To-day, while there are still some journals and reviewers who sin in these respects, the trend is strongly toward departmentalization and classification, which is quite as it should be.

This is not the place to attempt a conclusive statement of the rules of good reviewing; nevertheless, a few suggestions from the viewpoint of the reader may be in order. Perhaps the first and greatest requirement of the detective story review is that it should never under any circumstances give the plot away. The reasons for this rule would seem sufficiently obvious: yet it *has* been done! It is well, too, that the reviewer should have some knowledge of and liking for this sort of literature. As Chesterton pointed out somewhere, no one would think of handing a book of poetry for review to a critic who dislikes or is indifferent to poetry; and the reviewer who holds a similar position with regard to so specialized a genre as the detective story is equally incapable of producing a useful estimate. Likewise, the reviewer must be prepared to submerge his personal predilections *within* the form to the tastes of his readers. For example: he may happen to have little enthusiasm for, let us say, the hard-boiled school, but he must remember that this is the favorite literary diet of thousands of readers, and for their sake he must attempt to distinguish good examples of this type of writing from the bad. The conscientious reviewer will also endeavor to classify each book clearly as to the general division into which it falls, so that those readers whose tastes lie in special directions may be advised or warned, as the case may be. He will similarly state prominently the name of the sleuth and any continuing significant characters, realizing that they will strike a helpful reminiscent note with many readers who do not attempt to keep authors' names in mind. If the detective story reviewer will observe these few special considerations, the canons of ordinary good taste and literary practice will take care of the rest. (For an able published discussion of this problem, see Clarence B. Boutell's informative article, "England's Other Crisis . . ." in the *Publishers' Weekly* for April 15, 1939.)

A survey of all the competent reviewers now doing yeoman work on behalf of readers of the police novel would be manifestly impossible, but awards for special merit must be pinned, in this country, on "Judge Lynch" of the *Saturday Review of Literature,* Isaac Anderson of the New York *Times Book Review,* Will Cuppy of the New York *Herald Tribune "Books,"* and "Jack Ketch" of the *Tribune's* daily book pages. . . . One is less familiar with the English scene, but word of the discriminating excellence of "Nicholas Blake" (C. Day Lewis) and "Torquemada" (the late Edward Powys Mathers) has penetrated even to these shores. (Shortly after the latter's untimely death, John Dickson Carr cryptically dedicated a novel to: "My father, Powys Mathers." The relationship, however, was presumably only spiritual.)

In short, little criticism can be offered of present-day detective story reviewing. It has made great strides in recent years and continues steadily to improve in method and quality.

Some Reading about the Detective Story

Material in Books

(Arranged alphabetically by authors. Where no qualifying comment is appended, the full work pertains to the subject.)

Berkeley, A., *The Second Shot* (London, Hodder, 1930; New York, Doubleday, Doran, 1931). See Foreword: a succinct statement of the author's "credo."

Cambiaire, C. P., *The Influence of Edgar Allan Poe in France* (New York, Stechert, 1927). Includes several chapters on the early history of detective fiction.

Carter, J., editor, *New Paths in Book-Collecting* [by several hands] (London, Constable, 1934). See Carter's own chapter on "Detective Fiction"; also available separately as *Collecting Detective Fiction* (Constable, 1938).

Chandler, F. W., *The Literature of Roguery* (Boston, Houghton, Mifflin, 1907). See "The Literature of Crime Detection."

Chesterton, G. K., *As I Was Saying* (London, Methuen; New York, Dodd, Mead, 1936). See "About Shockers."

——— *Come to Think of It* (London, Methuen, 1930; New York, Dodd, Mead, 1931). See "On Detective Story Writers."

——— *The Defendant* (London, R. B. Johnson; New York, Dodd, Mead, 1902). See "A Defense of Detective Stories."

——— *G.K.C. as M.C....* [ed. by P. J. de Fonseca] (London, Methuen, 1929). See "Detective Stories" [reprinted from Masterman, q.v.].

——— *Generally Speaking* (London, Methuen, 1928; New York, Dodd, Mead, 1929). See "On Detective Novels."

——— *The Man Who Was Chesterton* [comp. and ed. by R. T. Bond] (New York, Dodd, Mead, 1937). See "On Detective Novels."

——— *The Uses of Adversity* (London, Methuen, 1920; New York, Dodd, Mead, 1921). See "The Domesticity of Detectives."

——— See also Jepson, R. W.; Masterman, W. S.; Pritchard, F. H.; Rhode, J.

Connington, J. J. See Rhode, J.

Crouse, R., *Murder Won't Out* (New York, Doubleday, Doran, 1932). See particularly "The Murder of Mary Cecilia Rogers."

Depken, F., *Sherlock Holmes, Raffles, und Ihre Vorbilder: Ein Beitrag zur Entwicklungsgeschichte und Technik der Kriminalerzählung* (Heidelberg, C. Winter, 1914).

Detective Fiction: A Collection of First and a Few Early Editions (New York, The Scribner Bookstore, 1934). Catalogue; believed assembled by John Carter.

Epstein, H., *Der Detektivroman der Unterschicht* (Frankfurt-am-Main, Neuer Frankfurter Verlag, 1930).

Forbes, A. P., editor, *Essays for Discussion* (New York, Harper, 1931). See "Cold Chills of 1928" [by S. Strunsky].

Ford, C., *The John Riddell Murder Case: A Philo Vance Parody* (New York, Scribner, 1930). Parody-criticism.

Ford, F. M., *The March of Literature* (New York, Dial Press, 1938; London, Allen & Unwin, 1939). See particularly pp. 831-833.

Fosca, F., *Histoire et Technique du Roman Policier* (Paris, Éditions de la Nouvelle Revue Critique, 1937).

Freeman, R. A., *Dr. Thorndyke's Crime File* [omnibus; ed. by P. M. Stone] (New York, Dodd, Mead, 1941). Includes the author's "The Art of the Detective Story" and Thorndykiana by Freeman and P. M. Stone.
———— See also Rhode, J.

Gass, S. B., *The Criers of the Shops* (Boston, Marshall Jones, 1925). See "Desipere in Loco."

Hardy, T. J., *Books on the Shelf* (London, P. Allan, 1934). See "The Romance of Crime."

Hawthorne, J., editor, *The Lock and Key Library* (New York, Review of Reviews Co., 1909). See Introduction ("Riddle Stories").

Hitchcock, A. See Wright, L.

Hogarth, B., *Writing Thrillers for Profit* ... (London, A. & C. Black, 1936).

Honce, C., *Mark Twain's Associated Press Speech* (New York, privately printed, 1940).
———— *A Sherlock Holmes Birthday* (New York, privately printed, 1938).

Houghton, S. G., and Olson, U. G., editors, *The Writer's Handbook* (Boston, The Writer, Inc., 1936). See "The Detective Story" [by V. W. Mason].

Jepson, R. W., editor, *New and Old Essays: 1820-1935* (London and New York, Longmans, 1937). See "A Defense of Detective Stories" [by G. K. Chesterton].

Jesse, F. T., *Solange Stories* (London, Heinemann, 1931; New York, Macmillan, 1931). See Foreword.

Knox, R. A., editor, *The Best [English] Detective Stories of 1928* (London, Faber, 1929; New York, Liveright, 1929). See Introduction, which includes the editor's "decalogue" of detective story commandments.

Landmarks in Medicine: Laity Lectures (New York, Appleton-Century, 1939). See "Dr. Watson and Mr. Sherlock Holmes" [by H. S. Martland].

Leacock, S., *Here Are My Lectures and Stories* (New York, Dodd, Mead, 1937; London, Lane, 1938). See "Murder at $2.50 a Crime."

—— *Too Much College* ... (New York, Dodd, Mead, 1939; London, Lane, 1940). See "Twenty Cents Worth of Murder."

Leonard, S. A., and Poole, R. C., editors, *Introducing Essays* (Chicago, Scott, Foresman, 1933). See "On the Floor of the Library" [by S. Strunsky].

Locard, E., *La Criminalistique, à l'Usage des Gens du Monde et des Manual Auteurs de Romans Policiers* (Lyon, J. Desvigne, 1937).

Lucas, E. V., *A Fronded Isle and Other Essays* (London, Methuen, 1927; New York, Doubleday, Doran, 1938). See "Murder and Motives."

—— *Only the Other Day* ... (London, Methuen, 1936; Philadelphia, Lippincott, 1937). See "My Murder Story."

Macgowan, K., editor, *Sleuths: Twenty-Three Great Detectives of Fiction and Their Best Stories* (New York, Harcourt, Brace, 1931). See Introduction and "Who's Who" accounts of detectives preceding each story.

MacLean, M. S., and Holmes, E. K., compilers, *Men & Books* (New York, R. R. Smith, 1930). See "Detectives in Fiction"; "The Professor and the Detective" [by M. Nicolson].

Martland, H. S. See *Landmarks in Medicine.*

Mason, V. W. See Houghton and Olson.

Masterman, W. S., *The Wrong Letter* (London, Methuen, 1926; New York, Dutton, 1926). See Preface [by G. K. Chesterton].

Matthews, B., *Inquiries and Opinions* (New York, Scribner, 1907). See "Poe and the Detective Story."

Meet the Detective [by several English writers] (London, Allen & Unwin, 1935). In which a number of leading craftsmen talk about their sleuths; reprints of B.B.C. broadcasts.

Messac, R., *Le "Detective Novel" et l'Influence de la Pensée Scientifique* (Paris, H. Champion, 1929).

Milne, A. A., *By Way of Introduction* (London, Methuen, 1929; New York, Dutton, 1929). See "Introducing Crime."
———— *If I May* (London, Methuen, 1920; New York, Dutton, 1921). See "The Watson Touch."
———— See also Rhode, J.
Morland, N., *How to Write Detective Novels* (London, Allen & Unwin, 1936).
Murder Manual: A Handbook for Mystery Writers (East San Diego, Calif., Wight House Press, 1936). Hints, chiefly for the "pulp" market.
Nash, O., *The Face Is Familiar* (Boston, Little, Brown, 1940). See "Don't Guess, Let Me Tell You," the author's famous tribute to the Had-I-But-Known school, reprinted from *The New Yorker*.
Nicolson, M. See MacLean, M. S.
Noyes, E. S., *Readings in the Modern Essay* (Boston, Houghton, Mifflin, 1933). See "On Detective Novels" [by G. K. Chesterton].
Overton, G. M., *American Nights Entertainment* (New York and London, Appleton, 1923). See "A Breathless Chapter."
Pearson, E. L., *Books in Black or Red* (New York and London, Macmillan, 1923). See "With Acknowledgements to Thomas De Quincey."
Peck, H. T., *Studies in Several Literatures* (New York, Dodd, Mead, 1909). See "The Detective Story."
Pence, R. W., editor, *Essays by Present-Day Writers* (New York, Macmillan, 1924). See "On the Floor of the Library" [by S. Strunsky].
Pritchard, F. H., editor, *Essays of To-day: An Anthology* (Boston, Little, Brown, 1924). See "A Defense of Detective Stories" [by G. K. Chesterton].
Queen, E., editor, *Challenge to the Reader: An Anthology* (New York, Stokes, 1936). See Introduction and afterwords to the individual stories.
Rawson, C., *Death From a Top Hat* (New York, Putnam; London, Collins, 1938). See first chapter for a tongue-in-cheek critique.

Rhode, J., editor, *A Detective Medley* (London, Hutchinson, 1939); as *Line-Up* (New York, Dodd, Mead, 1940). Story anthology interspersed with essays by members of the Detection Club, including Rhode, A. A. Milne, G. K. Chesterton, J. J. Connington, R. A. Freeman ["The Art of the Detective Story"].

Roberts, K. L., *For Authors Only and Other Gloomy Essays* (New York, Doubleday, Doran, 1935). See "For Authors Only."

Rosenbach, A. S. W., *A Book Hunter's Holiday* (Boston, Houghton, Mifflin, 1936). See "The Trail of Scarlet."

Sayers, D. L., editor, *Great Short Stories of Detection, Mystery, and Horror* (London, Gollancz, 1928); as *The Omnibus of Crime* (New York, Payson & Clarke, 1929). See Introduction.

————, editor, *Great Short Stories of Detection, Mystery, and Horror: Second Series* (London, Gollancz, 1931); as *The Second Omnibus of Crime* (New York, Coward-McCann, 1932). See Introduction.

————, editor, *Great Short Stories of Detection, Mystery, and Horror: Third Series* (London, Gollancz, 1934); as *The Third Omnibus of Crime* (New York, Coward-McCann, 1935). See Introduction.

————, editor, *Tales of Detection* (London, Dent [Everyman's Library], 1936). See Introduction.

Seaborne, E. A., editor, *The Detective in Fiction: A Posse of Eight* (London, G. Bell & Sons, 1931). See Introduction.

Starrett, V., *Books Alive* (New York, Random House, 1940). See particularly "From Poe to Poirot."

———— *The Private Life of Sherlock Holmes* (New York, Macmillan, 1933; London, Nicholson, 1934).

———— editor, *Fourteen Great Detective Stories* (New York, Modern Library, 1928). See prefatory essay, "Of Detective Literature."

Stone, P. M. See Freeman, R. A.

Strunsky, S., *Sinbad and His Friends* (New York, Holt, 1921). See particularly "On the Floor of the Library."

———— See also Forbes, A. P.; Leonard, S. A.; Pence, R. W.

Thomson, H. D., *Masters of Mystery: A Study of the Detective Story* (London, Collins, 1931).

Van Dine, S. S., *Philo Vance Murder Cases* [omnibus] (London and New York, Scribner, 1936). Includes the author's "Twenty Rules for Writing Detective Stories."

Warren, D., editor, *What is a Book?* ... (Boston, Houghton, Mifflin, 1935; London, Allen & Unwin, 1936). See "On Crime Fiction" [by V. Williams].

Wells, C., *The Technique of the Mystery Story* (Springfield, Mass., Home Correspondence School, 1913, rev. ed., 1929). See also Prefaces to her several anthologies.

White, T. M., *How to Write for a Living* (New York, Reynal & Hitchcock, 1937). See "The Detective Story."

Williams, V. See Warren, D.

Wright, L., editor, *The Pocket Book of Great Detectives* (New York, Pocket Books, 1941). See Introduction [by A. Hitchcock].

Wright, W. H., *The Great Detective Stories* (New York, Scribner, 1927). See Introduction.

Wrong, E. M., *Crime and Detection* (London and New York, Oxford University Press, 1926). See Introduction.

MATERIAL IN MAGAZINES

(American publications unless otherwise noted)

Adams, J., "The Detective-Fiction Game" (*Overland Monthly*, August, 1932).

Adams, J. D., "Speaking of Books—" (New York *Times Book Review*, March 30, 1941).

Armstrong, M. T., "The Detective Story" (*Editor*, May, 1906).

Baring, M., "From the Diary of Sherlock Holmes" (*Eye-Witness* [London], November 23, 1911; same *Living Age*, January 20, 1912).

Beattie, A. B., "Whet Your Wits on a Clue" (*Survey*, July 15, 1930).

Becker, M. L., "The Readers' Guide" (*Saturday Review of Literature*, November 27, 1926; March 25, 1933).

Benét, S. V., "Bigger and Better Murders" (*Bookman*, May, 1926).

Benét, W. R., "Here's to Crime" (*Saturday Review of Literature*, February 18, 1928).

Bishop, J. P., "Georges Simenon" (*New Republic*, March 10, 1941).

"The Blood and Thunder Yen" (*Literary Digest*, June 21, 1930).

Boardman, F. W. See *The Pleasures of Publishing*.

Books. See New York *Herald Tribune "Books."*

Boutell, C. B., "England's Other Crisis: How Howard Spring ...Wrestled with Mystery Fiction" (*Publishers' Weekly*, April 15, 1939).

Boynton, H. W., "Adventures in Riddles" (*Bookman*, May, 1919).

——— "In Behalf of the Puzzle Novel" (*Bookman*, November, 1923).

Brisbane, P., "A Poll of Mystery Fans" (*Publishers' Weekly*, August 10, 1940).

——— and Carpenter, C., "Mouthpiece for Murder" (*Publishers' Weekly*, March 15, 1941).

Broun, H., "Sherlock Holmes and the Pygmies" (*Woman's Home Companion*, November, 1930).

Cahuet, A., "Les Romans Policiers au Front" (*L'Illustration* [Paris], March 9, 1940).

Campinchi, C., "Le Crime et le Mystère d'Edgar Poe à Geo. London" (*Les Annales Politiques et Littéraires* [Paris], July 15, 1931).

Carpenter, C. See Brisbane, P.

Casey, R. J., "Oh, England! Full of Sin: As Discovered by a Chronic Reader of English Detective and Mystery Stories" (*Scribner's Magazine*, April, 1937).

Chastaing, M., "Le Roman Policier et Vérité" (*Journal de Psychologie* [Paris], April-June, 1938).

Chesterton, C., "Art and the Detective" (*Temple Bar* [London], October, 1906; same *Living Age*, November 24, 1906).

Chevalley, A., "Letter From France" (*Saturday Review of Literature*, December 13, 1930).

"The Chinese Apathy Toward Crime Detection" *Literary Digest,* September 23, 1933).

"Chronicle and Comment" [on detective stories, pp. 106-107] (*Bookman,* October, 1900).

Colbron, G. I., "The Detective Story in Germany and Scandinavia" (*Bookman,* December, 1909).

Collins, H., "Stooges for Fictional Detectives" (*Saturday Review of Literature,* January 25, 1941).

———— "Your Literary I.Q.: Famous Detectives" (*Saturday Review of Literature,* November 25, 1939; June 29, 1940).

Connolly, C., "Deduction From Detectives" (*New Statesman and Nation* [London], December 5, 1931).

Coxe, G. H., "Starting That Mystery Book" (*Writer,* December, 1940).

"Crime and the Reader" (*Nation,* February 13, 1908).

"Crime in Current Literature" [Signed "A. C."] (*Westminster Review* [London], April, 1897).

"Crime in Fiction" (*Blackwood's* [Edinburgh], August, 1890).

"Crime Should Be Credible" (*Saturday Review* [London], October 8, 1932).

Cummings, J. C., "Detective Stories" (*Bookman,* January, 1910).

Cushing, C. P., "Who Reads These Mystery Yarns?" (*Independent,* April 9, 1927).

Dane, C., "The Best Detective Story in the World" (*Bookman,* October, 1932).

Darwin, B., "Multiple Murder" (*Nation* [London], August 18, 1928).

Davis, F. C., "Mysteries Plus" (*Writer,* October, 1940).

Denbie, R. See Waite, J. B.

"Detective Stories" (*Atlantic Monthly,* April, 1898).

"Detectiveness in Fiction" (*Nation,* August 15, 1912).

"Detectives" (*Saturday Review* [London], May 5, 1883).

"Detectives in Fiction: A Study of Literary Fashions" (*Times Literary Supplement* [London], August 12, 1926; same *Living Age,* September 18, 1926).

Dodd, M. E., "The Crime Club" (*Saturday Review of Literature,* April 28, 1928).

Edgar, G., "The Unromantic Detective" (*Outlook* [London], December 3, 1910; same *Living Age*, December 24, 1910).

Elwin, M., "The Psychology of The Thriller" (*Saturday Review* [London], August 26, 1933).

Ewart, S. T., "Murder in (and of) a Library" (*Library World* [London], November, 1937).

Farrar, J., "Have You a Detective in Your Home?" (*Century*, May, 1929).

Field, L. M., "Philo Vance & Co.: Benefactors" (*North American Review*, March, 1933).

"$5,000,000 Worth of Crime" (*Publishers' Weekly*, July 24, 1937).

"Fluctuat," "Sur le Roman Policier" (*L'Europe Nouvelle* [Paris], April 2, 1938).

Frank, W., "The Mystery Tale" (*New Republic*, October 13, 1936).

Freeman, R. A., "The Art of the Detective Story" (*Nineteenth Century and After* [London], May, 1924).

Gerould, K. F., "Men, Women, and Thrillers" (*Yale Review*, June, 1930).

———— "Murder for Pastime" (*Saturday Review of Literature*, August 3, 1935).

"A Grave Literary Crisis" (*Saturday Review* [London], February 22, 1930).

Gruber, F., "The Mystery Writer Can Make Money" (*Publishers' Weekly*, April 5, 1941).

Hankiss, J., "Littérature 'Populaire' et Roman Policier" (*Revue de Littérature Comparée* [Paris], July, 1928).

Hardy, A. E. G., "... Émile Gaboriau" (*National Review* [London], July, 1884).

Harwood, H. C., "The Detective Story" (*Outlook* [London], January 1, 1927).

———— "Holiday Homicide" (*Saturday Review* [London], August 17, 1929).

Haycraft, H., "Dictators, Democrats, and Detectives" (*Saturday Review of Literature*, October 7, 1939; same *Spectator* [London], November 17, 1939; translated *Kort en Goed* [Johannesburg], April, 1940).

Haycraft, H., "From Poe to Hammett: A Foundation List of Detective Fiction" (*Wilson Library Bulletin,* Feb., 1938).

Hendricks, D., "Red Herrings Are Bad Business" (*Publishers' Weekly,* July 5, 1941).

Horwill, H. W., "London Letter" (New York *Times Book Review,* August 20, 1939; frequent discussion of the detective story in other issues).

Hutchinson, H. G., "Detective Fiction" (*Quarterly Review* [London], July, 1929).

Hyatt, R., "Who Done It? Detectives in Fiction" (*Wilson Library Bulletin,* June, 1940; additions by M. D. Brooks, October, 1940, and A. Burtch, January, 1941).

Jarrett, C., "Jane Austen and Detective Stories" (*Saturday Review of Literature,* December 7, 1935).

Jennings, E., "Mystery Story Solution Wanted" (*Library Journal,* October 15, 1931).

Johnston, C., "The Detective Story's Origin" (*Harper's Weekly,* February 12, 1910).

Kehl, M. M., "A Mystery Story Collection" (*Library Journal,* February 1, 1938).

Kellett, E. E., "Marginal Comments" (*Spectator* [London], February 26, 1937).

"Ketch, J.," "Selected Detective Fiction" (*Scribner's Magazine,* December, 1936).

Kimball, M. W. See Waite, J. B.

Knox, R. A., "10 Rules for a Good Detective Story" (*Publishers' Weekly,* October 5, 1929).

Kunitz, S. J., "Crime of the Century" (*Wilson Library Bulletin,* May, 1941).

Langenbrucher, E. and others, " 'Geistes' Blitze aus Kriminal-Romanen" (*Die Buchbesprechung* [Leipzig], Jahrg. 3, 1939).

Leacock, S., "The Irreducible Detective Story" (*Golden Book,* May, 1932).

———— "Twenty Cents Worth of Murder" (*Saturday Review of Literature,* July 8, 1939).

Lemmonier, L., "Edgar Poe et les Origines du Roman Policier en France" (*Mercure de France* [Paris], October 15, 1935).

Little, J. T., "The Mystery Story in the Hospital" (*Libraries,* October, 1929).

Long, J., "Guilty as Hell, But—" (*The Writer,* March, 1941).

"A Long Way After Poe" (*Nation,* September 19, 1907).

"Looking Backward: Detective Stories" (*Literary Review,* November 24, 1923).

Loveman, A., "Clearing House: Some Scientific Detective Stories That Are Scientific" (*Saturday Review of Literature,* July 13, 1935).

Lucas, E. V., "The Search" (*Outlook* [London], September 22, 1906; same *Living Age,* December 8, 1906).

"Lynch, J.," "Blotter for 1939" (*Saturday Review of Literature,* December 30, 1939; same condensed *Publishers' Weekly,* January 20, 1940).

——— "Come Sweet Death" (*Saturday Review of Literature,* December 7, 1940).

——— "Spring Comes to Life with Death" (*Saturday Review of Literature,* April 5, 1941).

McCarthy, M., "Murder and Karl Marx: Class-Conscious Detective Stories" (*Nation,* March 25, 1936).

MacDonell, A. G., "The Present Convention of the Mystery Story" (*London Mercury,* December, 1930).

McElroy, C. F., "The Cliché of the Mystery Writers" (*Saturday Review of Literature,* January 13, 1940).

McGill, V. J., "Henry James: Master Detective" (*Bookman,* November, 1930).

Marcel, G., "Romans Policiers" (*L'Europe Nouvelle* [Paris], October 1, 1932).

Marion, D., "The Detective Novel" (*Living Age,* November, 1939; translated from *La Nouvelle Revue Française* [Paris] —date of issue not found).

Mason, A. E. W., "Detective Novels" (*Nation* [London], February 7, 1925).

Matthews, B., "Poe and the Detective Story" (*Scribner's Magazine,* September, 1907).

Maugham, W. S., "Give Me a Murder" (*Saturday Evening Post,* December 28, 1940).

Maurice, A. B., "The Detective in Fiction" (*Bookman*, May, 1902).

Mierow, C. C., "Through Seas of Blood" (*Sewanee Review*, January, 1933).

Millar, A. M., "The Detective in Literature" (*Humberside* [Manchester, England], October, 1938).

Mochrie, M., "They Make Crime Pay" (*Delineator*, February, 1937).

Morand, P., "Réflexions sur le Roman Detective" (*Revue de Paris*, Tome 2, 1934).

Morley, C., "Granules From an Hour Glass" (*Saturday Review of Literature*, March 10, 1928).

———— "Mystery-Detective Stories of an Earlier Vintage" (*Saturday Review of Literature*, January 13, 1940).

Morley, S. G. "Adjectives and Whodunits" (*Saturday Review of Literature*, May 3, 1941).

"Murder Market" (*Time*, February 28, 1938).

"Murder Most Foul: Ingenious Means of Murder Devised by Mystery Story Writers" (*Readers' Digest*, October, 1936).

"Mysteries in The Theatre" (*Literary Digest*, September 16, 1922).

"Mystery in Fiction and Real Life" (*Saturday Review* [London], November 28, 1885; same *Critic*, January 2, 1886).

Nelson, J., "Judge Lynch of the *Saturday Review's* 'Criminal Record'" (*Publishers' Weekly*, August 5, 1939).

"The New School of Murder Mystery" (*Literary Digest*, September 1, 1934).

"A New Thrill for Armchair Detectives: With a Crimefile of Clues ..." (*Literary Digest*, October 3, 1936).

New York *Herald Tribune* "*Books*," July 16, 1933 and July 29, 1934. Two special crime-story numbers with reviews and special articles by several hands.

Nicolson, M., "The Professor and the Detective" (*Atlantic Monthly*, April, 1929).

"The Noble Art of Mystery" (*Nation*, September 4, 1927).

O'Faoláin, S., "Give Us Back Bill Sykes" (*Spectator* [London], February 15, 1935).

"On the Floor of His Library" [by S. Strunsky?] (*Nation*, October 15, 1916).

"On Intellectual Thrillers" (*Bookman*, March, 1933).

O'Neill, D., "Too Many Murders" (*Saturday Review of Literature*, February 11, 1939).

O'Riordan, C., "Vicious Circle" (*New Statesman* [London], June 28, 1930).

Orr, C., "Miss Clink and Mr. Crump Talk Mysteries" (*Publishers' Weekly*, July 20, 1929).

Osborne, E. A., "Collecting Detective Fiction" (*Bookman* [London], February, 1932).

Page, C. H., "Poe in France" (*Nation*, January 14, 1909).

"The Passing of the Detective in Literature" (*Academy* [London], December 30, 1905; same *Living Age*, February 17, 1906).

Paul, E., "Whodunit" (*Atlantic Monthly*, July, 1941).

Pearson, E., "Perfect Murder" (*Scribner's Magazine*, July, 1937).

——— "Spring Three One Hundred" (*Outlook*, August 3, 1927).

——— See also Walbridge, E. F.

Philmore, R. and Yudkin, J., "Inquest on Detective Stories" (*Discovery* [London], April, September, 1938).

The Pleasures of Publishing, April 14, 1941 (New York, Columbia University Press). A survey of the preferences and prejudices of several hundred detective story addicts, conducted and compiled by F. W. Boardman, Jr.; same condensed *Publishers' Weekly*, April 26, 1941.

Portugal, E., "Death to the Detectives" (*Bookman* [London], April, 1933).

Powys, J. C., "Crime Wave in Fiction" (*World Today* [London], September, 1929).

Priestley, J. B., "On Holiday With the Bodies" (*Saturday Review* [London], July 3, 1926).

"Printed Murder is Valued at $5,000,000 a Year" (*News-Week*, June 19, 1937).

"Quincunx," "In General: The Cult of Detective Stories" (*Saturday Review* [London], December 6, 1930).

"Quiz, Q.," "Mental Holidays" (*Christian Century,* July 25, 1934).

——— "A Resolution and a Protest" (*Christian Century,* February 8, 1939).

"Read 'Em and Creep" (*Publishers' Weekly,* July 20, 1929).

Reeve, A. B., "In Defense of the Detective Story" (*Independent,* July 10, 1913; same condensed *Literary Digest,* August 2, 1913).

Rendall, V., "Reply" [to J. B. Priestley, *supra*] (*Saturday Review* [London], July 10, 1926).

Rhodes, H. T. F., "The Detective in Fiction—and in Fact" (*Cornhill Magazine* [London], January, 1938).

Rinehart, M. R., "The Repute of the Crime Story" (*Publishers' Weekly,* July 20, 1929).

Robbins, L. H., "They Get Away With Murder" (New York *Times Magazine,* November 17, 1940).

Roberts, D. M., " 'The Red-Headed League' and 'The Rue Morgue' " (*Scholastic,* February 26, 1938).

Roberts, K. L., "For Authors Only" (*Saturday Evening Post,* September 24, 1932).

Rodell, M. F., "Murder for Rent, Murder for Sale" (*Publishers' Weekly,* February 15, 1941).

Rogers, C., "We Dare You to Read the First Three Pages" (*World's Work,* January, 1925).

Rosenbach, A. S. W., "The Trail of Scarlet" (*Saturday Evening Post,* October 1, 1932).

Rutledge, W. A., "Detective Fiction" (*The Quill,* May, 1941).

Rutter, F., "Detectives in Fiction" (*Bookman* [London], July, 1925).

Sayers, D. L., "Aristotle on Detective Fiction" (*English* [London], Vol. I, No. 1, 1936).

——— "The Present Status of the Mystery Story" (*London Mercury,* November, 1930).

——— "The Sport of Noble Minds" (*Saturday Review of Literature,* August 3, 1929).

"A School of Detective Yarns Needed" (*Literary Digest,* September 23, 1922).

Scott-James, R. A., "Detective Novels" (*London Mercury,* February, 1939).

Seagle, W., "Murder, Karl Marx, and McCarthy: A Reply to M. McCarthy" [*supra*] (*Nation,* April 15, 1936).

Seldes, G., "Diplomat's Delight" (*Bookman,* September, 1927).

———— "Van Dine and His Public" (*New Republic,* June 19, 1929).

"Sherlock Holmes and After" (*Saturday Review of Literature,* July 19, 1930).

"Shifting the Apology" (*Saturday Review of Literature,* September 11, 1926).

Simpson, H., "Down Among the Dead Men" (*Bookman* [London], December, 1924).

Sparrell, A., "Fiction and Cookery: An Interview With Carolyn Wells" (*Christian Science Monitor Magazine,* October 21, 1939).

Sprague, P. W., "A Plea for Mystery Relief" (*Atlantic Monthly,* June, 1933).

Steel, K., "A Literary Crisis" [reply to "Quiz, Q.," *supra*] (*Christian Century,* May 17, 1939).

Steeves, H. R., "A Sober Word on the Detective Story" (*Harper's,* April, 1941).

Stern, P. V. D., "The Case of the Corpse in the Blind Alley" (*Virginia Quarterly Review,* Spring, 1941).

Stevenson, B. E., "Supreme Moments in Detective Fiction" (*Bookman,* March, 1913).

Stolper, B. J. R., "Who Done It?" (*Scholastic,* October 22, 1938).

Stone, P. M., "An American View of English Detective Fiction" (*Bookman* [London], July, 1932).

———— "Contemporary Detective Fiction" (*Reading and Collecting,* July, August, September, 1937).

———— "Long Life—To Some Detectives: A Reply to E. Portugal" [*Supra*] (*Bookman* [London], June, 1933).

Stout, R., "Watson Was a Woman" (*Saturday Review of Literature,* March 1, 1941).

———— "We Mystery Writers Don't Kid Ourselves" (*Publishers' Weekly,* December 28, 1940).

Strachey, E. St. J., "The Golden Age of English Detection" (*Saturday Review of Literature*, January 7, 1939).

Taylor, F. S., "The Crux of a Murder" (*Spectator* [London], April 9, 1937); same as "Corpus Delicti: Secret Disposal of the Body" (*Living Age*, July, 1937).

Taylor, I. S., "Just Mysteries—and Proud of It" (*Publishers' Weekly*, February 22, 1941).

"Throw Out the Detective" (*Saturday Review of Literature*, December 1, 1928).

Tiffany, H. R., "Pacifying the Public with Mysteries" (*Publishers' Weekly*, August 24, 1935).

"Too Many Corpses in Detective Fiction" (*Literary Digest*, February 27, 1932).

Ullman, A. G., "Making Crime Pay" (*Publishers' Weekly*, July 7, 1934).

——— "Servicing the Mystery Fan" (*Publishers' Weekly*, August 18, 1934).

"The Ultimate Source of Sherlock Holmes" (*Bookman*, April, 1908).

Van Dine, S. S., "I Used to be a Highbrow But Look at Me Now" (*American Magazine*, September, 1928).

——— See also Waite, J. B.

Véry, P., "Murder on Parnassus: The Literature of the Future" (*Living Age*, April, 1935).

"Voracious Readers' Swiftly Changing Tastes Keep Publishers on the Jump" (*Literary Digest*, January 2, 1937).

Waite, J. B., "If Judges Wrote Detective Stories" [with reply by R. Denbie] (*Scribner's*, April, 1934).

Waite, J. B., and Kimball, M. W., "A Lawyer and a Mystery Writer Trade Blows" (*Bookman*, August, 1929; same condensed *Literary Digest*, October 26, 1929 [together with reply by S. S. Van Dine]).

Walbridge, E. F., and Pearson, E. L., "Who Killed Cock Robin?" (*New York Libraries*, May, 1931).

Wallace, E., "The Mystery Story Today and Yesterday" (*Bookman* [London], December, 1929).

Ward, C., "The Pink Murder Case by S. S. Veendam" (*Saturday Review of Literature*, November 2, 1929).

Weber, W. C., "Murder Will Out" (*Saturday Review of Literature*, August 15, September 24, 1932; February 25, 1933).

—— "A Survey of Sleuths" (*Publishers' Weekly*, January 30, 1937).

—— "Thrillers" (*Saturday Review of Literature*, June 18, 1932).

Wells, C., "The Detective Story's Place in Literature" (*World Review*, January 21, 1929).

Wells, W. H., "New Blood Whets More Customers' Appetites for Murder" (*Publishers' Weekly*, August 13, 1938).

"What the Lure of the Detective Story?" (*Literary Digest*, January 24, 1931).

Whipple, L., "Nirvana for Two Dollars" (*Survey*, May 1, 1929).

Williams, H. L., "The Germ of the Detective Novel" (*Book-Buyer*, November, 1900).

Williams, V., "Detective Fiction" (*Bookman*, July, 1928).

—— "The Detective in Fiction" (*Fortnightly Review* [London], September, 1930).

—— "Gaboriau: Father of the Detective Novel" (*National Review* [London], December, 1923).

—— "Putting the Shocks into Shockers" (*Bookman*, November, 1927).

Wilson, A. D., "Crime and the Stage" (*Spectator* [London], September 10, 1936).

Wimsatt, W. K., Jr., "Poe and the Mystery of Mary Rogers" (*Publications of the Modern Language Association of America*, March, 1941).

Wodehouse, P. G., "About These Mysteries" (*Saturday Evening Post*, May 25, 1929).

Woods, K. P., "Renaissance of Wonder" (*Bookman*, December, 1899).

Woollcott, A., "The President's Crime Shelf" (*Cosmopolitan*, April, 1941; same condensed *Readers' Digest*, April, 1941).

Wright, L., "Murder for Profit" (*Publishers' Weekly*, April 10, 1937).

—— "Mysteries Are Books" (*Publishers' Weekly*, January 25, 1941).

Wright, W. H., "The Detective Novel" (*Scribner's Magazine,*
November, 1926).
——— "How I Got Away with Murder" (*Readers' Digest,*
July, 1936).
Wyndham, H., "The Lure of the Crime Book" (*Saturday Re-
view* [London], July 8, 1933).

CHAPTER XIV

A Detective Story Bookshelf

> Even if the output of detective stories stopped tomorrow, the vogue has been long enough and prolific enough for the production of a body of literature which the Taines and Saintsburys of the future will not be able to ignore, even should they wish.—JOHN CARTER, *New Paths in Book-Collecting*

THE popular conception of a book-collector presumes an individual of vast wealth and unlimited leisure, versed in "points," prices, and bibliophilic lore and language. Such collectors exist, as well as others of more modest means but equal knowledge. But there is also another type of collector: the plain reader who enjoys accumulating books he has read and liked, blissfully unaware of their pecuniary worth, neither knowing nor caring whether he possesses invaluable "firsts" or cheap reprints. It is to such readers, unpretentious detective story fans who may care to assemble for their own pleasure "cornerstone" libraries of the best and most influential writing in the medium, that this chapter is addressed.* If the suggestions

---

* "Professionals" are referred to John Carter's admirable chapter on detective story collecting in *New Paths in Book-Collecting* (Constable, London, 1934), where they will find all they need to know about points and rarities—and discriminating criticism besides.

offered here should additionally be found useful in public and institutional libraries, so much the better.

The list which follows, then, is primarily a "readers' list." It does not pretend to be complete, but only an outline, a framework, which may be expanded by each reader at will. At most, it attempts to present a *suggestive* selection of the recognized "high spots."

The arrangement of the list is approximately chronological, according to each author's initial appearance in the genre. In numerous cases the books selected for mention are also the authors' maiden efforts, but there has been no slavish adherence to this principle: for such an arbitrary requirement would too often subordinate really outstanding achievement to mere chronological priority. Dorothy Sayers' *Nine Tailors* and Agatha Christie's *Roger Ackroyd,* for example, must find high place on any list of the great detective novels; yet they were not their respective creators' first works by many years. (Item: the "author date" given is frequently earlier than the date of first book publication, because of prior known magazine appearance. Poe, who begins the list, is a case in point.)

In general it has been considered sufficient to include only a single book per author; but here again some flexibility has been allowed where special circumstances have supervened. E.g., Miss Sayers has been accorded one WIMSEY novel and one particularly distinctive non-WIMSEY novel; Freeman Wills Crofts can be adequately represented only by the immortal *Cask* (in which INSPECTOR FRENCH does *not* appear—its sole flaw, by the way) and by a second title to give that most meticulous of policemen space on our shelves; the unique method of R. Austin Freeman's *Singing Bone* and its influence on other writers simply means that it must stand beside the epochal *Red Thumb Mark* as an equal; nothing less than the complete HOLMES saga will do; we have been unfair to Gaboriau unless we allow him both M. LECOQ and PÈRE TABARET; and so on.

That these multiple mentions make necessary further curtailment of a list already restricted is perhaps unfortunate. But there is some consolation in E. M. Wrong's remark (made of short detective stories, but applicable to the whole form) that a selection of the truly great examples of the craft might "limit the choice to three or four authors only." Happily, we are not under *quite* so rigid a necessity—yet the present compiler firmly believes that a list of the influential "milestones" of the form, limited as it must be to a relatively small group of authors, will be found of greater point and value than a numerically wider tabulation which would admit additional craftsmen of undoubted competence but of little developmental significance.

But, though the list is avowedly chronological in outline, it may be truthfully said that no authors or titles have been included for historical reasons *only*. To be sure, we must admit Gaboriau, Anna Katharine Green, and Arthur B. Reeve, even though they have few readers to-day—for surely every one will concede that they played developmental rôles which transcend the merely historical. But here will be found no unreadable Hanshews or *Hansom Cabs;* no demi-detection of the Dick Donovan school; no counterfeit police memoirs. Such agenda are the proper concern of the specialist, and it has not been difficult to exclude them from a purely general listing.

A considerably more painful decision was that which

called for the outlawing, for our purposes, of the "border-liners"—the Buchans, Hornungs, McNeiles, Beedings, Kevernes, and all the host of excellent writers who have *approached* detection without quite attaining it in the strict sense of the term. To admit them, for whatever reasons of personal enjoyment, would be to open the flood-gates beyond any hope of repair. A sole exception has been made in favor of the group typified by Francis Iles, Mrs. Belloc Lowndes, and Richard Hull—though less on the grounds that the school of writing they represent is essentially an inverted form of the detective story, which it is, than for the powerful influence they have exercised in recent years on the more conventional police novel.

Dates of publication appearing in the listings, unless otherwise noted, are those of original publication in the country of origin, to the best of the compiler's ability and information. There has been no attempt, however, to give publishers or prices; for in many if not most instances the "ordinary" collector will be limited to reprints and re-issues, which are available for the majority of titles.... Occasional informational notes have been appended to the individual titles when some really useful purpose would seem to be served, but there has been no pretense of comprehensive annotation. . . . Names of detectives have been given in the column provided for that purpose only when they have some color of claim to the designation (and even then some of them have been questioned); no book characters have been singled out and "created" sleuths merely to satisfy an arbitrary requirement.

Finally, if the list as a whole has been restricted to the "high spots," the limitation has been applied with doubled intensity to the works and authors of the latest decade. Only a bare handful of names will be found for this period: those whom critical or popular acclaim has raised above their fellows beyond any possibility of doubt. This additional restraint has been enforced equally for the reason that to-day's output is too large, too recent, and too varied for accurate classification at this time; and because it is here that the reader himself is best able to make his own selections and assert his own preferences.

A Readers' List of Detective Story "Cornerstones"

Author's Date *	Author	Title and Date of Book	Detective
1841	Edgar Allan Poe	*Tales,* 1845	Auguste Dupin
1853	Charles Dickens	*Bleak House,* 1853	Inspector Bucket
——	——————	*The Mystery of Edwin Drood,* 1870	Datchery [?]
1866	Émile Gaboriau	*L'Affaire Lerouge,* 1866	Père Tabaret
——	——————	*Monsieur Lecoq,* 1869	Monsieur Lecoq
1868	Wilkie Collins	*The Moonstone,* 1868	Sergeant Cuff
1878	Anna Katharine Green	*The Leavenworth Case,* 1878	Ebenezer Gryce
1887	A. Conan Doyle	*A Study in Scarlet,* 1887; *The Sign of the Four,* 1890; *The Adventures of Sherlock Holmes,* 1892; *The Memoirs of Sherlock Holmes,* 1894; *The Hound of the Baskervilles,* 1902; *The Return of Sherlock Holmes,* 1905; *The Valley of Fear,* 1915; *His Last Bow,* 1917; *The Case-book of Sherlock Holmes,*	Sherlock Holmes

* *i.e.,* approximate date of each author's first appearance in the field.

Author's Date *	Author	Title and Date of Book	Detective
1887	A. Conan Doyle	1927. Available in one volume as *The Complete Sherlock Holmes,* 1936 [U. S.]	SHERLOCK HOLMES
1891	Israel Zangwill	*The Big Bow Mystery,* 1891	GEORGE GRODMAN, EDWARD WIMP [?]
1894	Arthur Morrison	*Martin Hewitt: Investigator,* 1894	MARTIN HEWITT
1902	Baroness Orczy	*The Old Man in the Corner,* 1909	THE OLD MAN IN THE CORNER
1906	G. R. Benson [later Lord Charnwood]	*Tracks in the Snow,* 1906	JAMES CALLAGHAN [?]
1906	Robert Barr	*The Triumphs of Eugène Valmont,* 1906	EUGÈNE VALMONT
1906	Jacques Futrelle	*The Thinking Machine,* 1907 (later re-issued as *The Problem of Cell 13*)	PROFESSOR AUGUSTUS S. F. X. VAN DUSEN ("The Thinking Machine")
1907	Maurice Leblanc	*The Eight Strokes of the Clock,* 1922 [U. S] (the best LUPIN adventures *as detective*)	ARSÈNE LUPIN
1907	Gaston Leroux	*The Mystery of the Yellow Room,* 1908 [U.S.]	JOSEPH ROULETABILLE
1907	R. Austin Freeman	*The Red Thumb Mark,* 1907	DR. JOHN THORNDYKE
		The Singing Bone, 1912	
1907	Mary Roberts Rinehart	*The Circular Staircase,* 1908	JAMIESON [?]
1907	Carolyn Wells	*The Clue,* 1909	FLEMING STONE
1910	A. E. W. Mason	*At the Villa Rose,* 1910 (but most readers prefer *The House of the Arrow,* 1924)	HANAUD
1910	Arthur B. Reeve	*The Silent Bullet,* 1912	PROFESSOR CRAIG KENNEDY

* *i.e.,* approximate date of each author's first appearance in the field.

Author's Date *	Author	Title and Date of Book	Detective
1911	G. K. Chesterton	*The Innocence of Father Brown*, 1911	FATHER BROWN
1911	Melville Davisson Post	*Uncle Abner: Master of Mysteries*, 1918	UNCLE ABNER
1912	Mrs. Belloc Lowndes	*The Lodger*, 1913	
1913	E. C. Bentley	*Trent's Last Case*, 1913 [first U. S. title: *The Woman in Black*]	PHILIP TRENT
1914	Ernest Bramah	*Max Carrados*, 1914	MAX CARRADOS
1918†	J. S. Fletcher	*The Middle Temple Murder*, 1918	FRANK SPARGO [?]
1920	Freeman Wills Crofts	*The Cask*, 1920	INSPECTOR BURNLEY, GEORGES LA TOUCHE
——	——————	*Inspector French's Greatest Case*, 1924	INSPECTOR JOSEPH FRENCH
1920	Agatha Christie	*The Murder of Roger Ackroyd*, 1926	HERCULE POIROT
1920	H. C. Bailey	*Call Mr. Fortune*, 1920	DR. REGINALD FORTUNE
——	——————	*The Red Castle* [*Mystery*], 1932	JOSHUA CLUNK
1921	Eden Phillpotts	*The Grey Room*, 1921 [U. S.]	PETER HARDCASTLE [?]
1921	Frederick Irving Anderson	*The Book of Murder*, 1930	DEPUTY PARR, OLIVER ARMISTON, ORLO SAGE
1922	A. A. Milne	*The Red House Mystery*, 1922	ANTONY GILLINGHAM
1923	G. D. H. Cole	*The Brooklyn Murders*, 1923 (later works in collaboration with M. I. Cole)	SUPERINTENDENT HENRY WILSON
1923	Dorothy Sayers	*The Nine Tailors*, 1934	LORD PETER WIMSEY
——	—————— and Robert Eustace	*The Documents in the Case*, 1930	

* *i.e.*, approximate date of each author's first appearance in the field.
† Fletcher's fame dates from *The Middle Temple Murder*.

Author's Date *	Author	Title and Date of Book	Detective
1924†	Edgar Wallace	*The Mind of Mr. J. G. Reeder*, 1926 [U. S.: *The Murder Book of J. G. Reeder*]	J. G. REEDER
1924	Philip Mac-Donald	*The Rasp*, 1924	COLONEL ANTHONY GETHRYN
1925	John Rhode	*The Paddington Mystery*, 1925	DR. PRIESTLEY
1925	Anthony Berkeley	*The Poisoned Chocolates Case*, 1929	ROGER SHERING-HAM
——	[Francis Iles]	*Before the Fact*, 1932 (Francis Iles is Anthony Berkeley)	
1925	Earl Derr Biggers	*The House Without a Key*, 1925	CHARLIE CHAN
1925	Ronald A. Knox	*The Viaduct Murder*, 1925	MORDAUNT REEVES [?]
1926	S. S. Van Dine	*The Benson Murder Case*, 1926 (or *The "Canary" Murder Case*, 1927)	PHILO VANCE
1927	Frances Noyes Hart	*The Bellamy Trial*, 1927	
1928	R. A. J. Walling	*The Fatal Five Minutes*, 1932	PHILIP TOLEFREE
1928	Clemence Dane and Helen Simpson	*Re-enter Sir John*, 1932 (a better book than its predecessor)	SIR JOHN SAUMAREZ
1928	Margery Allingham	*Death of a Ghost*, 1934	ALBERT CAMPION
1929	Ellery Queen	*The Roman Hat Mystery*, 1929	ELLERY QUEEN, INSPECTOR RICHARD QUEEN
——	[Barnaby Ross]	*The Tragedy of X*, 1932 (Barnaby Ross "are" Ellery Queen)	DRURY LANE
1929	Dashiell Hammett	*The Maltese Falcon*, 1930	SAM SPADE
1929	Mignon G. Eberhart	*The Patient in Room 18*, 1929	LANCE O'LEARY

* *i.e.*, approximate date of each author's first appearance in the field.
† Date of MR. REEDER's first appearance.

Author's Date *	Author	Title and Date of Book	Detective
1930	David Frome	*The Hammersmith Murders*, 1930	EVAN [?] PINKERTON and INSPECTOR HUMPHREY BULL
1930	John Dickson Carr	*The Arabian Nights Murder*, 1936	DR. GIDEON FELL
——	[Carter Dickson]	*The Plague Court Murders*, 1934 (Carter Dickson is John Dickson Carr)	SIR HENRY MERRIVALE
1930 [?]	Georges Simenon	*The Patience of Maigret*, 1940 [U. S.]	INSPECTOR MAIGRET
1931	Phoebe Atwood Taylor	*The Cape Cod Mystery*, 1931 (As "Alice Tilton" Miss Taylor also writes the hilarious LEONIDAS WITHERALL stories)	ASEY MAYO
1933	Erle Stanley Gardner	*The Case of the Sulky Girl*, 1933	PERRY MASON
1934	Rex Stout	*Fer de Lance*, 1934	NERO WOLFE
1934	Ngaio Marsh	*Overture to Death*, 1939	INSPECTOR RODERICK ALLEYN
1935	Richard Hull	*The Murder of My Aunt*, 1935	
1935	Nicholas Blake	*The Beast Must Die*, 1938	NIGEL STRANGEWAYS
1936	Michael Innes	*Lament for a Maker*, 1938	INSPECTOR JOHN APPLEBY
1936	Eric Ambler	*A Coffin for Dimitrios*, 1939	CHARLES LATIMER [?]
1938	Mabel Seeley	*The Listening House*, 1938	LIEUTENANT PETER STROM [?]

* *i.e.* approximate date of each author's first appearance in the field.

II

The rise of detective story anthologies (i.e., collections of short tales by several hands, as distinguished from collections of stories by a single author) is of comparatively recent origin.

Frederic Dannay, an authority on the subject, though better known to the reading public as half of the Ellery Queen collaboration, believes that no work approaching the definition was published before 1895; and that in all, good and bad, no more than seventy-five separate anthologies touching on detection have come from the presses. Mr. Dannay also makes the interesting estimate that no more than 400 volumes *all told* of short detective stories have ever been printed. This is a surprisingly low total when one recalls that the brief narrative was the chosen form of so many of the early writers. To-day, of course, fewer short detective tales are being written and published than a generation or even a decade ago, because of increased technical and marketing obstacles (a point discussed in a previous chapter).

It is a reasonable inference, therefore, that both the detective short story and collections of it have seen their most verdant days, at least in a quantitative sense. But the conscientiously prepared anthology has long offered one of the least expensive and most convenient and pleasurable means of studying any field of literature. For these reasons a selected list of some of the better of such works in the line of our present interest, readily available to American readers, will be given here.

But first a few preliminary comments may be helpful. Although the early anthologies of such compilers as Julian Hawthorne, J. L. French, J. W. McSpadden, and Carolyn Wells (out of several) must be recognized as at least partly detival in nature, and though they doubtless played an influential rôle in creating the vogue, the era of really significant work in this field is limited to a short period of ten or at most fifteen years.

At the top of the list for purposes of serious study, we must clearly place the three Dorothy Sayers *Omnibuses* and Willard Huntington Wright's *The Great Detective Stories,* representing, respectively, in their selections the analytical and historical approaches to the subject, as do the prefatory essays in each case (discussed in the previous chapter).

E. M. Wrong's collection for the Oxford University Press is perhaps more noteworthy for its introduction than for the choice of tales.* It presents, however, a pleasant enough standard selection in convenient pocket size; as do Vincent Starrett's similar volume for the Modern Library, and Lee Wright's more recent "Pocket Book" collection.

Eugene Thwing's *The World's Best 100 Detective Stories* (in ten diminutive volumes) places a refreshing emphasis on contemporary writing—in contradiction of its misleading title—at a surprisingly low cost for the amount of good reading provided.

Indubitably, the two most entertaining anthologies are Kenneth Macgowan's *Sleuths* and Ellery Queen's *Challenge to the Reader.* The former offers a mock-serious "Who's Who" biography of each of the detectives rep-

---

* Because the title-page of this work is inexcusably vague on the subject of editorship, some American bibliographers have held a reasonable doubt whether it should be listed under Mr. Wrong's name. However, careful study of the Preface and Introduction would seem to indicate that he did select the stories which he introduced, and the volume is accordingly ascribed to him in the present listing. A second series of the same title (published in England only) which appeared after Mr. Wrong's death is probably not of his editing. It is, incidentally, definitely inferior to the first volume.

resented; while the latter is built on a particularly engaging idea: the names of well known investigators are changed (but correctly revealed at the ends of the stories) so that the book is what the title implies, a challenge to each reader to test his own ability to recognize his heroes by their methods and mannerisms.

The writer of the present book has succumbed to advice to include in the list two anthologies of his own making, solely because they are the only collections, to this date, of bona fide detective stories compiled especially for younger readers.

Though not quite anthologies in the dictionary definition, several entertaining volumes prepared in collaboration by the members of the distinguished Detection Club, of London, are given space for their undoubted interest to every advanced devotee. (It is by means of these anthologies that this unique no-dues association maintains its premises at 31 Gerrard Street free of cost to any individual member, including an extensive professional library.)

A number of excellent English collections of more general nature, however, have had to be omitted because they have not been published in America and are virtually unobtainable under present conditions. A single exception has been made for Dorothy Sayers' "Everyman's Library" collection—a selection of such outstanding merit that it simply can not be passed up. With only this exception, all volumes listed, it is believed, are available in American print to-day either in their original editions or in reprint.

As this short summary shows, much excellent work has been done in the field. But it is no disparagement of existing efforts to say that the truly definitive anthology of short detective stories remains to be made. Such a compilation may never be achieved. It must, at the least, await clarification of international copyright relations and a new and more coöperative realization on the part of certain agents and publishers that the conscientious anthologist is the friend and servant, not the enemy, of the author. (Lest self-interest be suspected in these remarks, let it be added that the present writer has neither the qualifications to undertake such a work, nor the slightest intention of attempting it!)

A Selected List of Detective Story Anthologies

(Arranged alphabetically by compilers; U. S. dates,
titles, publishers given)

General

Macgowan, Kenneth, *Sleuths: Twenty-Three Great Detectives of Fiction and Their Best Stories* (New York, Harcourt, Brace, 1931).

Queen, Ellery, *Challenge to the Reader: An Anthology* (New York, Stokes, 1938).

Sayers, Dorothy, *The Omnibus of Crime* (New York, Payson & Clarke, 1929).

——— *The Second Omnibus of Crime* (New York, Coward-McCann, 1932).

——— *The Third Omnibus of Crime* (New York, Coward-McCann, 1935).

——— *Tales of Detection* (London, Dent [Everyman's Library], 1936).

Starrett, Vincent, *Fourteen Great Detective Stories* (New York, Modern Library, 1929).

Thwing, Eugene, *The World's Best 100 Detective Stories* (New York, Funk & Wagnalls, 1929).

Wright, Lee, *The Pocket Book of Great Detectives* (New York, Pocket Books, 1941).

Wright, Willard Huntington, *The Great Detective Stories* (New York, Scribner's, 1927).

Wrong, E. M., *Crime and Detection* (New York, Oxford University Press [World's Classics], 1926).

Juvenile

Haycraft, Howard, *The Boys' Book of Great Detective Stories* (New York, Harper, 1938).

—— *The Boys' Second Book of Great Detective Stories* (New York, Harper, 1940).

"Specialties"

Allingham, Margery, and others, *Six Against Scotland Yard* (New York, Doubleday, Doran, 1936).

Detection Club of London, *The Floating Admiral* (New York, Doubleday, Doran, 1932).

—— *Ask a Policeman* (New York, Morrow, 1933).

Rhode, John [for the Detection Club], *Line-Up* (New York, Dodd, Mead, 1940).

CHAPTER XV

Dictators, Democrats, and Detectives *

> Why was there no flowering [of the detective
> story] under the Roman Empire, when an urban
> population sought amusement in the butchery of
> the circus, and might have been more cheaply ap-
> peased by stories of law-breaking and discovery?
> Perhaps a faulty law of evidence was to blame.
> —E. M. WRONG.

I

A FEW months before the outbreak of the Second World
War, press dispatches from totalitarian Italy announced
to the outside world that the works of Agatha Christie
and Edgar Wallace, the two English detective story
writers most popular in Italian translation, had been
banned from the country by decree of the Fascist party.
No reason was stated for the decision. But early in 1941
a more explicit action was reported from the Third Reich,
where the Nazi party ordered the withdrawal of *all* imported detective fiction from German bookshops. As
spokesman for the party line, the *Deutsche Allgemeine
Zeitung* was quoted in angry denunciation of this "illegitimate offspring" of English literature. Detective
stories, the newspaper thundered, were nothing but "pure

* Reprinted, in part, from *The Saturday Review of Literature* (New
York); *The Spectator* (London); and *Kort en Goed* (Johannesburg).

liberalism," designed to "stuff the heads of German readers with foreign ideas."

These actions were dismissed by many citizens of free lands simply as further instances of the reasonless stupidity (once so amusing!) of dictatorships. But those readers who paused to recall the genesis, history, and very premises of detective fiction found little that was surprising in the edicts—save that they had been deferred so long. For the detective story is and always has been essentially a democratic institution; produced on any large scale only in democracies; dramatizing, under the bright cloak of entertainment, many of the precious rights and privileges that have set the dwellers in constitutional lands apart from those less fortunate.

"Detectives," wrote the late E. M. Wrong of Oxford in a notable dictum, "cannot flourish until the public has an idea what constitutes proof." It is precisely this close affinity between detection and evidence which accounts for the interrelation of the fictionized form and democracy. For, of all the democratic heritages, none has been more stubbornly defended by free peoples the world over than the right of fair trial—the credo that no man shall be convicted of crime in the absence of reasonable *proof,* safeguarded by known, just, and logical rules. The profession of detection thus owes its being directly to the fact that democracies require and scrutinize evidence; that they conscientiously attempt to punish the actual perpetrators of crime, not the first victims who come conveniently to hand. This state of affairs prevails not only because the citizens of enlightened lands expect and demand fair play and impartial justice as a matter of right, but also because it is the only method by which governments that rule by consent rather than by force can adequately curb and control crime. Hence detection, hence detectives—hence the detective story.

Conversely, it is easy to understand why detection, as distinct from espionage, has played little part in despotisms of either the ancient or the modern variety. Where civil rights do not exist, where star chamber methods prevail, where "justice" is dispensed by self-constituted oligarchies, confident of their supreme wisdom and divine rightness on all occasions—even if the rules must be changed in the middle of the game!—there is obviously slight need or opportunity for methodical criminal investigation with accuracy and impartiality for its objectives. . . . Dictatorships, of course, would be delighted to have us misled by the surface similarity of democratic criminal investigation (object: impartial evidence for the legal determination of guilt) and their own gestapo and ogpu systems (object: rule by fear and intrigue). Actually the two are, suorum generum, the landmarks of opposite poles of civilization—and there are but few to-day who can remain wilfully blind to the fact.

It is equally comprehensible why despotic governments should seek to discourage the reading of imported detective stories, as in the Italian and German instances cited. For, obviously, no literary form so irrevocably wedded to the exercise of reason as the detective novel could conceivably be welcomed by predatory hegemonies, dependent on uncritical acceptance of propaganda for their very survival. The fuehrer principle and logical thought are simply no more compatible than oil and water! It was no accident that the first really spontaneous revulsion of democratic peoples against totalitarianism coincided with the perpetration of such shameless sophistries as the farcical Reichstag-fire trial and the fantastic Stalin-purge tribunals. This revulsion was not only a testimony of a greater humanity; it was a revelation as well of profound differences of mind. Millions who had been only vaguely aware of distantly unpleasant philosophies suddenly discovered themselves personally outraged by these mockeries of institutions so sacred in the republics that they have come to be taken for granted. ("These truths we hold to be self-evident. . . .")

But (the alert reader may object) why should virtually all detective stories worth the name be limited, as they have been, to England, France, America, and to a lesser extent the Scandinavian commonwealths? What, for instance, of the Central European republics between 1918 and the Brown Plague—or, for that matter, of the pre-1914 Teutonic empires which, for all their military autocracy, developed some excellent police organizations and even occasional civil liberalism? Why did none of these produce significant detective fiction? In the first place, aside from wide political considerations too complex to be discussed here, there is no guaranty that even centuries of democracy and competent criminal procedure will produce a corresponding literature in *every* race or land—any more than notable music or drama or art can be accurately forecast. To borrow a phrase from the law, the relationship between the roman policier and civil liberty is permissive, not mandatory. In the second place, there has always been a substantial and varying "time-lag" between responsible police systems and their fictional counterpart.

II

An eminent devotee of detective fiction, the recent Lord Chief Justice of England, Lord Hewart of Bury, has suggested somewhere in his delightful obiter dicta that "the detective story, as distinct from the crime story, flourishes only in a settled community where the readers' sympathies are on the side of law and order, and not on the side of the criminal who is trying to escape from justice."

This is another way of saying what has been set forth in the preceding paragraphs. It is an expression of the same fundamental contradiction between the We and They in government—the distinction, again, between government by consent and government by force. When the government is Our government, Our sympathies are on the side of the law We made. When the government is Their government, Our sympathies are instinctively with the lone wretch ("there but for the grace of God go I") whom They are hunting down. Tyranny hatches not only rebels, but a subsequent literature of roguery: thus Robin Hood and his "blood" brothers in benevolent crime. When a government is truly popular, the Robin Hoods are few and far between. The brief American glorification of the gangster had its origin in the lifetime of an unpopular law; when the law was repealed, the sentimentalism quickly evaporated. We still have lovable rascals in the literatures of the democracies, but they grow notably fewer with the passing of time. That they will ever completely disappear is unlikely—sympathy for the underdog is a democratic trait, too. Perhaps the very preference of detective story readers for the amateur who reaches the solution ahead of the official police is an unconscious rationalized survival, a last, vestigial, inverted remnant of the Robin Hood instinct.

Dorothy Sayers must have had something of the sort in mind when she wrote that the modern fictional detective is the "true successor of Roland and Lancelot"; and presumably most Anglo-Saxon readers look at the matter in a similar light. So long as our hero is on the side of the angels, what boots it if pompous officialdom be pricked a little? It will do them good, teach them to be on their toes next time! But it is curiously revealing that this same emphasis on the amateur, with his freedom to think, act, and criticize, constitutes one of the most violent of the stated German objections to the detective story. There is, when one comes to think of it, good reason for the outcry from the apostles of the "New Order." As the New York *Times* said in comment on the Nazi fulminations: "Who ever heard of a German amateur student of crime punching holes in the official explanation of the Reichstag fire?" If one were so disposed, something quite profound might be added at this point about the wide gulf between the kind of mentality which sees Might and Right as inseparable—and the free mind which dares proclaim that they have no relation whatsoever!

But we wander afield. The significant thing to know and remember is that detection and the detective story definitely thrive in proportion to the strength of the democratic tradition and the essential decency of nations; while the closer governments approach legalized gangsterism and rule-by-force, the less likely we are to find conscientious criminal investigation or any body of competent detective literature.

Wars, it has been said in a somewhat tarnished phrase,

have been won on the playing fields of Eton. By the same hyperbolic and still rather magnificent license, one might reasonably depict the titanic events in progress as these lines are written in terms of a struggle between civilizations which find fictive release and recreation in the wholesome atmosphere of Baker Street and Scotland Yard—and conflicting concepts of life and living that can have no use for a literary form so instinct with logic, fair play, justice, and denial of force. The point may seem a trivial one, but it symbolizes inherent boundaries of the mind that by no means stop with the Atlantic Ocean. When the countrymen of SHERLOCK HOLMES and LECOQ, of ROULETABILLE and FATHER BROWN, of PHILIP TRENT and POIROT, accepted the challenge of the too grimly real Moriarty of Europe, little wonder that no neutrality of the spirit was possible in the land of DUPIN, UNCLE ABNER, and CHARLIE CHAN!

CHAPTER XVI

The Future of the Detective Story

The detective in literature is hardly more than fifty years old, but already he is passing into decay. He has enjoyed extraordinary popularity, and may even claim to be the one person equally beloved by statesmen and errand boys. His old achievements enthrall as ever. But he makes no new conquests. . . . From henceforth he retires to limbo with the dodo and the District Railway's trains. He carries with him the regret of a civilized world.—"The Passing of the Detective in Literature," *London Academy,* December 30, 1905.

I

THE demise, or at least the decline, of the detective story has been erroneously predicted so many times that, by process of antithesis, an equally unwarranted assumption of its indestructibility has been created. Even the most devoted friends of the medium, however, must concede that two possible perils lie in its path. The one, that the day may yet arrive when internal exhaustion will summon the bankruptcy accountant, exactly as unfriendly critics have been prophesying for many years past. The other, that a form of writing at once so closely allied with a specific way of life and law, and at the same time so frankly recreational in its purposes, is particularly at the mercy of the kind of external events and forces tragically prevalent in large areas of the world's surface as these paragraphs are penned.

The first hazard—if it in fact exists—may conceivably be overcome by intelligence and labor if it is recognized in time; the second is a danger not to be controlled or ameliorated by any efforts of authors, editors, publishers, or booksellers.

Confining our attention, then, as we must, to the first possibility: it seems reasonable to say that the immediate prospect of self-exhaustion of the form is no greater and no less to-day than it has been at any time during the past twenty-five years. On the debit side, we must acknowledge that the number of basically original themes (if not the combinations and variations of them) available to the detective story is inevitably declining under the combined pressure of time and increased production. On the credit side stands the marvelous advance which the form has recorded in technique and literary stature in the last two decades.

It is conceivable, of course, that even this new skill may not stave off forever a point of eventually diminishing returns, but such a point is not likely to be reached in current lifetimes. And when and if it be reached, the probability is that the police novel will merely be diverted into some new and as yet unthought-of channel. As Vincent Starrett suggests (not without apprehension, one notes with approval) we may even some day have novels *about* detectives "as we now have novels about clergymen and physicians and peanut vendors."

To predict the unequivocal doom of the detective story from internal causes is, in fact, like forecasting the disappearance of the love story, the historical novel, the epic poem, or the drama. Such predictions have not been lacking in literary history, and each one of these fundamental forms has indeed undergone periods of stagnation and disfavor—only to reëmerge, often in new garb. Although the detective tale may not be "fundamental" in quite the same sense, it has nevertheless come to fill a particular niche and need in modern life that seemingly can not be satisfied by any other literary form now extant.

Mention has already been made of the accelerated demand for detective stories in the bomb-shelters of London. In America, book-sellers and librarians report a like increase at times of national crisis; while only recently so rigorously intellectual a journal as the *New Republic* has admitted reviews of detective fiction to its columns for the first time, in the stated belief that this form of fiction has a useful function to fulfil in days of doubt and distress. These instances are only a few of numerous straws in the wind, indicative of the solid position the ratiocinative crime novel occupies in contemporary existence.

Not that—to be quite fair—there are *no* good arguments on the other side. A most intelligent minority report has, in fact, been recently filed by Philip Van Doren Stern under the appropriate title "The Case of the Corpse in the Blind Alley." Published in the *Virginia Quarterly Review* for Spring 1941, on the hundredth anniversary of Poe's "Murders in the Rue Morgue," this able critique sees the modern police novel doomed in its second century by its own readers. With many of Mr. Stern's thoughtful contentions—that the urgent want of the crime story to-day is not novelty of apparatus but novelty of approach, that a return to first principles, to simplicity and plausibility, is needed, as well as closer attention to character and literary merit—one can only express unqualified agreement. But his central thesis, that the detective story is currently being stifled by a small group of dictatorial readers who would throttle all attempts at originality, seems less capable of sustained proof.

"Heaven help the writer who tries to give [these readers] anything but the old familiar brand!" cries Mr. Stern. Unhappily, there *are* such bigoted readers as he describes, and every book-seller knows them only too well. Still, one question may be pertinent. If the situation perceived by Mr. Stern is as prevalent as he thinks, how are we to account for the warm success of virtually every original writing talent to enter the field in recent years; how explain the jubilant reception accorded such authors who dared to strike out in new directions as—to name but a selected few out of many—Francis Iles, Dashiell Hammett, Dorothy Sayers, Margery Allingham, Nicholas Blake, Michael Innes, Richard Hull, Selwyn Jepson, Mabel Seeley, Raymond Postgate? These, and many like them, are authors who have done exactly the things Mr. Stern says ought to be done—and if present information is correct the reading public is eating them up! So perhaps there is some hope after all.

II

Assuming, then, the continuance of the detective story for as long as external circumstances permit the writing and publication of any such purely recreational literature, what will be its future shape?

One of the best and keenest American fashioners of the form has stated his considered private opinion to the present writer that significant structural alterations are inevitable and overdue—though he confesses his inability to predict their nature. There is much in the past history of the genre to support such a view. The Poe-Gaboriau formula was virtually extinct when Conan Doyle came along to resurrect and reclothe it in more colorful garb. Later, when the romantic apparel supplied by Doyle had begun to wear embarrassingly thin, opportune succor arrived from such master craftsmen as R. Austin Freeman, E. C. Bentley, Dorothy Sayers, Francis Iles, S. S. Van Dine, Dashiell Hammett (only a sampling is possible), who produced in their several fashions a more naturalistic and believable type of tale, better suited to modern life. If we accept this "cycle" theory, and recollect as well that all the previous changes went unrecognized until some years after their occurrence, it is even possible that the seeds of a new movement are already present in the contemporary detective story—only none of us has the wit to perceive them!

But an equally plausible case exists for the belief, held in other quarters, that the medium has now reached its essential maturity, and that future development will chiefly take the form of intensification and improvement of the several lines now in existence, rather than the creation of new lines. Certainly it must be said for this contention that the detective story of to-day, representing as it does so many diverse styles, already possesses sufficient variety as to need no drastic alteration, in the sense that earlier styles wore themselves out and had to be supplanted. The very number of avenues now open to the writer, the liberalization of conventions, the relaxation of the old rigid molds, have all decreased the likelihood of any major new development (or so this school of thought holds) by rendering it unnecessary.

Time alone will show which line of belief is correct. Conceivably, actuality may lie somewhere between the two viewpoints.

Of the several types of the police novel now in favor, it would seem that two or three have overstayed their time, at least in their present guise.

This is probably true of the "character" detective story, so highly regarded in England in recent years. Excellent and influential as this subdivision of the genre has been, the warning signals are not lacking that it has gone about as far as it can go without leaving the boundaries of detection behind. The literacy and conviction which it has contributed (and no influence in recent years has been more salutary) will without doubt live on, but the style itself is likely to be modified into something, for instance, not far removed from the naturalistic novels of Ngaio Marsh.

On the American side of the water, the related "screwball" and "hard-boiled" schools in their extreme forms give evidence of approaching exhaustion and may be expected gradually to eventuate into some less strenuous pattern. No other example than Rex Stout's fine NERO WOLFE stories is required to prove that such a modification can be achieved both painlessly and profitably.

The "Had-I-But-Known" school of stagy feminine romantics has, of course, been dead in the minds of discriminating readers for some length of time. It is only the editors who have failed to discover the fact, and presumably the exceeding weariness of the public will reach even their ears before long!

On the other hand, we shall probably see increased activity in such experimental divisions as the stylized story and the crime tour de force; though it should be remembered that comparatively few writers can succeed in these media, so that the development can not be numerically large under any circumstances.

But all these are essentially sub-developments, sidelines, of the main issue. The major portion of all detective story writing may be expected to continue, as it always has, in the field of the "straightaway" or deductive police novel—as currently exemplified, let us say, by Ellery Queen in America and John Dickson Carr (under his two names) in England. Yet the very existence, however temporary, of the more experimental "side-line" forms will inevitably force the routine police novel into intensified effort to retain its laurels—which is all to the good. A public which has tasted exotic cookery may not object to returning to plain fare for its daily sustenance, but it will demand tastier preparation of that fare. There can be no turning back now to the slovenly writing, the banal formulas, that were considered "good enough" for the detective story a generation ago. To hold its own, the roman policier of the future will need all the artful aids utilized by the "legitimate" fiction-writer—compact, coherent plot; liveliness of style, dialogue, and characterization; literacy; humor—if it is to satisfy an increasingly intelligent and critical audience.

As for that favorite bugaboo of the professional viewers with alarm (or sometimes malice), that the detective story may some day run out of material: it should be necessary to point only to the history of the last fifty years and the manner in which a rapidly changing world has taken care of this phase of the problem. Surely, an increasingly H. G. Wellsian universe will not fail to provide the crime novel with fresh and as yet unsuspected devices and situations. Thus shall new clichés take the place of old! More seriously, readers will continue to be—let us say—readers, and to hold individual preferences, while authors will, in the manner of authors, continue to supply their wants.

Finally, to reiterate a thought touched on previously, by sheer compulsion of world events the future of the detective story may well lie in America. If this should prove to be the case, the present book can conclude its major argument on no more useful note than a plea to American publishers: to study the form seriously; to insist on at least the same standards which they require of their general fiction (and adherence to the special rules as well); to eschew cheap and shoddy craftsmanship, even at the sacrifice of immediate profit. By doing so they will, in the long view, benefit themselves no less than a vast and intelligent section of the reading public and a department of literature which has amply won its right to respect and consideration.

CHAPTER XVII

A Comprehensive Detective Story Quiz

The answers are on page 332. To play strictly fair, the reader will not look at the answers until he has completed all the questions, for some of the material overlaps. Scoring: give yourself 1 point for each part of a question—*a, b, c,* etc.—answered correctly. A perfect score would be 125 points; anything above 75 points is good; and 100 or more points makes you a specialist!

QUESTIONS

1. How well do you know your detectives? What famous sleuths would you expect to find at the following addresses: (*a*) 110A Piccadilly; (*b*) East 38th Street; (*c*) Punchbowl Hill; (*d*) West 87th Street; (*e*) Golders Green; (*f*) Brockley Road; (*g*) West 35th Street; (*h*) 5A King's Bench Walk; (*i*) No. 1 Adelphi Terrace; (*j*) No. 33, Rue Dunôt?

2. If you were to attend a convention of fictional detectives, how many could you recognize by their appearance or mode of dress? With what sleuths are the following articles of wearing apparel, facial decoration, or accoutrement usually associated: (*a*) deer-stalker cap; (*b*) umbrella, square derby, mutton-chop whiskers; (*c*) umbrella, round hat with shovel brim; (*d*) rabbit-skin waistcoat; (*e*) green research-case; (*f*) large black hat with

flopping brim, pirate mustache, *two* canes; (*g*) No. 8 hat; (*h*) gold spectacles, white tie, *mince redingote?*

3. With what detectives do you associate the following hobbies: (*a*) roses; (*b*) rare coins; (*c*) vegetable marrows; (*d*) orchids; (*e*) mathematics?

4. The "Watson" convention goes all the way back to AUGUSTE DUPIN's nameless and marveling friend, and continues to this day. To what famous sleuths do the following individuals play Watson (either as narrators or simply as "stooges"): (*a*) Julius Ricardo; (*b*) Walter Jameson; (*c*) Brett ("a journalist"); (*d*) Sainclair; (*e*) Captain Arthur Hastings; (*f*) Dr. Christopher Jervis; (*g*) Archie Goodwin; (*h*) Farrar; (*i*) Hutchinson Hatch; (*j*) Polly Burton; (*k*) Louis Carlyle?

5. Certain verbal expressions, likewise certain statements of theory, have come to be identified with particular fictional sleuths. Name the detectives suggested by each of the following (approximately rendered) phrases or thoughts: (*a*) "Oh, my aunt!"; (*b*) "I have a criminal mind"; (*c*) "I'm the Old Man!"; (*d*) "little gray cells"; (*e*) "Two and two make four, not some of the time, but *all* of the time"; (*f*) "There is such a thing as being *too* profound."

6. Names (question contributed). (*a*) What famous detective was known only by his *first* name? (*b*) What famous detective was known only by his *last* name? (*c*) What famous detective had *no* name? (*d*) What famous detective had the *most* names?

7. What had the following in common? Give specific information in each case: (*a*) Dr. Alfred Swayne Taylor;

(*b*) Dr. Otto H. Schultze; (*c*) Chang Apana; (*d*) Inspector Whicher; (*e*) Inspector Field; (*f*) Dr. Joseph Bell?

8. Eccentricity—despite all denials—has always played an important part in the delineation of fictional sleuths, beginning with DUPIN's predilection for candlelight and continuing down through HOLMES' cocaine to NERO WOLFE's milder addiction to beer and PHILO VANCE's Régie cigarettes. Name the detectives denoted by the following idiosyncrasies: (*a*) tying and unraveling complicated knots in a piece of string; (*b*) singing hymns and sucking boiled sweets; (*c*) a gold toothpick and strong cigars; (*d*) indoor target practice; (*e*) snuff.

9. The following are the culprits in seven classic detective novels. Name the detective who matched wits with each culprit and give the name of the case in which the test of skill occurred; (*a*) Ada Greene; (*b*) Dr. James Sheppard; (*c*) Frédéric Larsan; (*d*) Godfrey Ablewhite; (*e*) James Trueman Harwell; (*f*) Nathaniel B. Cupples; (*g*) Jefferson Hope.

10. The "least-likely-person" theme is rather out of favor to-day (some one has remarked that the only remaining gambit is to have the *reader* commit the crime!), but it once played a legitimate rôle in the detective story, and some highly ingenious variations were developed. Name the novels or stories in which the following were the culprits (in case of short stories, give yourself full credit if you can name the author): (*a*) the detective; (*b*) the narrator of the story; (*c*) the judge at the trial; (*d*) an animal; (*e*) a dead man.

11. Like the "least-likely-person" theme, the "unexpected means" is frowned on in the better circles to-day, chiefly because the devices invented have become so increasingly far-fetched. But in its heyday the fashion led to the construction of some remarkably adroit murder-methods. Name the novels or stories in which the following "weapons" were instrumental in inducing death (take full credit if you can name the authors of short stories): (*a*) the sun; (*b*) the peal of bells; (*c*) an air-bubble; (*d*) an icicle; (*e*) insects.

12. Returning to our detectives: under what names are the following sleuths better known: (*a*) Professor Augustus S. F. X. Van Dusen; (*b*) Adrian Van Reypen Egerton Jones; (*c*) Edmund Jones; (*d*) Max Wynn; (*e*) Astrogen Kerby; (*f*) Prince Rénine; (*g*) E. Entwistle; (*h*) Joseph Josephine; (*i*) "Tir-Au-Clair"?

13. A moment with famous pseudonyms and other disguises of authors. Under what names are the following writers better known to the readers of their detective stories: (*a*) Mrs. Zenith Brown; (*b*) Frederic Dannay and Manfred B. Lee; (*c*) Godfrey Rathbone Benson; (*d*) Willard Huntington Wright; (*e*) John L. Palmer and Hilary A. St. G. Saunders; (*f*) John Innes Mackintosh Stewart; (*g*) Richard Wilson Webb and Hugh Callingham Wheeler; (*h*) Dorothy Feilding?

14. Your next job is to unscramble the following eight pairs of well known sleuths and re-arrange them in eight *new* pairs; each new pair to be the product of a single author (under one or more names) or team of collaborators: (*a*) Dr. Gideon Fell—Joshua Clunk; (*b*) Asey Mayo

—Montague Egg; (c) Ellery Queen—Père Tabaret;
(d) Reginald Fortune—Sir Henry Merrivale; (e)
Perry Mason—Colonel Primrose; (f) Lord Peter
Wimsey—Leonidas Witherall; (g) M. Lecoq—
Drury Lane; (h) Mr. Pinkerton—Douglas Selby.

15. Too tough? Then try this easy one. The following
twenty detectives—all top-rankers of the past or present
—have been scrambled as to first and last names. Your
job is to unscramble them and give each his correct name:
(a) Fleming Alleyn; (b) Philo Campion; (c) Philip
Carrados; (d) Sir John Chan; (e) Nigel Dupin; (f)
Max Gethryn; (g) Nero Gryce; (h) Hercule
Holmes; (i) Ebenezer Kennedy; (j) Albert Lupin;
(k) Auguste Poirot; (l) Arsène Rouletabille; (m)
Craig Saumarez; (n) Charlie Sheringham; (o) Joseph Spade; (p) Sherlock Stone; (q) Roderick
Strangeways; (r) Anthony Trent; (s) Sam Vance;
(t) Roger Wolfe.

16. (a) What was Professor Moriarty's given name?
(b) What was Dr. Watson's given name? (c) What is
Mr. Pinkerton's given name?

17. (a) What have Randolph Mason and Perry
Mason in common, aside from their mutual surname?
(b) What famous detective has eleven children? (c)
Name at least three detectives who are blind. (d) What
detectives, if any, have died?

18. (a) What was the date of Arthur B. Reeve's *Adventures of Craig Kennedy?* (b) Have any detectives
served more than one author?

19. Can you identify the author of the following: "If we had only known then what we know now these terrible events would never have occurred. . . . It was a beautiful spot, but it soon became a place of dread and horror. That night I had the feeling that some presence, unseen and malignant, was following me. . . . I nerved myself to climb the rickety stairs to the attic from which the faint, cat-like footsteps came, but it was empty and the floor lay thick with ancient dust. It was so dark I couldn't see the door through which I entered. There wasn't a sound, yet a sixth sense told me I was not alone. Some one in that eerie room was waiting for me. I was sick with terror as I heard the door slowly close, and the faint click of the lock told me I was a helpless prisoner in that grim chamber of tragedy. . . . As I watched, transfixed with terror, the curtain moved and a hand, thin and like the claw of some evil bird, slowly reached for the gun on my table. If I had only thought to mention this experience next morning so much tragedy could have been avoided, but it slipped my mind completely."

Answers

1. (*a*) Lord Peter Wimsey; (*b*) Philo Vance; (*c*) Charlie Chan; (*d*) Ellery Queen and Inspector Richard Queen; (*e*) Mr. Pinkerton; (*f*) J. G. Reeder; (*g*) Nero Wolfe; (*h*) Dr. John Thorndyke; (*i*) Dr. Gideon Fell; (*j*) Auguste Dupin.

2. (*a*) Sherlock Holmes; (*b*) J. G. Reeder; (*c*) Father Brown; (*d*) "Old Ebbie"; (*e*) Dr. Thorndyke; (*f*) Dr. Fell; (*g*) Professor Augustus, etc. Van Dusen ("The Thinking Machine") (this hat

size figures importantly in the classic "Problem of Cell 13"); (*h*) M. Lecoq.

3. (*a*) Sergeant Cuff; (*b*) Max Carrados; (*c*) Hercule Poirot; (*d*) Nero Wolfe; (*e*) Dr. Priest‚ ley.

4. (*a*) M. Hanaud; (*b*) Craig Kennedy; (*c*) Martin Hewitt; (*d*) Joseph Rouletabille; (*e*) Hercule Poirot; (*f*) Dr. Thorndyke; (*g*) Nero Wolfe; (*h*) Philip Tolefree; (*i*) The Thinking Machine; (*j*) The Old Man in the Corner; (*k*) Max Carrados.

5. (*a*) Either Philo Vance or Reggie Fortune is correct; (*b*) J. G. Reeder; (*c*) Sir Henry Merrivale (who is also perennially being "burned" and lives in constant fear of entombment in the House of Lords); (*d*) Hercule Poirot (if you missed this one, you might as well quit!); (*e*) "The Thinking Machine"; (*f*) Auguste Dupin.

6. (*a*) Uncle Abner; (*b*) Far, far too many detectives belong to this class, but the proper answer surely is —Father Brown; (*c*) The Old Man in the Corner; (*d*) Top honors go to Arsène Lupin, whose aliases pass description or count; a close second would be Thomas W. Hanshew's Hamilton Cleek, whose names were exceeded numerically only by his "Forty Faces," so well known to boys a generation ago.

7. All the individuals named were the "originals" (or so reputed in some quarters) of famous fictional sleuths, to wit: (*a*) Taylor of Dr. Thorndyke; (*b*) Schultze of Craig Kennedy; (*c*) Apana of Charlie Chan (but Biggers denied it); (*d*) Whicher of Sergeant Cuff; (*e*)

Field of INSPECTOR BUCKET; (*f*) you guessed it—SHER-
LOCK HOLMES!

8. (*a*) Baroness Orczy's nameless OLD MAN IN THE
CORNER; (*b*) JOSHUA CLUNK; (*c*) JIM HANVEY; (*d*)
SHERLOCK HOLMES; (*e*) INSPECTOR RICHARD QUEEN.

9. (*a*) PHILO VANCE in *The Greene Murder Case* (no
excuses!); (*b*) HERCULE POIROT in *The Murder of
Roger Ackroyd;* (*c*) JOSEPH ROULETABILLE in *The Mys-
tery of the Yellow Room* (and subsequent novels); (*d*)
SERGEANT CUFF in *The Moonstone;* (*e*) EBENEZER
GRYCE in *The Leavenworth Case;* (*f*) PHILIP TRENT in
Trent's Last Case; (*g*) SHERLOCK HOLMES in *A Study in
Scarlet.*

"Never, gentlemen, fail to observe *everything*!"

10. (*a*) One of the earliest tales in which the detective
was named as the culprit was Robert and Marie Connor
Leighton's *Michael Dred: Detective* (1899). Perhaps the
best known example is Gaston Leroux's *Mystery of the
Yellow Room;* another notable case was the dramatized
version of Mary Roberts Rinehart's *Circular Staircase* as
The Bat. There are several other instances of this device.
(*b*) The classic example, of course, is Agatha Christie's
Murder of Roger Ackroyd; among several others may
be mentioned Anthony Berkeley's *The Second Shot* and
Virgil Markham's *Death in the Dusk.* (*c*) Melville Davisson Post's UNCLE ABNER short story, "Naboth's Vine-
yard." (*d*) Poe's "The Murders in the Rue Morgue" was
the first of several such tales; Doyle's "Speckled Band"
and *Hound of the Baskervilles* must also be named. (*e*)
"The Finger of Death," a remarkable COLWIN GREY
story by Arthur J. Rees condensed from the novel *The*

Unquenchable Flame (1926). Read it for yourself in the original volume or in *The World's Best 100 Detective Stories,* edited by Eugene Thwing, to discover how the deed was accomplished (somewhat indirectly, it is true).

11. (*a*) Melville Davisson Post's most famous story, "The Doomdorf Mystery"; (*b*) Dorothy Sayers' *The Nine Tailors;* (*c*) again Dorothy Sayers: *The Dawson Pedigree* (English title: *Unnatural Death*) but the device had been used earlier, though far less plausibly, by Thomas W. Hanshew in one of the CLEEK stories; (*d*) "The Tea Leaf" by Edgar Jepson and Robert Eustace; (*e*) "The Cyprian Bees" by Anthony Wynne.

12. (*a*) "THE THINKING MACHINE"; (*b*) "AVERAGE" JONES; (*c*) "JUPITER" JONES; (*d*) MAX CARRADOS; (*e*) "ASTRO"; (*f*) ARSÈNE LUPIN; (*g*) "OLD EBBIE"; (*h*) JOSEPH ROULETABILLE; (*i*) PÈRE TABARET.

13. (*a*) "David Frome" and "Leslie Ford"; (*b*) collaborators under two pseudonyms: "Ellery Queen" and "Barnaby Ross"; (*c*) Lord Charnwood (the original edition of *Tracks in the Snow,* written before his elevation to the peerage, was signed G. R. Benson); (*d*) "S. S. Van Dine"; (*e*) collaborators as "Francis Beeding"; (*f*) "Michael Innes"; (*g*) collaborators under the pseudonyms "Q. Patrick," "Patrick Quentin," and "Jonathan Stagge"; (*h*) "A. E. Fielding."

14. (*a*) DR. GIDEON FELL—SIR HENRY MERRIVALE (by John Dickson Carr and his alter ego "Carter Dickson"); (*b*) ASEY MAYO—LEONIDAS WITHERALL (by Phoebe Atwood Taylor and her other self, "Alice Tilton"); (*c*) ELLERY QUEEN—DRURY LANE (by "Ellery

Queen" and "Barnaby Ross," the two pseudonyms covering the same collaborating team; (*d*) REGINALD FORTUNE —JOSHUA CLUNK (by H. C. Bailey); (*e*) PERRY MASON—DOUGLAS SELBY (by Erle Stanley Gardner); (*f*) LORD PETER WIMSEY—MONTAGUE EGG (by Dorothy Sayers); (*g*) M. LECOQ—PÈRE TABARET (by Émile Gaboriau); (*h*) MR. PINKERTON—COLONEL PRIMROSE (by "David Frome" and "Leslie Ford," both pseudonyms of the same writer).

15. (*a*) FLEMING STONE; (*b*) PHILO VANCE; (*c*) PHILIP TRENT; (*d*) SIR JOHN SAUMAREZ; (*e*) NIGEL STRANGEWAYS; (*f*) MAX CARRADOS; (*g*) NERO WOLFE; (*h*) HERCULE POIROT; (*i*) EBENEZER GRYCE; (*j*) ALBERT CAMPION; (*k*) AUGUSTE DUPIN; (*l*) ARSÈNE LUPIN; (*m*) CRAIG KENNEDY; (*n*) CHARLIE CHAN; (*o*) JOSEPH ROULETABILLE; (*p*) SHERLOCK HOLMES; (*q*) RODERICK ALLEYN; (*r*) ANTHONY GETHRYN; (*s*) SAM SPADE; (*t*) ROGER SHERINGHAM.

16. (*a*) Probably "James"; but he also had a brother named James, which has led Vincent Starrett to support the late William Gillette's contention that the word for the unspeakable Professor was "Robert." (*b*) "John H.," according to ample testimony. But on one occasion at least Mrs. Watson addressed him as "James," thereby hinting at a possible unsung Scandal in Bohemia.* It has been the fashion to blame Watson's bumbling memory for the numerous discrepancies of the Moriarty nature. But when one considers the personal implications of the pres-

---

* This was one of the principal circumstances adduced by Rex Stout in support of his brilliant but outrageous thesis that "Watson Was a Woman," perpetrated first upon the membership of the Baker Street Irregulars and later on the readers of the *Saturday Review of Literature*.

ent matter—together with the doctor's celebrated vagueness as to the location of his war-time injury—it seems just possible that one A. Conan Doyle may have been at fault. (*c*) "Evan," according to the latest advices; but in his first appearance in print he was addressed by his author as "David." Doyle doesn't stand alone!

17. (*a*) Both are lawyers. (*b*) CHARLIE CHAN. (*c*) Ernest Bramah's MAX CARRADOS, Clinton Stagg's THORNLEY COLTON, and Baynard H. Kendrick's CAPTAIN DUNCAN MACLAIN are three who come readily to mind; there have been others. (*d*) Leaving out of consideration SHERLOCK HOLMES's purported demise at the Reichenbach, the most celebrated instance would seem to be the case of T. S. Stribling's HENRY POGGIOLI (who, however, survived his own passing in a fashion quite different from HOLMES, and which the reader can only be advised to investigate for himself in the final episode of *Clues of the Caribbees*). Ben Ray Redman's DR. HARRISON TREVOR also came to a mortal end, but inasmuch as he figured in only one, though notable, story ("The Perfect Crime") he can scarcely qualify.

18. (*a*) If your answer is "I don't know"—count it as correct. Neither does any one else, for this is one of the "lost books" of detection that have given collectors so many headaches. Reeve listed this work, up to the time of his death, in his *Who's Who in America* biography as a separate publication under date of 1910; but there never was such a volume issued between covers. The explanation is probably this: the first series of CRAIG KENNEDY short stories appeared in magazine form about 1910-11 under the generic title "Adventures of Craig

Kennedy" and was later collected in book form as *The Silent Bullet* (1912). By listing *both* titles without explanation, Reeve (probably quite unintentionally) gave the impression of two separate works. This is a matter in which many otherwise conscientious authors are curiously careless. The late Willard Huntington Wright was one of the worst offenders, filling his *Who's Who* sketches with titles of entirely non-existent books (not only "works in progress" but earlier manuscripts that never achieved physical publication) both under his own name and under his alias, "S. S. Van Dine." ... All of which, of course, brings to mind the famous lost chapters of the HOLMES saga, on the subject of which so many delightful speculative essays have been written; but these were definitely apocryphal from the beginning, and no one has spent presumably valuable time trying seriously to trace their publication. (*b*) Yes, several. Du Boisgobey, you will remember, so admired his master Gaboriau that he wrote a novel continuing M. LECOQ's adventures. In our own time BULLDOG DRUMMOND, RAFFLES, and COMMISSIONER SANDERS (all a trifle beyond our proper field, it is true) have undergone reincarnations at the hands of new authors by arrangement with the respective estates of their original inventors; while a long list of Hollywood scenarists have carried the exploits of CHARLIE CHAN far beyond the original saga as conceived by the late Earl Derr Biggers. One of the clearest cases would seem to be the appearance of INSPECTOR FURNEAUX in the works both of Louis Tracy and "Gordon Holmes"; but the latter was a pseudonym which sometimes covered Tracy and M. P. Shiel, and sometimes Tracy alone. Similarly, there are those among the cognoscenti who swear that DR. FELL and SIR HENRY MERRIVALE are the same character, with and without mustache. But here again the sleuths in question are the creations of one author writing under two names. SHERLOCK HOLMES, as scarcely needs be said, has been the subject of an endless number of burlesques and travesties, including prominently those by Maurice Leblanc and John Kendrick Bangs. Among modern writers in this vein, Leo Bruce's AMER PICON and LORD PLIMSOLL would seem to be but thin disguises for POIROT and PETER WIMSEY, respectively; there are other similar instances. And we should not overlook the Detection Club's matchless tour de force of a few years ago entitled *Ask a Policeman,* in which several eminent English craftsmen, with results both amusing and brilliant, traded sleuths and styles.

19. Sorry, you're wrong! But take full credit if you made a guess. As a matter of record, this passage was not taken from any of the writers you may have had in mind, but from a "comic supplement," where it was intended to represent a story written by a sixteen-year-old. (Mr. Milquetoast was fooled, too!) Quotation by permission of H. T. Webster, creator of the "Timid Soul" cartoons.

CHAPTER XVIII

Who's Who in Detection

Being a Quick Finding-List of the Best Known Sleuths of
Fiction; Together With Some of Their Principal
Watsons, Assistants, Antagonists, and
Familiars *

A

Name of Character	*Name of Author*
ABBOTT, (SERGEANT) FRANK . . .	Patricia Wentworth
ABBOTT, PATRICIA	Mary Roberts Rinehart
ABBOTT, SAMMY	James R. Langham
ABBOTT, (MRS.) SAMMY (ETHEL) . .	James R. Langham
ABLEWHITE, GODFREY	Wilkie Collins
ABNER, (UNCLE)	Melville Davisson Post
ACKROYD, ROGER	Agatha Christie

* This compilation has been made purposely to solve the plight of the reader who (as so frequently occurs) can recall the name of a favorite character, but not of the author; and the alphabetizing is accordingly by characters. But, with a little more effort, the right-hand column may be scanned to meet the less frequent situation where the name of the author is recalled, but not that of a character. . . . To make the listing as widely useful as possible, it has not been restricted to detectives in a puristic or police sense, but has admitted many names which belong to detection by courtesy only. Full names and professional rank have been given insofar as the curious reticence of some authors in these matters has permitted. In a list of such dimensions some errors and omissions have undoubtedly occurred. The compiler and publishers will be happy to have any such brought to their attention.

340

Name of Character	*Name of Author*
ADAMS, ADELAIDE ("THE OLD BATTLE-AX")	Anita Blackmon
ADAMS, ANTHONY	Timothy Brace
ADAMS, PETER	Forrester Hazard
ADAMS, (NURSE) ("MISS PINKERTON")	Mary Roberts Rinehart
AINSLEY, JOHN	Arthur Somers Roche
ALLAIN, (INSPECTOR) PIERRE	Bruce Graeme
ALLAN, (SHERIFF) ROCKY	Virginia Rath
ALLEN, JANET. See BARRON, (MRS.) PETER.	
ALLEN, PETER	Lindsay Anson
ALLENBY, (MAJOR) ROGER	Van Wyck Mason
ALLEYN, (CHIEF INSPECTOR) RODERICK	Ngaio Marsh
ALLWRIGHT, (SUPERINTENDENT) DUDLEY	Philip MacDonald
AMAYAT	H. De Vere Stacpoole
AMBER, JOAN (later MRS. REGINALD FORTUNE)	H. C. Bailey
AMOUR. See SAINT-AMOUR.	
ANDERSON, PIKE	Carl M. Chapin
ANDREWS, (INSPECTOR)	H. C. McNeile ("Sapper")
"ANGEL OF THE LACE CURTAINS, THE." See WOLFF.	
ANSTRUTHER, (SIR) GEORGE	Carter Dickson
APPLEBY, (INSPECTOR) JOHN	Michael Innes
ARBUTHNOT, (HON.) FREDDY	Dorothy Sayers
ARCHER, JILL	Stephen Ransome
ARCHER, MAXWELL	Hugh Clevely
ARMISTON, OLIVER	Frederick Irving Anderson
ARMSTRONG, (ASSISTANT COMMISSIONER) (SIR) HERBERT	John Dickson Carr

Name of Character	*Name of Author*
ARNOLD, INSPECTOR HENRY . . .	Miles Burton
ARNOLD, ROBERT	Constance & Gwenyth Little
ASHLEY, T.	George Allan England
ASHWIN, (DR.) JOHN	Anthony Boucher
"ASTRO." See KERBY.	
(AUNTS) SUNDAY, THURSDAY, WEDNESDAY. See WEEKE.	
AUSTEN, (CHIEF INSPECTOR) WILLIAM	Anne Hocking

B

BABBING, WALTER	Harvey J. O'Higgins
BAGBY, GEORGE	George Bagby
BAHL. See DE BAHL.	
BAILEY, CARLETON	Joseph Cottin Cooke
BAILEY, HILARY DUNSANY III ("DUNSANY BROOKE")	Hilea Bailey
BAILEY, HILEA	Hilea Bailey
BAINES, SCATTERGOOD	Clarence Budington Kelland
BAKER, DIANE	Leslie Ford
BANCROFT, CHARLES DUKE	Melville Burt
BARING, MARTELLA (later LADY SAUMAREZ)	Clemence Dane & Helen Simpson
BARKER, RONALD	George Gibbs
"BARNETT, JIM." See LUPIN.	
"BARNEY, DETECTIVE." See COOK, BARNEY.	
BARR, RONALD	Robert Murphy
BARRON, PETER	Ruth Darby
BARRON, (MRS.) PETER (*née* JANET ALLEN)	Ruth Darby
BARRY, HERBERT	Edwin Baird

Name of Character	*Name of Author*
BARTLETT, HAL	Lawrence Dwight Smith
BARTON, SUSAN	Robert George Dean
BASKERVILLE, (SIR) HENRY . . .	Sir Arthur Conan Doyle
BASKERVILLE, JOHN. See STAPLETON.	
BASS, (INSPECTOR)	George Selmark
BASTION, (PROFESSOR) LUTHER . .	Gavin Holt
BATHGATE, NIGEL	Ngaio Marsh
BATHURST, ANTHONY	Brian Flynn
"BATTLE-AX, THE OLD." See ADAMS, ADELAIDE.	
BEAGLE, AMANDA	Torrey Chanslor
BEAGLE, LUTIE	Torrey Chanslor
BEAUMONT, NED	Dashiell Hammett
BECK, PAUL	M. McDonnell Bodkin
BEEDEL, (INSPECTOR)	Ernest Bramah
BEEF, (SERGEANT) WILLIAM . . .	Leo Bruce
BELL, (SUPERINTENDENT)	H. C. Bailey
BELLAMY, (PROFESSOR) AKERS . .	George Goodchild
BELMAN, MARGARET (later MRS. J. G. REEDER)	Edgar Wallace
BENCOLIN, HENRI	John Dickson Carr
BENEDICT, BILL	Bryant Ford
BENNETT, GEOFFREY (LORD BROGH-VILLE)	George Worthing Yates
BENSKIN, PETER	E. Phillips Oppenheim
BENSON, PHILIP	M. E. Corne
BENSON, (MRS.) PHILIP (*née* ELSIE RITTER)	M. E. Corne
BENTIRON, (DR.) THADDEUS . . .	Ernest M. Poate
BERESFORD, TOMMY	Agatha Christie
BERNADONE, (INSPECTOR) PETER . .	Frank P. Grady

Name of Character	*Name of Author*
BETTEREDGE, GABRIEL	Wilkie Collins
BIDDLE, (PROFESSOR) JAMES YEATES .	John Mersereau
"BIG NICK." See MORRO.	
BIGELOW, ANTONY	Burton E. Stevenson
BILES, (INSPECTOR)	Anthony Wynne
"BILL THE BLOODHOUND." See DAWSON.	
BIRDSONG, (DR.) TOM	Leslie Ford
BIRNICK, JIM	Thomas Polsky
BISHOP, ROBIN	Geoffrey Homes
BIXBY, ZEBEDIAH	Mike Teagle
BJELKE, (SUPERINTENDENT) . . .	Jonas Lie
BLACK, CARLOS	George Harmon Coxe
BLACK, HENRY ("LORD FORTWORTH")	Bertram Atkey
BLACK, (COLONEL) JARVIS	Peter Coffin
BLACK, REGINALD ("BEAUTY") . .	Edward Bonns
"BLACK, THE." See MORLAKE.	
BLACKBURN, JEFFERY	Max Afford
BLACKWOOD, RILEY	Vincent Starrett
BLAKE, FRANKLIN	Wilkie Collins
BLAKE, (CAPTAIN) KENWOOD . . .	Carter Dickson
BLAKELEY, (DR.) FREDERICK HOLMES	Ernest M. Poate
BLAKELEY. See also DOWELL-BLAKELEY.	
BLATCHINGTON, EVERARD	G. D. H. & M. I. Cole
BLIGH, (CHIEF INSPECTOR) . . .	E. C. Bentley
BLISS, (SUPERINTENDENT)	Edgar Wallace
"BLUE MASK, THE." See MANNERING.	
BLYTHE, MAXWELL	Judson P. Philips
BONDURANT, (INSPECTOR) VICTOR . .	James G. Edwards
"BONES." See TIBBITS.	
BONNER, THEODOLINA ("DOL") . .	Rex Stout
BOOM	Marion Randolph
BORDEN, HILARY	Richard Keverne
BOREL, NARCISSE	Eugène Sue
BOUNTY, (SHERIFF) PETER	Todd Downing

Name of Character	*Name of Author*
BOXRUUD, (SHERIFF) CARL . . .	Mabel Seeley
BRACEGIRDLE, MILLICENT	Stacy Aumonier
BRADE, SIMON	Lady Harriette R. Campbell
BRADLEY, (MRS.) ADELA	Gladys Mitchell
BRADLEY, (INSPECTOR) LUKE . . .	Hugh Pentecost
BRADSHAW, NOEL	Madeleine Johnston
BRADY, (INSPECTOR) FRANKLIN . .	Allan McRoyd
BRAGG, (INSPECTOR) JOHN	Henry Wade
BRAND, DELIA	Rex Stout
BRAND, HELENE (later MRS. JAKE JUSTUS)	Craig Rice
BRAND, MARK ("THE COUNSELLOR") .	J. J. Connington
"BRANDT, DIRK." See KINGSTON, MICHAEL.	
"BRANDT, HENDRIK." See HAMBLEDON, THOMAS ELPHINSTONE.	
BRANT, MASON	Nevil Monroe Hopkins
BRAXTON (COLONEL)	Melville Davisson Post
BREDON, MILES	Ronald A. Knox
BREDON. See also WIMSEY.	
"BRENDAN, GEORGE." See WOAR.	
BRENDEL, ERNST	J. C. Masterman
BRENNAN, (CHIEF) TIM	Clarissa Fairchild Cushman
BRETT, JEFFREY	Leonard Ross
BRETT, MARCUS	Mrs. Baillie Reynolds
BRETT, REGINALD	Louis Tracy
BRETT	Arthur Morrison
BRICKLEY, BELLA	Hulbert Footner
BRIDIE, (INSPECTOR) IAN	Margery Allingham
BRIERCLIFFE, RONALD	Francis Beeding
BRISCOE, (CHIEF) MIKE	Charles Saxby

Name of Character	*Name of Author*
BRISTOW, (CHIEF INSPECTOR) WILLIAM	Anthony Morton
BROCKETT, MATILDA	Carolyn Byrd Dawson
BROGHVILLE, (LORD). See BENNETT.	
"BROOKE, DUNSANY." See BAILEY.	
BROOKE, LOVEDAY	C. L. Perkis
BROWN, (DR.) JIMMY	Henry Harrison Kroll
BROWN, (FATHER)	G. K. Chesterton
BRUCE, CLAUDE	Gordon Holmes
BRUFF, MATTHEW	Wilkie Collins
BRUSH, (DR.) LUCAS	Frank Dudley
BUCK, (SERGEANT) PHINEAS T. . . .	Leslie Ford
BUCKET, (INSPECTOR)	Charles Dickens
BUDD, BARNABAS	John Brophy
BUDD, (SUPERINTENDENT) ROBERT .	Gerald Verner
BULL, (SIR) GEORGE	Milward Kennedy
BULL, (INSPECTOR) J. HUMPHREY .	David Frome
BULMER, (SERGEANT) THOMAS . . .	Wilkie Collins
BUNCE, (DR.) NATHANIEL	E. M. Curtiss
BUNN, SMILER	Bertram Atkey
"BUNNY." See MANDERS.	
BUNTER, MERVYN	Dorothy Sayers
BURKE, GERALD	Benge Atlee
BURKE, JERRY	Asa Baker
BURKE, (CHIEF)	Robert Orr Chipperfield
BURKE, (INSPECTOR)	Cortland Fitzsimmons
BURMAN, (INSPECTOR) CHEVIOT . .	G. Belton Cobb
BURNHAM, "BREEZE"	Sinclair Gluck
BURNLEY, (INSPECTOR)	Freeman Wills Crofts
BURNS, LARRY	Sloane Callaway
BURR, JASON	David Kent
BURTON, MARY J. ("POLLY") . . .	Baroness Orczy

Name of Character	*Name of Author*
Butterworth, Amelia	Anna Katharine Green
Byrd, Horace	Anna Katharine Green

C

Caine, (Inspector) Fred	Charles G. Givens
Calhoun, Bert	Weed Dickinson
Callaghan, James	Lord Charnwood
Callaghan, "Slim"	Peter Cheyney
Camberwell, Ronald	J. S. Fletcher
Campbell, Humphrey	Geoffrey Homes
Campbell, Quessy	Gail Stockwell
Campenhaye, Paul	J. S. Fletcher
Campion, Albert	Margery Allingham
Cardani, Paul	Joseph T. Shaw
Cardby, Mick	David Hume
Carlyle, Louis	Ernest Bramah
Carner, Mary	Zelda Popkin
Carpenter, (Colonel) Rutherford B.	Alice Tilton
Carrados, Max (born Max Wynn)	Ernest Bramah
Carruthers, (Inspector) John	John Dickson Carr
Carter, Philip	Florence Ryerson & C. C. Clements
Carver, Bruce	Denis Allen
Carver, Margot	Esther Haven Fonseca
"Catalyst Club, The"	George Dyer
Caution, "Lemmy"	Peter Cheyney
Cavendish, Georgia. See Strangeways, (Mrs.) Nigel.	
Chadlington, (Colonel)	V. L. Whitechurch
Chan, Charlie	Earl Derr Biggers
Chance, Christopher ("Kit")	Stephen Ransome

Name of Character	*Name of Author*
COBB, (INSPECTOR)	Jonathan Stagge
COCHET, ARMAND ("THE WHITE EAGLE")	Arthur Somers Roche
COFFIN, PETER	Peter Coffin
COHEN, MARTY	Emmett Hogarth
COLT, (COMMISSIONER) THATCHER .	Anthony Abbot
COLTON, THORNLEY	Clinton H. Stagg
CONNERS, LE DROIT	Samuel Gardenshire
COOK, BARNEY	Harvey J. O'Higgins
COOL, (MRS.) BERTHA	A. A. Fair
CORDRY, JASON	James O'Hanlon
CORNFORD, (INSPECTOR)	Milward Kennedy
CORNISH, ALEXANDER	John August
CORNISH, KAY	Virginia Hanson
COTTON, GUNSTON	Rupert Grayson
"COUNSELLOR, THE." See BRAND.	
COWPER, JOHN	Francis Beeding
COYLE, DANNY	Judson P. Phillips
CRABTREE, JOHN CARTER	Leslie Ford
CRAGG, SAM	Frank Gruber
CRAINE, PAUL	Eugene P. Healey
CRANE, WILLIAM ("BILL")	Jonathan Latimer
CREED, JOHN	Anthony Marsden
CREEVY, (COLONEL) WINSTON . . .	Jeremy Lord
CREIGHTON	F. Britten Austin
"CRIME DOCTOR, THE." See DOLLAR.	
CROSBY, HERBERT	Mary Semple Scott
CROSBY, MARK	Eleanor Blake
CROSS, (INSPECTOR)	John Donavan
CROW	George Norsworthy
CROW, ANDERSON	George Barr McCutcheon
CRUSIT, MYRA	Joseph C. Lincoln
CUFF, (SERGEANT)	Wilkie Collins
CUMBERLEDGE, HUBERT	Grant Allen

Name of Character	*Name of Author*
CUPPLES, NATHANIEL BURTON . . .	E. C. Bentley
CURRY, ELEANOR	March Evermay
CURTIS, LYLE	Emma Lou Fetta
CYR, (DR.) JACQUES	Donald Q. Burleigh

D

D——, (MINISTER)	Edgar Allan Poe
"D.A., THE." See SELBY.	
DAGGART, BRINTON	Mark Saxton
DAGOBERT	Baldwin Groller
DALE, JIMMY ("THE GRAY SEAL") .	Frank L. Packard
DALE, KENNETH	Raymond Allen
DAMMAN, (CAPTAIN)	Mark Saxton
DANAVAN, MAT	James Warner Bellah
DANTRY, (CAPTAIN) NICK	John Hunter
DARE, SUSAN	Mignon G. Eberhart
DARRELL, JEFFREY	Harry Stephen Keeler
DARROW, (INSPECTOR) CAESAR . . .	John Mason Bigelow
DARYL, MIDDLETON	Edward Acheson
DATCHERY, DICK	Charles Dickens
"DAUBREUIL, PAUL." See LUPIN.	
DAVENANT, P. J.	Lord Frederic Hamilton
DAVENPORT, ANNE. See McLEAN, (MRS.) HUGH.	
DAWLE, (SUPERINTENDENT) . . .	Henry Wade
DAWSON, PETER J.	Harry Stephen Keeler
DAWSON, (CHIEF INSPECTOR) WILLIAM (*alias* "BILL THE BLOODHOUND," "CHOLMONDELEY JONES") . . .	Bennet Copplestone

Name of Character	*Name of Author*
DE BAHL, (BARON) ALEXIS ("THE FOX")	Valentine Williams
DELEVAN, DANNY	Frederick C. Davis
DEMING, RICHARD	R. L. F. McCombs
DENE, DORCAS	George R. Sims
DENE, (SIR) JOHN	H. H. Jenkins
DENE, TREVOR	Valentine Williams
DENNY, HAL	Lucian Austin Osgood
DENVER, GERALD CHRISTIAN WIMSEY (VISCOUNT ST. GEORGE) (16TH DUKE)	Dorothy Sayers
DENVER, HONORIA LUCASTA WIMSEY (DOWAGER DUCHESS) (*née* DELAGARDIE)	Dorothy Sayers
"DEPARTMENT OF QUEER COMPLAINTS." See MARCH.	
"DETECTIVE BARNEY." See COOK, BARNEY.	
DIAVOLO, DON	Stuart Towne
DILLON, (SHERIFF) STEVE	Anna Katharine Green
"DISHER"	Will Scott
DIX, CONSTANTINE	Barry Pain
DIX, FRANCIS	Mary E. Wilkins Freeman
DJUNA	Ellery Queen
DODD, CEDRIC	Kenneth Livingston
DODD, SEPTIMUS	Sutherland Scott
DOLLAR, (DR.) ("THE CRIME DOCTOR")	E. W. Hornung
DOLLOPS	T. W. Hanshew
DONAQUE, (MONSIEUR)	Arthur Train
DONNY, (SHERIFF) PETE	Mignon G. Eberhart
DONOVAN, CLAUDE ("HARVARD") . .	Judson P. Phillips
DONOVAN, DICK	Dick Donovan
DONOVAN, (LIEUTENANT) JEROME .	Elizabeth Dean
DOONH, LANGA	R. T. M. Scott

Name of Character	*Name of Author*
DOOWINKLE, JOHN ("D.A.") . . .	Harry Klingsberg
DORNFELL, (INSPECTOR)	J. J. Connington
DOWELL-BLAKELEY, (CAPTAIN) LEIGH	Edward Acheson
DOYLE, PATRICK MICHAEL	Audrey Newell
DRACULA, (COUNT)	Bram Stoker
DRAKE, CALLIE	Constance & Gwenyth Little
DRAKE, DEXTER	Elsa Barker
DRAKE, PAUL	Erle Stanley Gardner
DRANSFIELD, (CHIEF INSPECTOR) . .	Frank King
DRAPER, (SERGEANT)	John Rhode
DRED, MICHAEL	Marie and Robert Leighton
DREW, MAJOR ADAM	Virginia Hanson
DRIFFIELD, (SIR) CLINTON	J. J. Connington
DROOD, EDWIN	Charles Dickens
DRUMMOND, (CAPTAIN) HUGH ("BULL-DOG")	H. C. McNeile ("Sapper") [and Gerard Fairlie]
DUBOURG, PAULINE	Edgar Allan Poe
"DUCHARME, (PROFESSOR) PAUL." See Valmont.	
DUCKETT, GEORGE	Valentine Williams
DUFF, JOHN	Harvey J. O'Higgins
DUFFY, (LIEUTENANT)	Burton E. Stevenson
DUKOVSKI	Anton Chekhov
DULUTH, PETER	Patrick Quentin
DUNCAN, HUGH	A. E. Fielding
DUNCAN, MATT	H. H. Holmes
DUNCAN, ROBBIE	Dan Billany
DUNDAS, MICHAEL	Virginia Rath
DUNDEE, JAMES F. ("BONNIE") . .	Anne Austin
DUNEEN, DULCIE (later MRS. ARTHUR HASTINGS)	Agatha Christie
DUNLAP, CONSTANCE	Arthur B. Reeve

Name of Character	*Name of Author*
DUNN, (SIR) PETER ("SERGEANT SIR PETER")	Edgar Wallace
DUPIN, C. AUGUSTE	Edgar Allan Poe
DUVEEN, MICHAEL	Eden Phillpotts
DURKIN, (LIEUTENANT) DAN . . .	Arthur M. Chase
DUSEN. See VAN DUSEN.	
DYKE, TOBY	E. X. Ferrars

E

"EAGLE, THE WHITE." See COCHET.	
"EBBIE, OLD." See ENTWISTLE.	
EDWARDES, (SERGEANT)	Mary E. Wilkins Freeman
EDWARDS, JANE AMANDA	Charlotte Murray Russell
EDWARDS, KATHIE	Eleanor Blake
EGERTON, SCOTT	Anthony Gilbert
EGG, MONTAGUE	Dorothy Sayers
EGO, (INSPECTOR)	G. R. Malloch
EMIL. See TISCHBEIN.	
"ENGEL, GEORGE." See WOLFF.	
ENTWISTLE, EBBIE ("OLD EBBIE") .	F. A. M. Webster
ESSINGTON, MANDELL	J. Storer Clouston
ESTABROOK, ROBERT	Louis Dodge
EVANS, HOMER	Elliot Paul

F

FAIRBANKS, HENRY ("HANK") . .	Elizabeth Dean
FAIRFORD, (INSPECTOR) TOM . . .	G. D. H. and M. I. Cole
"FALCON, THE"	Drexel Drake
FARLING, HORNSBY	C. F. Nicolet

Name of Character	*Name of Author*
FRAMPTON, (INSPECTOR) ANDREW . .	T. Arthur Plummer
FRENCH, (LIEUTENANT) BILL . . .	Christopher Hale
FRENCH, (INSPECTOR) JOSEPH . . .	Freeman Wills Crofts
FRIKER, (INSPECTOR) PAUL . . .	Mignon G. Eberhart
FROBISHER, TIMOTHY	Constance and Gwenyth Little
FROST, (INSPECTOR)	H. Maynard Smith
FU MANCHU, (DR.)	Sax Rohmer
FURNEAUX, (INSPECTOR) C. F. . . .	Louis Tracy
FYTTON, BERNARD	J. D. Beresford

G

G——, (PREFECT)	Edgar Allan Poe
GABRIEL, BILL	Lawrence G. Blochman
GAMADGE, HENRY	Elizabeth Daly
GANIMARD, (CHIEF INSPECTOR) . .	Maurice Leblanc
GANNS, PETER	Eden Phillpotts
GANTT, BERNARD ("BARNEY") . . .	John Stephen Strange
GARDELLA, (INSPECTOR)	Judson P. Phillips
GARET, FONTAINE	Evelyn Cameron
GARTH	Harrison J. Holt
GAUNT, JEREMY	Marion Randolph
GAUNT, JOHN	Carter Dickson
GAYLORD, JAN	Mary Hastings Bradley
GETHRYN, (COLONEL) ANTHONY RUTHVEN	Philip MacDonald
GEVROL, (INSPECTOR) ("GENERAL") .	Émile Gaboriau
GHOST, WALTER	Vincent Starrett
GIBBS, GRUMPY	Bliss Lomax
GIBBS, JAMES AUGUSTUS ("JAG") . .	Means Davis

Name of Character	*Name of Author*
GIBSON, CHRIS	Ione Montgomery
GILLESPIE, (DR.) LEONARD	Max Brand
GILLINGHAM, ANTONY	A. A. Milne
GILMOUR, (INSPECTOR)	MacLeod Winsor
GLASS, (CONSTABLE)	Georgette Heyer
GLASS, JOEL	Marco Page
GLASS, (MRS.) JOEL (GERDA) . . .	Marco Page
GLOVER, (INSPECTOR)	March Evermay
GLUCK, (BARON)	Virgil Markham
GOADE, NICHOLAS	E. Phillips Oppenheim
GODAHL, "THE INFALLIBLE" . . .	Frederick Irving Anderson
GODFREY, JIM	Burton E. Stevenson
GOODWIN, ARCHIE	Rex Stout
GORDON, FANNY	Edith Macvane
GORE, (SHERIFF) ("PANAMINT PETE")	Charles Saxby and Louis Molnar
GORE, (COLONEL) WYCKHAM . . .	Lynn Brock
GOTT, (DR.) GILES ("GILBERT PENTREITH")	Michael Innes
GOWER, (SERGEANT)	Henry Wade
GRADY, (LIEUTENANT) FRANCIS BYRON	Ione Sandberg Shriber
GRANBY, (COLONEL) ALISTAIR . . .	Francis Beeding
GRANT, TONY	Paul McGuire
GRAY, COLIN	Mark Channing
"GRAY SEAL, THE." See DALE.	
GREEN, CHARLES	Arthur M. Chase
"GREEN SHADOW, THE"	Herman Landon
GREER, JAMES	Newton Gayle
GREGORY, (LIEUTENANT)	Medora Field
GREGSON, (INSPECTOR) TOBIAS . .	Sir Arthur Conan Doyle
GRENDON, PAUL	Frank King
GREY, COLWIN	Arthur J. Rees

Name of Character	*Name of Author*
"GREY PHANTOM, THE"	Herman Landon
GRIDDLE, L. F. ("SCOOP")	Thomas Polsky
GRIEF, (INSPECTOR)	Norman Forrest
GRIFFITH, WILLIAM	Robert George Dean
GRIM, JAMES SCHYLER ("JIMGRIM") .	Talbot Mundy
GRODMAN, GEORGE	Israel Zangwill
GRUNDT, (DR.) ADOLF ("CLUBFOOT")	Valentine Williams
GRYCE, EBENEZER	Anna Katharine Green
GUBB, PHILO	Ellis Parker Butler

H

"H.M." See MERRIVALE.	
HADLEY, (SUPERINTENDENT) DAVID .	John Dickson Carr
HAILEY, (DR.) EUSTACE	Anthony Wynne
HAKI, (COLONEL)	Eric Ambler
HALE, MAXFIELD CHAUNCEY . . .	George Harmon Coxe
HALE, SPENCER	Robert Barr
HALEY, ED	Weed Dickinson
HALL, PETE	S. Cole
HALSTEAD, ARTHUR	William Edward Hayes
HAMBLEDON, THOMAS ELPHINSTONE ("TOMMY") (*alias* "HENDRIK BRANDT," "KLAUS LEHMANN") . .	Manning Coles
HAMMERSLEY, CYRIL	George Gibbs
HAMMOND, (LIEUTENANT)	Charlotte Murray Russell
HAMMOND, (SHERIFF) TIM	Carolyn Byrd Dawson
HANAUD	A. E. W. Mason
HAND, CHRISTOPHER	Stanley Hart Page
HANNASYDE, (SUPERINTENDENT). .	Georgette Heyer
HANNAY, RICHARD	John Buchan

Name of Character	*Name of Author*
HANSLET, (SUPERINTENDENT) . . .	John Rhode
HANSON, (CAPTAIN) MARK . . .	Joseph C. Lincoln
HANVEY, JAMES H. ("JIM") . . .	Octavus Roy Cohen
HARDCASTLE, PETER	Eden Phillpotts
HARDING, (INSPECTOR)	Georgette Heyer
HARRISON, CLAY	Clifton Roberts
HARTY, (SERGEANT) CASS	Joel Y. Dane
HARVEY, GAIL	George Gibbs
HARVEY, PAUL	Robert Orr Chipperfield
HARWELL, JAMES TRUEMAN	Anna Katharine Green
HASTINGS, (CAPTAIN) ARTHUR . . .	Agatha Christie
HASTINGS, JEFFERSON	James Hay, Jr.
HASTINGS, JIMMY	Charles G. Given
HASTINGS, SPENCER	Philip MacDonald
HATCH, (PROFESSOR) CYRUS . . .	Frederick C. Davis
HATCH, HUTCHINSON	Jacques Futrelle
HATCH, (COMMISSIONER) MARK . .	Frederick C. Davis
HATTON	J. D. Beresford
HAWKES, "A. B. C."	C. E. Bechhofer Roberts
HAZARD, ERIC	Lee Crosby
HAZELL, THORPE	Victor L. Whitechurch
HAZZARD, (SIR) CHRISTOPHER ("KIT")	Richard Keverne
HEADCORN, (CHIEF INSPECTOR) . .	Alice Campbell
"HEADLAND, GEORGE." See CLEEK.	
HEATH, (SERGEANT) ERNEST . . .	S. S. Van Dine
HECK, BRIAN YOUNG	Bruce Graeme
HEINSHEIMER, (INSPECTOR) AUGUST .	Zelda Popkin
HEMINGWAY, (SERGEANT)	Georgette Heyer
HENNESSY, (INSPECTOR)	G. D. H. and M. I. Cole
HERN, ROWLAND	Nicholas Olde
HERRICK, A. Z.	Whitman Chambers

Name of Character	*Name of Author*
HERRIDGE, LISSA VICKERS	Constance and Gwenyth Little
HERRIVELL, (SIR) RICHARD . . .	John Bentley
HERROLD, (DR.) JOHN	Means Davis
HEWITT, MARTIN	Arthur Morrison
HICKS	F. A. M. Webster
HICKS, ALFRED	R. C. Woodthorpe
HIERONOMO, ANNE	Dorothy Cameron Disney
HIGGINS, (INSPECTOR) CUTHBERT . .	C. F. Gregg
HIGHWAY	Garnett Weston
HITE, QUINNY	Richard Burke
HOBART, (LIEUTENANT)	Ione Montgomery
HOLLIDAY, HIRAM	Paul Gallico
HOLM, PATRICIA	Leslie Charteris
HOLMES, MYCROFT	Sir Arthur Conan Doyle
HOLMES, SHERLOCK *	Sir Arthur Conan Doyle
HOLTZ, NICHOLAS	Alexander Laing
"HOMICIDE HANNAH." See VAN DOREN.	
HOPE, JEFFERSON	Sir Arthur Conan Doyle
HOPKINS, (INSPECTOR) STEPHEN . .	David Burnham
HOPLEY, VICTOR	H. C. Bailey
HORNLEIGH, (INSPECTOR)	Hans Wolfgang Priwin
HOWARD, GRAHAM	E. H. Clements
HOWARD, TONY	Arthur Applin

* For a remarkable listing of the complete personae of the HOLMES tales, the reader is recommended to Edgar W. Smith's privately printed *Appointment in Baker Street* (New York, Pamphlet House, 1938); available also in *221B: Studies in Sherlock Holmes,* edited by Vincent Starrett (New York, Macmillan, 1940). In the present compilation, space is given to only a handful of the more prominent or recurrent figures in a detective, criminal, or domestic sense.

Name of Character	*Name of Author*
HOWARD, WALLACE	Frederica De Laguna
HUDSON, (MRS.)	Sir Arthur Conan Doyle
HULL, (MISS) "SCRAPS"	Ione Montgomery
HUMBLETHORNE, (INSPECTOR) . . .	Lord Gorell
HUNT, ELSIE MAE	Aaron Marc Stein
HUNT, FREDERICK	Lillian Day and Norbert Lederer
HUNTER, ANTHONY ("TONY") . .	Robert George Dean
HUNTER, JIMMY	Mary Stimson
HUXFORD, REX	Cromwell Gibbons
HYER, HENRY ("HANK")	Kurt Steel
HYLAND, TERRY	Reginald Davis

I

"INFALLIBLE GODAHL." See GODAHL.	
IPSWITCH, (INSPECTOR)	Reginald Davis
IXELL, BARRON	Oscar Schisgall

J

JACKSON, (INSPECTOR)	David Lindsay
JACKSON, (LIEUTENANT) A. . . .	Anthony Boucher
JAMESON, WALTER	Arthur B. Reeve
JAMIESON	Mary Roberts Rinehart
JAMIESON, (SUPERINTENDENT) . . .	Anthony Berkeley
JAPP, (INSPECTOR)	Agatha Christie
"JEANNIOT, (CAPTAIN)." See LUPIN.	
JELLIPOT	Sidney Fowler
JENKINS, HEPZIBAH ("'HAPPY'") . .	Henry Barnard Safford
JENNINGS, EZRA	Wilkie Collins

Name of Character	*Name of Author*
JERVIS, (INSPECTOR)	Q. Patrick
JERVIS, (DR.) CHRISTOPHER . . .	R. Austin Freeman
JERVOIS, (CAPTAIN) GERALD . . .	J. Russell Warren
"JIMGRIM." See GRIM.	
JOHN, (SIR). See SAUMAREZ.	
JOHNSTONE	C. E. Bechhofer Roberts
JOLY, (INSPECTOR)	Arthur Sherburne Hardy
"JONAH & CO." See MANSEL.	
JONES, ADRIAN VAN REYPEN EGERTON ("AVERAGE")	Samuel Hopkins Adams
JONES, (INSPECTOR) ATHELNEY . .	Sir Arthur Conan Doyle
"JONES, CHOLMONDELEY." See DAWSON.	
JONES, "CURLY"	David Knox Patton
JONES, (SHERIFF) DAVEY	F. W. Bronson
JONES, EDMUND ("JUPITER") . . .	Timothy Fuller
JONES, "MEDDLESOME" [MEDDLESTON?]	Sir Basil Thomson
JONES, XENIUS ("X")	Harry Stephen Keeler
JONQUELLE ("PREFECT OF POLICE OF PARIS")	Melville Davisson Post
JORDAN, DAN	Harlan Reed
JORDAN, JACK	William Du Bois
JORDAN, TIMOTHY	Edgar Wallace
JOSEPHINE, JOSEPH. See ROULETABILLE.	
"JUST MEN, THE"	Edgar Wallace
JUSTUS, JAKE	Craig Rice

K

| KANE, DORIS . . . . | George Gibbs |
| KANE, FRED . . . . | Charles Saxby |

Name of Character	*Name of Author*
KAPLIN, (INSPECTOR)	H. De Vere Stacpoole
KAZ. See VON KAZ.	
KEATE, (NURSE) SARAH	Mignon G. Eberhart
KELLY, JOE	Robert Avery
KELTON, MATTHEW	Richard Connell
KENDALL, (INSPECTOR)	Jefferson Farjeon
KENNEDY, (PROFESSOR) CRAIG . . .	Arthur B. Reeve
KENT, WALLY	Charlotte Murray Russell
KERBY, ASTROGEN ("ASTRO") . . .	Gelett Burgess
KERRIGAN, PETER	Esther Haven Fonseca
KERRIGAN, PETER	Neil Gordon
KETCHAM, JOHN	Frank P. Grady
KILDARE, (DR.) JAMES	Max Brand
KILL. See VAN KILL.	
KING, BILL	B. J. Maylon
KING, (INSPECTOR) CHARLES . . .	Joseph L. Bonney
KING, PETER	Cortland Fitzsimmons and John Mulholland
KINGSTON, MICHAEL (*alias* "DIRK BRANDT," "BILL SAUNDERS") . .	Manning Coles
KIRBY, JOSEPH ("JOE")	Dwight V. Babcock
KIRK, ASHTON	John T. McIntyre
KLAW, MORIS	Sax Rohmer
KNOX, (HON.) ALGERNON	E. Phillips Oppenheim
KOA, KOMAKO	Max Long
KOMAKO. See KOA.	
KORAVITCH, (CAPTAIN) IVAN . . .	Victor L. Whitechurch
KRAMER, AUGUST FRANKFURTER ("GUS")	Cedric Worth
KROOK, (DR.)	Arthur Mallory

Name of Character	*Name of Author*
KUELZ, OSCAR	Erich Kästner
KYRA. See SOKRATESCO.	

L

LAKE, STAN	Whitman Chambers
LAM, DONALD	A. A. Fair
LAMB, (INSPECTOR)	Patricia Wentworth
LAMB, (SERGEANT) JOHN	John Donavan
LAMB, MARTIN	Anthony Boucher
LANDERVORNE, (SIR) JOHN	John Dickson Carr
LANE, DRURY	Barnaby Ross
LANE, JAMES	Florence Ryerson & C. C. Clements
LANG, SOPHIE	Frederick Irving Anderson
LANYARD, MICHAEL ("THE LONE WOLF")	Louis Joseph Vance
LARKIN, GLEN	Lawrence G. Blochman
LARRABEE, (LIEUTENANT) KIRK . .	Adam Bliss
LARSAN, FRÉDÉRIC	Gaston Leroux
LASH, SIMON	Frank Gruber
LATHAM, (MRS.) GRACE	Leslie Ford
LATIMER, CHARLES	Eric Ambler
LA TOUCHE, GEORGES	Freeman Wills Crofts
LAVENDER, JAMES ELIOT ("JIMMIE") .	Vincent Starrett
LE BRETON, (DR.) MILES	John Esteven
LECOQ	Émile Gaboriau
LEE, JUDITH	Richard Marsh
LEFARGE	Freeman Wills Crofts
LEGRAND, WILLIAM	Edgar Allan Poe
"LEHMANN, KLAUS." See HAMBLEDON, THOMAS ELPHINSTONE.	

Name of Character	*Name of Author*
LOVEAPPLE, (MISS)	Ethel Lina White
LOWELL, BILL	Whitman Chambers
LUCIAS, (CAPTAIN) BEN	Royce Howes
LUDLOW, JOHNNY	Mrs. Henry Wood
LUGG	Margery Allingham
LUMSDEN, ARCHIE	Max Saltmarsh
LUPIN, ARSÈNE (*alias* "JIM BARNETT," "PAUL DAUBREUIL," "CAPTAIN JEANNIOT," "PRINCE RÉNINE," "HORACE VELMONT," etc.)	Maurice Leblanc
LYLE, SAMUEL	Arthur Crabb
LYNCH, BERTRAM	John W. Vandercook
LYSON, (CAPTAIN)	E. Phillips Oppenheim

M

MCBRIDE, REX	Cleve F. Adams
MCC., J. J.	Ellery Queen
MCCARTHY, CATHY	Melville Burt
MCCARTHY, (INSPECTOR) TIMOTHY .	Isabel Ostrander
MCCOUN, (SERGEANT) PATRICK . .	Richard M. Baker
MACDONALD, (CHIEF INSPECTOR) . .	E. C. R. Lorac
MACDONALD, (MISS) LYNN . . .	Kay Cleaver Strahan
MCDUFF, (INSPECTOR) ANGUS . . .	John Mersereau
MACDUFFY, (INSPECTOR) ANGUS . .	Edwin Balmer and Philip Wylie
MCGARRAH, (INSPECTOR)	C. C. Nicolet
MCGEE, SQUILLER	A. A. Archer
MACGILLICUDY	Robert George Dean
MCGOVERN, (SERGEANT)	Lillian Day and Norbert Lederer
MACGOWAN, (LIEUTENANT) WILL . .	Shirley and Adele Seifert
MCGRAW, (INSPECTOR)	Gelett Burgess

Name of Character	*Name of Author*
MACGREGOR, ECHO. See WARE, (MRS.) ANTHONY.	
M'GUIRE, (INSPECTOR) ALOYSIUS . .	J. Russell Warren
MCINTYRE, (CHIEF) ("MAC") . . .	M. E. Corne
MCKEE, (INSPECTOR) CHRISTOPHER .	Helen Reilly
MCKELVIE, GRAYDON	Marion Harvey
MACLAIN, (CAPTAIN) DUNCAN . .	Baynard H. Kendrick
MCLEAN, (CHIEF INSPECTOR) . . .	George Goodchild
MCLEAN, (LIEUTENANT-COMMANDER) HUGH	Margaret Tayler Yates
MCLEAN, (MRS.) HUGH (*née* ANNE DAVENPORT) ("DAVVIE") . . .	Margaret Tayler Yates
MACLEVY, OSCAR	Bruno Fischer
MACNAB, ALASTAIR	James Ronald
MACNAB, FRANCIS	John A. Ferguson
MCNEILL, (DR.) JEFFREY	Theodora DuBois
MCNEILL, (MRS.) JEFFREY (ANNE) .	Theodora DuBois
MACOMBER, ELISHA	Kathleen Moore Knight
MCQUEEN, MICKEY	Harvey J. O'Higgins
MACVEIGH, (CAPTAIN) ANDY . . .	Sue MacVeigh
MACVEIGH, (MRS.) ANDY (SUE) . .	Sue MacVeigh
MADDEN, (CHIEF) JEROME	Thomas Polsky
MAHAN, BETTY	Timothy Fuller
MAIGRET, (INSPECTOR)	Georges Simenon
MALAND, (SHERIFF) ERIC	Mabel Seeley
MALLETT, (INSPECTOR) JOHN . . .	Cyril Hare
MALONE, JOHN J.	Craig Rice
MALTBY, EDWARD	Jefferson Farjeon
"MAN IN THE CORNER." See "OLD MAN IN THE CORNER, THE."	
"MAN OF FORTY FACES, THE." See CLEEK.	

Name of Character	*Name of Author*
MANCHU. See FU MANCHU.	
MANDERS, "BUNNY"	E. W. Hornung [and Barry Perowne]
MANDERSON, (MRS.) MABEL (DOMECQ) (later MRS. PHILIP MARSHAM TRENT)	E. C. Bentley
MANNERING, JOHN ("THE BLUE MASK")	Anthony Morton
MANNERS, HARTLEY	Charles I. Dutton
MANSEL, JONAH	Dornford Yates
MANSON, HELEN	Harvey J. O'Higgins
MAPPIN, AMOS LEE	Hulbert Footner
MARCH, (COLONEL)	Carter Dickson
MARCH, LARRY	Whitman Chambers
MARKHAM, JOHN F.-X.	S. S. Van Dine
MARKHAM, PHILIP	Lawrence W. Meynell
MARLOW, DICK	John Bentley
MARLOW, NICHOLAS	Eric Ambler
MARLOWE, PHILIP	Raymond Chandler
MARLOWE, SARAH	Patricia Wentworth
MARPLE, JANE	Agatha Christie
MARPLES, ROGER	Francis Beeding
MARQUIS, (SIR) HENRY	Melville Davisson Post
MARSH, EMMA	Elizabeth Dean
MARSHALL, GARY	George Harmon Coxe
MARSHALL, TERENCE	H. H. Holmes
MARTIN, (INSPECTOR)	Wallace Jackson
MARTIN, (INSPECTOR) GEORGE . .	Francis Beeding
MARTIN, (COMMODORE) REID . . .	Nard Jones
"MASK, THE BLUE." See MANNERING.	
MASON, PERRY	Erle Stanley Gardner
MASON, RANDOLPH	Melville Davisson Post
MASSEY, OLIVER	Henry C. Beck

Name of Character	*Name of Author*
MASTERS, (CHIEF INSPECTOR) HUMPHREY	Carter Dickson
MATTINGLY, (LIEUTENANT) . . .	Norman Stanley Bortner
"MAURAVANIA, PRINCE OF." See CLEEK.	
MAWSON, JAMES LEVITT	Ralph Henry Barbour
MAXWELL, JUSTICE	Edgar Wallace
MAYHEW, (LIEUTENANT) STEPHEN .	D. B. Olsen
MAYNARD, GARRETT	Howard Swiggett
MAYO, ASEY	Phoebe Atwood Taylor
MEAD, (LIEUTENANT) VALENTINE . .	J. Storer Clouston
MEATYARD, (INSPECTOR)	Stanley Casson
MEECH, "SPIDER"	Clifford Orr
MENZIES, (CHIEF INSPECTOR) WEIR .	Frank Froest
MEREDITH, (SIR) JOHN (formerly CHIEF INSPECTOR)	Francis Gérard
MEREFIELD, HAROLD	John Rhode
MERLINI	Clayton Rawson
MERRIMAN, JOHN	Milward Kennedy
MERRIMAN, (MRS.) JOHN (JOAN) . .	Milward Kennedy
MERRION, DESMOND	Miles Burton
MERRIVALE, (SIR) HENRY ("H. M.") .	Carter Dickson
"METICULOUS MICHAEL." See MORLANT.	
METZ, FRED	Allan McRoyd
MEYNARD, KATHEREN LUTETIA (later MRS. HAZLITT WOAR)	George Worthing Yates
MIDWINTER, (INSPECTOR) BERTRAM .	Harrington Hext
MILDENHALL, CHARLES	E. Phillips Oppenheim
MILES, PHILIP	James Remington McCarthy
MILLER, "DOC"	Herman Petersen
MILLER, JOSEPH	Augusta Groner

Name of Character	*Name of Author*
MILTON, HENRY ARTHUR ("THE RINGER")	Edgar Wallace
MINOT, SAM	Freeman Dana
MIQUET, CARYL (later BARONESS VON KAZ)	D. and H. Teilhet
"MISS MONTANA." See LEONARD.	
MITCHELL, (CHIEF INSPECTOR) . .	Freeman Wills Crofts
MOLLY, (LADY)	Baroness Orczy
MONROE, CRETE	Dwight Marfield
"MONTANA, MISS." See LEONARD.	
MOON, COTTON	Rufus King
MOONEY, JERRY	Terry O'Neil
MOORE, (INSPECTOR)	Torrey Chanslor
MOREL	Frederick Irving Anderson
MORESBY, (CHIEF INSPECTOR) . . .	Anthony Berkeley
MORGAN, (INSPECTOR)	Oswald Crawfurd
MORGAN, CHRISTOPHER	Sinclair Gluck
MORGAN, OSCAR	Geoffrey Homes
MORIARTY, (PROFESSOR) JAMES [ROBERT?]	Sir Arthur Conan Doyle
MORLAKE, JAMES ("THE BLACK") .	Edgar Wallace
MORLANT, (SERGEANT) MICHAEL ("METICULOUS MICHAEL") . . .	Frank King
MORPHEW, HARRIET	Mary Allerton
MORRIS, HUGH	William and Herman L. Targ
MORRO, ("BIG") NICK	Prosper Buranelli
MORSTON, MARY. See WATSON, (MRS.) JOHN H.	
MORTIMER, (DR.) JAMES	Sir Arthur Conan Doyle
MOTO, T. A.	J. P. Marquand
MOTT, DAISY JANE	Jennifer Jones

Name of Character	*Name of Author*
Mott, Lucie	E. Phillips Oppenheim
Muller, Joe	G. I. Colbron and A. Groner
Mulligan, Tim	Aaron Marc Stein
Mumm, Wolfgang Amadeus . . .	J. C. Snaith
Murch, (Inspector) W.	E. C. Bentley
Murdock, Kent	George Harmon Coxe
Murdock, Rachel	D. B. Olsen
Myrl, Dora	M. MacDonnell Bodkin

N

Narkom, (Superintendent) Maverick	T. W. Hanshew
Nash, Aubrey	Tech Davis
Newberry, Millicent	Jeanette Lee
Noonan, (Inspector)	Willard Rich
North, Gerald	Frances and Richard Lockridge
North, (Mrs.) Gerald (Pamela) .	Frances and Richard Lockridge
North, (Major) Hugh (formerly Captain)	Van Wyck Mason
North, Richard	Pearl Foley
Northeast, (Inspector) Guy . .	Joanna Cannan
"November Joe"	Hesketh Prichard

O

Oates, (Superintendent) Stanislaus	Margery Allingham
O'Banion, (Chief) Tim	Sloane Callaway
O'Breen, Fergus	Anthony Boucher
O'Brien, Patrick	Inez Haynes Irwin
O'Brien, Pierre	Whitman Chambers

Name of Character	*Name of Author*
O'DAY, CHAUNCEY	Audrey Gaines
ODOM, (SHERIFF) HIRAM	Marjorie Boniface
O'DONALD, (INSPECTOR) TIM . . .	Cortland Fitz- simmons and John Mulholland
O'HEARN, TIM	Ben Ames Williams
OKEWOOD, (MAJOR) FRANCIS . . .	Valentine Williams
"OLD BATTLE-AX, THE." See ADAMS, ADELAIDE.	
"OLD EBBIE." See ENTWISTLE.	
"OLD GENERAL, THE." See WHARTON.	
"OLD MAN IN THE CORNER, THE" . .	Baroness Orczy
O'LEARY, LANCE	Mignon G. Eberhart
O'MALLEY, (OFFICER)	William B. MacHarg
O'MORE, MARY	Whitman Chambers
"ORATOR, THE." See RATER.	
ORMOND, (INSPECTOR) DANIEL . . .	John Brophy
ORR, NAN	Anita Boutell
O'SULLIVAN, JOHNNY	Jerome Odlum
OURNEY, MAL	Raoul Whitfield
OWEN, (SERGEANT) BOBBY	E. R. Punshon

P

PAGE, SUSAN	Dorothy Cameron Disney
("PAPA") PONTIVY. See PONTIVY.	
PARDOE, (INSPECTOR) DAN	Dorothy Bowers
PARKER, (CHIEF INSPECTOR) CHARLES	Dorothy Sayers
PARKINSON	Ernest Bramah
PARMELEE, BILL	Percival Wilde
PARR, (DEPUTY)	Frederick Irving Anderson
PATTERSON, (DR.)	Harrison R. Steeves
PEARSON, (CHIEF INSPECTOR) ANDREW WILLIAM	Eric Shepherd

Name of Character	*Name of Author*
POE, CHRISTOPHER	Robert Carlton Brown
POGGIOLI, (PROFESSOR) HENRY . . .	T. S. Stribling
POINTER, (CHIEF INSPECTOR) . . .	A. E. Fielding
POIROT, HERCULE	Agatha Christie
POLTON, NATHANIEL	R. Austin Freeman
POND	G. K. Chesterton
PONTIVY, ("PAPA")	Bernard Newman
POOLE, (INSPECTOR) JOHN	Henry Wade
POPEAU, HERCULES	Mrs. Belloc Lowndes
PORTER, NIKKI	Ellery Queen
POTTS, (LIEUTENANT) HAKE . . .	Bryant Ford
POWEL, MIKE	James Francis Bonnell
POWEL, (P. O. INSPECTOR) THOMAS .	John Stephen Strange
PREECE, (SERGEANT)	J. S. Fletcher
PRENDERGAST, (DR.) MICHAEL . . .	G. D. H. and M. I. Cole
PRENTISS, (JUDGE)	Veronica Parker Johns
PRESCOTT, (CAPTAIN) LOUIS . . .	Josiah E. Greene
PRICE, (MRS.) CASSANDRA ("CASSIE") (*née* CARPENTER)	Alice Tilton
PRIEST, (JUDGE) WILLIAM	Irvin S. Cobb
PRIESTLEY, (DR.)	John Rhode
PRIMROSE, (COLONEL) JOHN T. . . .	Leslie Ford
PRINCE, HENRY	C. F. Gregg
"PRINCE OF MAURAVANIA." See CLEEK.	
"(PRINCE) RÉNINE." See LUPIN.	
(PRINCE) ZALESKI. See ZALESKI.	
PROUTY, (DR.) SAMUEL	Ellery Queen
PYM, (DEPUTY ASSISTANT COMMISSIONER) (MRS.) PALMYRA EVANGELINE	Nigel Morland
PYNE, PARKER	Agatha Christie

Q

Name of Character	Name of Author
"Q. Q." See QUAYNE.	
QUARLES, CHRISTOPHER	Percy Brebner
QUAYNE, QUENTIN. ("Q. Q.")	F. Britten Austin
QUEEN, ELLERY	Ellery Queen
QUEEN, (INSPECTOR) RICHARD	Ellery Queen
QUELL, PETER	William J. Makin
QUICK, ORSON	Kurt Steel
QUILL, (INSPECTOR) ADAM	Caryl Brahms and S. J. Simon
QUIN, HARLEY	Agatha Christie
QUINT, (LIEUTENANT) PETER D.	Hugh Austin

R

RACE, (CAPTAIN) CHARLES	Henry Wade
RACE, CHRISTOPHER	C. N. & A. M. Williamson
RADIGAN, (LIEUTENANT)	Hulbert Footner
RAFFLES, A. J.	E. W. Hornung [and Barry Perowne]
RAND, (COLONEL) THEODORE	Anthony Boucher
RANDOLPH, LUCY	Leslie Ford
RANKIN, (SERGEANT)	Timothy Fuller
RANKIN, TOMMY	Milton Propper
RAPHAEL, (DR.) LOUIS	Augustus Muir
RATER, (INSPECTOR) O. ("THE ORATOR")	Edgar Wallace
RAVENHILL, ANTHONY	R. Francis Foster
RAWLINS, (INSPECTOR) HUMPHREY	John Palmer
RAYMOND, EVERETT	Anna Katharine Green
REED, RUFUS	R. L. Goldman
REEDER, J. G.	Edgar Wallace

Name of Character	*Name of Author*
REESE, JOHNNY	Zelda Popkin
REEVES, MORDAUNT	Ronald A. Knox
"RÉNINE, (PRINCE)." See LUPIN.	
RENNERT, HUGH	Todd Downing
RENNETT, CARL	Edgar Wallace
REYNOLDS, CLAIRE	Helen Woodward & Frances Amherst
REYNOLDS, NANCY	Dorothy Cole Meade
RICARDO, JULIUS	A. E. W. Mason
RICE, STANLEY	Baynard H. Kendrick
RICHARDSON, (CONSTABLE) (later IN-SPECTOR and SUPERINTENDENT) . .	Sir Basil Thomson
RICHMOND, (MRS.) SALLY	Clarissa Fairchild Cushman
"RINGER, THE." See MILTON.	
RINGROSE, (INSPECTOR) JOHN . . .	Eden Phillpotts
RIPLEY, RAINBOW	Bliss Lomax
RIPPLE, (CHIEF INSPECTOR) . . .	John Victor Turner
RITCHIE, KAY	John Mersereau
RITTER, ELSIE. See BENSON, (MRS.) PHILIP.	
RIVIÈRE, (INSPECTOR) SIMON . . .	Claude Aveline
RODEN, (SHERIFF) JESS	A. B. Cunningham
ROGERS, (PROFESSOR) HUNTOON . .	Clifford Knight
ROLAND, (DR.) ANDREW	Ethel Fleming
ROLFE, SIMON	Joseph L. Bonney
ROSS, (SERGEANT)	G. Belton Cobb
ROULETABILLE, JOSEPH (born JOSEPH JOSEPHINE)	Gaston Leroux
ROYDEN, PHIL	Esther Haven Fonseca
RUDDOCK, (SERGEANT)	Francis Beeding
RUFF, PETER	E. Phillips Oppenheim

Name of Character	*Name of Author*
RUGGDALE, PAUL	Carl M. Chapin
RUMMEL, ("BEAU")	Ellery Queen
RUSBY, (INSPECTOR) MYLES . . .	Virgil Markham
RUSSELL, FRANKLIN	Richard M. Baker
RYDER, STEPHEN	Mary Hastings Bradley

S

SABER, JOEL	Gavin Holt
SAGE, MALCOLM	H. H. Jenkins
SAGE, (CONSTABLE) ORLO	Frederick Irving Anderson
SAINCLAIR	Gaston Leroux
"SAINT, THE." See TEMPLAR.	
SAINT-AMOUR, (LIEUTENANT) BOB .	Donald Clough Cameron
SALT, (SERGEANT)	Dorothy Bowers
SAMPSON, RICHARD HENRY	Richard Hull
SAMSON, (CAPTAIN)	Gavin Douglas
SANDERS, (COMMISSIONER)	Edgar Wallace [and Francis Gérard]
SANDERS, (DR.) JOHN	Anne Austin
SANDERS, (DR.) JOHN	Carter Dickson
SAUMAREZ, (SIR) JOHN (born JONATHAN SIMMONDS)	Clemence Dane and Helen Simpson
"SAUNDERS, BILL." See KINGSTON, MICHAEL.	
SAVOY, PAUL	Jackson Gregory
SAXON, PETER	Robert George Dean
SCARLETT, (DR.)	Alexander Laing
SCHMIDT, (INSPECTOR)	George Bagby
SCHMIDT, IMPERATOR	Robert George Dean
"SEAL, THE GRAY." See DALE.	

Name of Character	*Name of Author*
SEBASTIAN, (PROFESSOR)	Grant Allen
SEBRIGHT, (SUPERINTENDENT) . . .	F. Britten Austin
"SECRET SERVICE SMITH." See SMITH, AURELIUS.	
SEEGRAVE, (SUPERINTENDENT) . . .	Wilkie Collins
SELBY, (DISTRICT ATTORNEY) DOUGLAS ("THE D. A.")	Erle Stanley Gardner
SELFRIDGE, JASON	Frederick Irving Anderson
"SERGEANT SIR PETER." See DUNN.	
SEVREL, (EX-INSPECTOR) PAXTON . .	Cedric Worth
SEYMOUR, ANNE (later MRS. JOHN WEBB)	F. G. Presnell
"SHADOWERS, INC., THE"	David Fox
"SHAKESPEARE, BILL." See WITHERALL.	
SHAND, TONY	Willetta Anna Barber and R. F. Schabelitz
SHANE, PETER	Francis Bonnamy
SHANNON, DESMOND	M. V. Heberden
SHARPIN, MATTHEW	Wilkie Collins
SHAYNE, MICHAEL	Brett Halliday
SHEPPARD, (DR.) JAMES	Agatha Christie
SHERINGHAM, ROGER	Anthony Berkeley
SHOTT, (CHIEF INSPECTOR) . . .	Nigel Morland
SILENCE, (DR.) JOHN	Algernon Blackwood
SILVER, (INSPECTOR)	Henry Holt
SIMMONDS, JONATHAN. See SAUMAREZ.	
SIMS, (SUPERINTENDENT)	Francis D. Grierson
SINCLAIR, (SIR) ARTHUR	Walter S. Masterman
(SIR) JOHN. See SAUMAREZ.	
SLADE, (INSPECTOR) ANTHONY . . .	Leonard R. Gribble
SLADE, NICHOLAS	R. C. Woodthorpe
SLANE, (SIR) JASPER	E. Phillips Oppenheim

Name of Character	*Name of Author*
STANLEY, ANNE	Josiah E. Greene
STANLEY, BERT	Rufus King
STAPLETON, JOHN (principal *alias* of JOHN BASKERVILLE; also known as JOHN VANDELEUR)	Sir Arthur Conan Doyle
STARR, (DR.) COLIN	Rufus King
STEELE, JAMES	Dana Chambers
STEELE, STEPHEN	Kirke Mechem
STEVENS, (SUPERINTENDENT) WILLIAM	Bruce Graeme
STEWART, VALESKA (later MRS. ASTRO-GEN KERBY)	Gelett Burgess
STONE, FLEMING	Carolyn Wells
STOREY, MADAME ROSIKA	Hulbert Footner
STORKE, (DR.) ARCHIBALD	Anita Boutell
STORM, CARRIE	Audrey Gaines
STORM, CHRISTOPHER ("KIT") . . .	Willetta Ann Barber and R. F. Schabelitz
STORM, JACK	Dorothy Cameron Disney
STORM, (MRS.) JACK (LOLA) . . .	Dorothy Cameron Disney
STORM, LARRY	Hugh Pentecost
STORM, LEE	Edward Ronns
STRAKER, (INSPECTOR)	Wallace Jackson
STRANGE, VIOLET	Anna Katharine Green
STRANGEWAYS, (SIR) JOHN	Nicholas Blake
STRANGEWAYS, NIGEL	Nicholas Blake
STRANGEWAYS, (MRS.) NIGEL (*née* GEORGIA CAVENDISH)	Nicholas Blake
STREET, DELLA	Erle Stanley Gardner
STROGANOFF, VLADIMIR	Caryl Brahms and S. J. Simon
STROM, (LIEUTENANT) PETER . . .	Mabel Seeley

Name of Character	*Name of Author*
STUART, (MRS.) MOLLY	Delia Van Deusen
STUART, SALLY	Medora Field
SULLIVAN, BARRY	Judson P. Phillips
SULLIVAN, (INSPECTOR) JAMES . .	Virginia Rath
"SUREFOOT." See SMITH, "SUREFOOT."	
SURESNE, (INSPECTOR)	E. Phillips Oppenheim
SWEENEY, MICKEY	Lincoln Steffens
SWEETWATER, CALEB	Anna Katharine Green

T

TABARET, PÈRE ("TIR-AU-CLAIR") . .	Émile Gaboriau
TAIRLAINE, (DR.) MICHAEL . . .	Carter Dickson
TALBOT, PETER	Patricia Wentworth
TANCRED, (DR.) BENJAMIN . . .	G. D. H. and M. I. Cole
TANNER, (INSPECTOR)	Freeman Wills Crofts
TAYLOR, PETE	Robert D. Abrahams
TEAL, (CHIEF INSPECTOR) EUSTACE .	Leslie Charteris
TEMPLAR, SIMON ("THE SAINT") . .	Leslie Charteris
TEMPLE, EVELYN	Lord Gorell
TEMPLETON, PAUL	Richard Goyne
TERHUNE, WADE	Isabel Ostrander
THAMES, SYDNEY	Clinton H. Stagg
THEAKSTONE, (CHIEF INSPECTOR) FRANCIS	Wilkie Collins
"THINKING MACHINE, THE." See VAN DUSEN	
THOMAS, ETHEL	Cortland Fitz-simmons
THOMPSON, (SHERIFF) JAKE . . .	Evelyn Cameron
THOMPSON, (CHIEF INSPECTOR) JAMES	Peter Drax

Name of Character	*Name of Author*
THOMPSON, PAUL ANDREW	Robert George Dean
THORNDYKE, (DR.) JOHN EVELYN; M.D., F.R.C.P.	R. Austin Freeman
THORNE, (DR.) ABEL	Eden Phillpotts
THORNTON, BILL	Edison Marshall
THORPE, ANDY	Q. Patrick
TIBBITTS, (LIEUTENANT) FRANCIS AUGUSTUS ("BONES")	Edgar Wallace [and Francis Gérard]
TIERNEY, JAMES	John A. Moroso
TILBURY, MARGARET	Dorothy Cameron Disney
"TIR-AU-CLAIR." See TABARET.	
TISCHBEIN, EMIL	Eric Kästner
TOBIN, (INSPECTOR)	Dorothy B. Hughes
TOBY, (DR.) QUENTIN	Sturges Mason Schley
TODD, JERRY	Martin Joseph Freeman
TODHUNTER, LAWRENCE	Anthony Berkeley
TOLEFREE, PHILIP	R. A. J. Walling
TOPLITT, KINGSLEY	Gail Stockwell
TOR, NELSON	Barbara Malim
TOWER, (MRS.) BOYLSTON (DAISY) .	Freeman Dana
TOWNSEND, MATILDA	Arthur M. Chase
TRACY, PHILIP ("SPIKE")	Harriette Ashbrook
TRANT, LUTHER	Edgar Balmer and William MacHarg
TRANT, (LIEUTENANT) TIMOTHY . .	Q. Patrick
TRAVERS, LUDOVIC	Christopher Bush
TREADGOLD, HORACE B.	Valentine Williams
TRELAWNEY, EDWARD	Amelia Reynolds Long
TRENT, GREGORY	Adele Seifert
TRENT, PHILIP MARSHAM	E. C. Bentley
TREVOR, CAROLE	Judson P. Phillips

Name of Character	*Name of Author*
VAN DOREN, HANNAH ("HOMICIDE HANNAH")	Dwight V. Babcock
VAN DUSEN, (PROFESSOR) AUGUSTUS S.F.X.; PH.D., LLD., F.R.S., M.D., M.D.S. ("THE THINKING MACHINE")	Jacques Futrelle
VAN KILL, HENDRIK PETER MINUIT ("HAL")	Spencer Bayne
VANE, HARRIET (later LADY PETER WIMSEY)	Dorothy Sayers
VARDON, ROGER	Gerard B. Lambert
VAUTRIN	Honoré de Balzac
VELIE, (SERGEANT) THOMAS . . .	Ellery Queen
"VELMONT, HORACE." See LUPIN.	
VENABLE, CHARLES	C. St. J. Sprigg
VENNER	C. Hedley Barker
VERINDER, RACHEL	Wilkie Collins
VERREY, TONY	Vivian Meik
VINSEN, TAD ("SKIPPER")	T. Kenyon Cook
VON KAZ, (BARON) FRANZ MAXIMILIAN KARAGÔZ	D. & H. Teilhet
VON LEEUW, BENGAL	Lorenz Heller
VOSS, ABELARD	Donald Clough Cameron

W

WADE, (SERGEANT)	Jefferson Farjeon
WADE, HILDA	Grant Allen
WAGHORN, (INSPECTOR) JIMMY . .	John Rhode
WAIT, JACOB	Mignon G. Eberhart
WALDRON, ANTHONY V.	George Clinton Bestor
WALKER ("OF THE SECRET SERVICE")	Melville Davisson Post

Name of Character	*Name of Author*
WESTLAKE, (DR.) HUGH	Jonathan Stagge
WHARTON, (SUPERINTENDENT) GEORGE ("THE OLD GENERAL")	Christopher Bush
"WHISPERING MAN, THE"	Henry Kitchell Webster
WHITE, (INSPECTOR)	Gordon Holmes
WHITE, (LIEUTENANT) LACE . . .	Jeanette Covert Nolan
"WHITE EAGLE, THE." See COCHET.	
"WHITE FACE"	Edgar Wallace
WHITEHALL, (LIEUTENANT) . . .	Maurice Beam and Sumner Gritton
WHITING, (LIEUTENANT) PERCIVAL .	Jeremy Lord
WHITTAKER, CHRISTOPHER	Zelda Popkin
WHYTE, (PROFESSOR) CHATTIN ("CHAT")	W. C. Clark
WHYTE, (MRS.) CHATTIN (SARAH) .	W. C. Clark
WICKLEY, (MRS.) MABEL	Marjorie Boniface
WIGGINS	Sir Arthur Conan Doyle
WILLIAMS, "DOC"	Jonathan Latimer
WILLIAMS, RACE	Carroll John Daly
WILLING, (DR.) BASIL	Helen McCloy
WILLIS, (INSPECTOR)	Freeman Wills Crofts
WILSON, (EX-SUPERINTENDENT) HENRY	G. D. H. and M. I. Cole
WINDWARD, BRUCE	Stephen Bandolier
WIMP, EDWARD	Israel Zangwill
WIMSEY, (LADY) MARY (later MRS. CHARLES PARKER)	Dorothy Sayers
WIMSEY, (LORD) PETER DEATH BREDON	Dorothy Sayers
WIMSEY. See also DENVER.	
WINKLEY	Harriet Rutland

APPENDIX A

"The Purloined Letter" Controversy

DISCUSSION of this question in the main part of this volume concludes with the declaration, on page 20: "On the basis of these incontestable facts, it may now be stated for the first time beyond any reasonable doubt that the Philadelphia publication of 'The Purloined Letter' preceded the Edinburgh edition by approximately two months." For the general reader this is sufficient, and further pursuit of the subject would seem irrelevant. But the Poe-student and the bibliographer may conceivably care to follow the writer down a few of the by-paths and side-lines investigated in arriving at this conclusion. Therefore, at the confessed risk of belaboring a relatively slight point at best, a few "working notes" are set forth below, for the sake of the record and the information of the interested.

. . .

Poe's own references to the tale in correspondence can only be accepted as corroborative evidence of the provenance arrived at. On May 28, 1844, in a letter to James Russell Lowell, he mentioned the work as completed but as yet unsold. Writing again to Lowell on July 2 of the same year, in a paragraph listing his own preferences among his stories, he said: " 'The Purloined Letter,' *forth-*

coming in 'The Gift,' is perhaps the best of my tales of ratiocination." No mention, the reader will note, of *Chambers'*. Clearly, there is nothing here to suggest another and original version.

.   .   .

No single circumstance in the whole dispute has been the occasion of more unwarranted conclusion-jumping than a casual statement by the late Mr. James H. Whitty in his *Poeana* (1927) that he had "discovered among the remaining Poe manuscripts with the Griswold family, a manuscript copy of this Edinburgh version in Poe's autograph." Though this statement is frequently quoted and repeated, all efforts of the present writer to trace the alleged discovery further or to learn the present whereabouts of the purported document have failed; but no matter.

For no very logical reason, this announcement started the supporters of the *Chambers'* contention off in full and supposititious cry—though what possible bearing the document could have on the priority question it is difficult to perceive. Clearly, Whitty's reference to a "manuscript *copy*" seems significant. But even assuming the most unlikely situation—that the document he saw was a genuine manuscript of the tale as supplied by Poe to the editors of *Chambers'*, which in some miraculous way had found its way back across the ocean to America—the language of the prefatory note in the Edinburgh publication still makes it clear that such a manuscript could have been at most a *condensation* of the story as it previously appeared in *The Gift*: made perhaps by Poe at the Messrs. Chambers' request. What is much more likely, of course, is that

Chambers' made its own condensation; that Poe saw an issue of the magazine and made a copy by hand for his own convenience; and that this is what Whitty saw. The whole proposition is so far removed from the priority question that the only excuse for examining it here at all is the amount of thoughtless presumption it has occasioned in some not very critical quarters.... As for Mr. Whitty's opinion that the Edinburgh version (a bad job of editing if there ever was one, whoever may have been responsible!) was to be preferred to *The Gift* version, the less said the kinder.

Considering the extent and endurance of the misapprehension caused (quite unintentionally, one is sure) by Mr. Whitty's little aside, it would seem the clear public duty of the present owners of the document—whoever they may be and if it in fact exists—to come forward and propose its inspection by some reputable and unbiased Poe scholar, or committee of such scholars, so that the full circumstances may be published and the matter finally laid to rest. No permanent or unselfish interest can be served by further mystification.

. . .

It seems clear that Poe himself did not look upon the Edinburgh abridgment as the true or better version; else he would almost certainly have objected to Evert Duyckinck's inclusion of the Philadelphia draft in the 1845 *Tales*. He did not do so, although he had ample opportunity, and, in fact, outspokenly laid certain other editorial sins, real or imaginary, on Duyckinck's head. Under such circumstances, the omission of any complaint seems almost conclusive. Furthermore, Poe's personal copy ("the Lorimer Graham copy") of the 1845 *Tales,* with penciled annotations and corrections in his neat poet's calligraphy, is owned to-day by the Century Club of New York City. No single mark or note appears on the margins of "The Purloined Letter." This is scarcely the attitude of an irate author who feels that a "wrong draft" has been perpetuated!

.   .   .

There is even some indirect substantiation in the "Reverend" Griswold's employment of the Philadelphia version in the 1850 collected *Works.* Had the Edinburgh abridgment been considered the true original—or even an improvement—by Poe or any one else in his time, the opportunistic divine would scarcely have missed the chance to use it; since, if the Whitty report is correct, a manuscript-copy of some sort was in his possession. How Griswold, Poe's treacherous literary executor, misused his position to blacken the poet's memory and hocus poor, muddled "Muddie" Clemm of her "Eddie's" manuscripts and rights has been told at length elsewhere. But, as the late Professor Killis Campbell pointed out, he was as capable an *editor* (for all his personal knavery) as Poe could have named of those available at the time, save possibly Lowell.

.   .   .

Subsequent to the writer's investigation of this question, the Messrs. Charles F. Heartman and James R. Canny have also declared in favor of the Philadelphia publication in their *Bibliography of the First Editions of Edgar Allan Poe* (1940); though without elaborating their reasons. What is perhaps more important, the same work quotes a statement definitely placing the distinguished Poe scholar, Dr. Thomas Ollive Mabbott, on the Philadelphia side of the controversy.... Also, for what little it may be worth, the present writer's copy of *The Gift: 1845* bears on its fly-leaf a faded presentation inscription dated: "Boston Nov. 1844."

APPENDIX B

Sherlock Holmes' Name and Other Addenda

Valuable supplementary information concerning the genesis of SHERLOCK HOLMES' name has come at a late hour from the pen of Vincent Starrett, as published in the excellent *American Notes & Queries* for June, 1941 (from whence quotation is here made by special permission). But let Mr. Starrett speak for himself:

To the best of my knowledge there is no *direct* evidence that Conan Doyle surnamed his immortal detective after the American poet and physician. My own categorical statement to that effect, first made in an article entitled "Enter Mr. Sherlock Holmes" (*Atlantic Monthly,* July, 1932), and later included in *The Private Life of Sherlock Holmes* (N. Y., 1933), is a bold assumption—or deduction—based on a line in Sir Arthur's volume of bookly reminiscence, *Through the Magic Door* (London, 1907), in which, speaking of Oliver Wendell Holmes, he writes: "Never have I so known and loved a man whom I had never seen." The inference seemed clear to me at the time, and I still believe it to be justified. As far as I know, this claim of mine was the first suggestion anywhere that Doyle had named his detective after the American he most revered. All other similar assertions that I have seen have been subsequent to it, and have been, I believe, directly or indirectly, based on the statement in my book. If any earlier evidence exists, I shall be delighted to hear of it.

In the circumstances, it is at least conceivable that Oliver Wendell Holmes never dreamed that he had lent his name to the world's foremost private detective. Whether or not he ever read the stories I am unable to say. Doyle visited America in the late autumn of 1894, the year of Holmes's death, but failed to meet his favorite American. I have no evidence to suggest that the two men ever corresponded. If they did, the evidence must be found in the writings of Holmes the poet or Holmes the jurist; it is not in any published statement by Conan Doyle that I have seen.

While I am confessing, perhaps I should add that the story concerning Sherlock's given name—i.e., that Doyle once made thirty runs against a bowler named Sherlock and thereafter had a kindly feeling for the name—also appeared for the first time (in accessible form) in my *Private Life*. I found the statement years ago in an English newspaper interview with Doyle; but I could not now say where or when the item appeared. It is possible, I suppose, that the story is apocryphal; my memory, however, is entirely trustworthy as to its newspaper appearance. But it *is* a little odd, I think, that in his autobiography, *Memories and Adventures*, Conan Doyle has no clear word to say about the origin of either name.

.   .   .

It now appears that the first bow between covers of Baroness Orczy's OLD MAN IN THE CORNER (pp. 70-72) was *not* in the volume bearing his name, issued in 1909, but in an earlier and long forgotten tome entitled *The Case of Miss Elliott* which was published (in England only) in 1905. This of course brings the total number of books in which the OLD MAN figures to three. Nevertheless, the 1909 collection may accurately be called "first" in one sense of the word. As the opening story in the book makes amply clear, it is an assembling of the *earliest* OLD MAN tales, which in point of fact had begun to appear in magazines, as nearly as can now be determined, around 1902. *Miss Elliott* gives every internal evidence of being composed in haste and most likely "to order," and its failure to cross the ocean or be remembered to-day is entirely understandable. *The Old Man* is a far superior and more spontaneous work in every respect.

ILLUSTRATIONS

THE BIRTHPLACE OF THE DETECTIVE STORY

The center of these three brick houses (which were torn down several years ago) was the "Coates Street home" in Philadelphia where Poe resided during the writing of "The Murders in the Rue Morgue." (From an unpublished work, "Poe's Philadelphia Homes," by the late Dr. Ellis Paxson Oberholtzer. By kind permission of Mrs. Winona McBride Oberholtzer.)

THE FATHER OF THE DETECTIVE STORY

Edgar Allan Poe, from the "Whitman daguerreotype," now owned by Brown University. (By permission of the Library Committee.)

THE "REAL" DUPIN?

André Marie Jean Jacques Dupin (1783-1865), from a portrait by Émile Lassalle, 1839. Did he inspire both hero and villain?

1s.

GABORIAU'S
SENSATIONAL NOVELS
The Favourite Reading of Prince Bismarck.

THE
LEROUGE CASE.

LONDON: VIZETELLY & CO.
10, Southampton Street, Strand.

EMILE GABORIAU

The only likeness of Gaboriau known to survive to-day is
this medallion-engraving from the covers of the Vizetelly
(London) translations of his "Sensational Novels." This
unusually brilliant specimen of one of the great items in
detection collecting is reproduced here by the special courtesy of Ned Guymon, San Diego, California.

WILKIE COLLINS
From Thompson Cooper's *Men of Mark* (London, 1881).

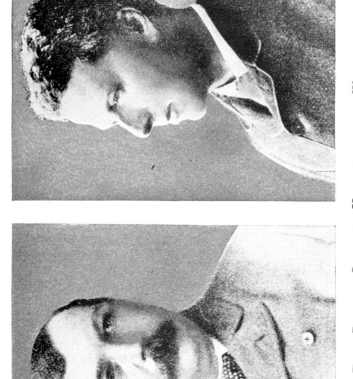

THEY BROUGHT SHERLOCK HOLMES INTO THE WORLD

(LEFT) Young Dr. A. Conan Doyle as he looked in the Southsea years. (RIGHT) An early portrait of Dr. Joseph Bell of Edinburgh, on whom Doyle founded his character. Note the distinctive Holmesian profile. (From *McClure's Magazine.*)

Two Sherlock Holmes Doorways

(LEFT) Doorway of Doyle House, Southsea, Portsmouth, through which Holmes first stepped
into the world in 1887. Courtesy of Portsmouth *Evening News*. (RIGHT) Doorway of the
present 111 Baker Street, London, most usually identified as the mythical "221-B" of the
"Sacred Writings." Photographed by the author.

ARTHUR MORRISON   ROBERT BARR
R. AUSTIN FREEMAN   A. E. W. MASON
G. K. CHESTERTON   ERNEST BRAMAH

ANNA KATHARINE GREEN   JACQUES FUTRELLE

MARY ROBERTS RINEHART   CAROLYN WELLS

MELVILLE DAVISSON POST   ARTHUR B. REEVE

FORTUNÉ DU BOISGOBEY   GASTON LEROUX
MAURICE LEBLANC   GEORGES SIMENON

E. C. Bentley   J. S. Fletcher

Agatha Christie   Dorothy Sayers

F. W. Crofts   H. C. Bailey

ANTHONY BERKELEY   EDGAR WALLACE
("FRANCIS ILES")

G. D. H. COLE   M. I. COLE

R. A. J. WALLING   JOHN RHODE

FREDERICK IRVING ANDERSON   EARL DERR BIGGERS

S. S. VAN DINE   DASHIELL HAMMETT

FREDERIC DANNAY   MANFRED B. LEE

("ELLERY QUEEN," "BARNABY ROSS")

MARGERY ALLINGHAM   MICHAEL INNES
JOHN DICKSON CARR   ERIC AMBLER
NICHOLAS BLAKE   NGAIO MARSH

REX STOUT   MIGNON EBERHART

LESLIE FORD   PHOEBE ATWOOD TAYLOR
("DAVID FROME")

MABEL SEELEY   ERLE STANLEY GARDNER

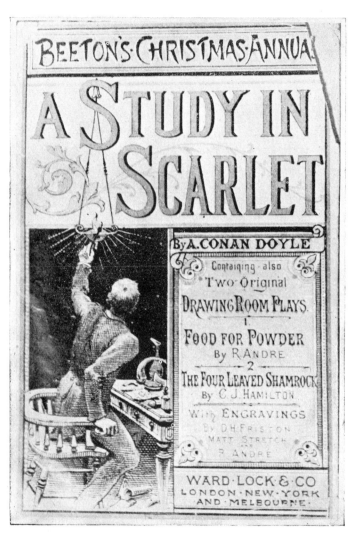

A Great Detection "High Spot"

Front wrapper of the first edition of *A Study in Scarlet.*
(From *The Private Life of Sherlock Holmes*, by permission of Vincent Starrett and The Macmillan Company.)

INDEX

See also "Who's Who in Detection," pages 340-386, and the bibliography of writings about the detective story on pages 279-297. These have *not* been repeated in the present index, because they are indexes themselves. Likewise, indexing has purposely been restricted to really informational references. Merely passing or casual mentions have not been included, in the belief that they only serve to confuse the reader.